JUMP START
Your Brain v2.0

JUMP START
Your Brain v2.0

How Everyone at Every Age
Can Be Smarter and More Creative

Doug Hall
with David Wecker

© 1995, 2008 by Doug Hall
All Rights Reserved
Published by Clerisy Press
Printed in the United States of America
Distributed by Publishers Group West
Second edition, first printing

Clerisy Press
1700 Madison Road
Cincinnati, OH 45206
www.clerisypress.com

Library of Congress Cataloging-in-Publication Data

Hall, Doug, 1959-
Jump start your brain 2.0 : everything you need to think smarter and
more creatively / Doug Hall.
p. cm.
Rev. ed. of: Jump start your brain. c1995.
ISBN-13: 978-1-57860-284-1
ISBN-10: 1-57860-284-X
1. Creative ability in business. 2. Success in business.
I. Hall,Doug, 1959- Jump start your brain. II. Title.

HD53.H35 2007
650.1--dc22

2007045324

Eureka! Institute, Inc.
3849 Edwards Road
Cincinnati, OH 45244
(513) 271-9911
DougHall@DougHall.com
http://www.eurekaranch.com
http://www.doughall.com

Various Jump Starts are © 1991-2007 by Doug Hall and are used with permission.

AcuPOLL and BrainScan are trademarks of AcuPOLL Research, Inc.,
and are used with permission.

Illustrations from Big Bird's Color Game © 1980 Children's Television Workshop
© 1980 Jim Henson Productions, Inc. Illustrations by Tom Cooke.
Reprinted by permission of Children's Television Workshop.

Edited by
SALEHA GHANI

Cover and interior designed by
STEPHEN SULLIVAN

By Doug Hall

Jump Start Your Business Brain
The Scientific Way to Make More Money

Meaningful Not Mindless Marketing
The Science of Sustained, Successful Marketing
(Editions also published as *Jump Start Your Marketing Brain*)

Also by

Making the Courage Connection
Finding the Courage To Journey from Fear to Freedom
Simon & Schuster

Jump Start Your Brain
Warner Books

By Roger Sweet and David Wecker

Mastering the Universe
He-Man and the Rise and Fall of a Billion-Dollar Idea

DEDICATION

This book is dedicated to my high school sweetheart, my best friend, my wife, the mother of our children, Debbie Hall— the only person on this good earth for whom I will make the ultimate sacrifice: at her bidding, I will wear a tie.

This book is written for the sixty-something man who told me he'd devoted 35 years to corporate America. After hearing my Jump Start Your Brain lecture in 2006, he realized how far he'd sunk into conformity; how he'd allowed himself to be pushed into a dull, gray, emotionally numb corner; how he'd adjusted his life to fit the day-to-day world and, finally, how he'd stopped dreaming. He told me he realized that he'd lost the fire.

But on that day,
he thought I might have helped him rekindle the fire.

It was one of those misty moments. I saw a man in the homestretch of life taking stock of where he'd been and what he'd done—an individual who, once upon a time, could have been anything he'd set his mind to be.

It doesn't matter if I sell 10 books or 10 million. What's important is that the message of hope, independence, imagination, and self-reliance makes a difference for you.

CONTENTS

WHY A "2.0" NEW EDITION?

"If you would not be forgotten as soon as you are dead and rotten, either write things worth reading or do things worth the writing."
– Ben Franklin

I bring you good news!

Creativity is not random. There are reproducible tools and tactics that can help you think smarter and more creatively about personal challenges.

I help people-executives, entrepreneurs, kids, teachers, and just plain folks-invent ideas for solving their problems 52 weeks a year using the Eureka! Way. In the 48 hours prior to this writing, I've used some of the methods detailed on these pages to help:

- A frustrated young woman find the courage to follow her dream.
- The owners of a small but spectacular restaurant invent ideas for attracting new customers and generate additional revenue.
- A VP at one of the world's most respected corporations create 75 choices for growth.
- The executive director of a non-profit discover ways for turning momentary positive momentum into stable long-term income growth.

For the past decade, my life and the world of the Eureka! Ranch has been focused on turning the art of creativity into a reliable, renewable science.

When creativity is conceived of as an art, it's ethereal and fickle; a slippery intangible. As creativity moves more toward being a science, it becomes more predictable and dependable, a trustworthy tool that can be wielded to yield real results.

Years of mining through mountains of data have unearthed a clear understanding of what works and what doesn't as far as enhancing the ability to generate ideas. The teachings on these pages are grounded in original research involving thousands of big companies, small companies and start-up entrepreneurs who have participated in Eureka! Ranch Inventing projects, as well as Eureka! Institute lectures and seminars. Everything you'll read about in here you can apply to your career and your life.

Warner Books, a division of Time Warner, published this book in its original form in January 1994. It became a creativity classic, reprinted by dozens of book clubs and international publishers.

As the years passed, my understanding of the creative process evolved. By measuring and analyzing over 6,000 invention teams and over 10,000 business-building ideas, I developed a new understanding of what drives success.

Simply speaking, this new material had to be incorporated into *Jump Start Your Brain*, so I contacted Warner Books with the news. They told me to cool my jets. They saw no problem, saying the book was selling.

But I was bothered. Finally, my frustration rose to action level. I called Time Warner and bought back the rights to the book. With the help of Richard Hunt, my publisher, I've recast this book based upon how my perceptions have been changed based on quantitative research.

Correcting past works is something my hero, Ben Franklin, America's first great inventor and entrepreneur, articulated in his epitaph:

> "Here lies the Body of B. Franklin Printer; like the cover of an old book, it's contents torn out, and stripped of its lettering and gilding, lies here, food for worms. But the work shall not be wholly lost: for it will, as he believed, appear once more, in a new & more perfect edition, corrected and amended by the author."

What's New?!

From a big picture perspective, the three most important changes from the first edition are:

1. FEAR, not lack of FUN, is the key issue.

The first edition declared, "Fun is Fundamental." Instead, there is another "f word" even more critical to creativity—fear.

But, when we measured real people inventing real ideas to solve real problems, we found that increasing levels of fun did not correlate with the production of more big ideas. We tried every manner of measurement and questioning to validate the importance of FUN. It didn't matter: increasing the fun factor was NOT as fundamental to creativity as was decreasing the fear factor.

What we discovered was that as the level of fear increased, the number of high quality ideas dropped. Fear could be the pressure to produce, the presence of a particularly scary boss, or simply not wanting to appear foolish or stupid.

2. Diversity is a much greater issue than I initially thought.

The first edition stated that diversity was an additive to stimulus when it came to creating ideas.

The data clearly shows that diversity delivers an exponential kick. When you connect with others who have different mindsets, experiences, and backgrounds, you realize a ginormous leap in your creativity. Diversity is not just about people-although people are a great way to connect with new ideas-diversity is about exploring, accepting, and adapting to fresh ideas and insights.

Diversity is so important that it cannot be left solely to those moments when you gather together for an ideation or brainstorming session. In recognition of the importance of diversity, this edition contains a bounty of ideas and advice for making connections with other people and other ideas.

3. Capitalist Creativity is about effectiveness, not "liking."

Eureka! Ranch research found that the classic customer service measure of "liking" or "how much did you enjoy the exercise" had no correlation with actual success levels. Instead, results directly tie to the direct and blunt question-how effective was this exercise at generating ideas that fulfill our objective?"

Enjoyment and effectiveness are two different things. A creative exercise could be difficult and challenging, yet still very effective. Alternatively, an exercise could be fun and enjoyable yet result in meaningless ideas.

In this edition, we have edited the creativity techniques, the "Jump Starts," to include only those proven effective at creating big ideas. The fun-yet-not-effective exercises are gone. Only the real stuff that really works remains.

Every account you'll read here is essentially true in terms of the events they describe, however, I have taken the liberty to make two modifications to historical accounts:

- Certain identities or products have been hidden in the interest of client confidentiality ... or to protect the guilty. This is a book about hope, faith, and believing in yourself. You won't find tales tattled here.
- As Ben Franklin often did, I've editorialized a few stories, adding a joke here or a twist there to make a point. My intent is to teach and inspire—not to brag or bore.
- Richard Saunders lives. As with the first edition, these pages are sprinkled liberally with quotes from friends, colleagues and associates. Here and there, I've included nuggets that came to me on a moonlit night from one Saunders, which by odd coincidence was Ben Franklin's pen name. Although I can't prove conclusively that it's the same Saunders, I can believe it so. It's a free country.

Jump Start Your Brain

The title sums up the corporate mission of this book and my companies. The intent here is to help you get the maximum horsepower from your particular combination of imagination and intellect. My mission is to help you turn your dreams into reality.

This little piggy went to market,
This little piggy stayed home.
The first little pig had a wicked good idea,
The second little pig had none.
And the first little pig laughed,
Hee, hee, hee, hee,
All the way to the bank.
– Richard Saunders

So here it is: the new edition on the Eureka! Way. It's what I am. Just as with the first book, it's all I know-and all I've come to know about thinking smarter and more creatively. You hold in your hands my life's work on personal creativity. On these pages is what I've learned from nearly 40 years of real world entrepreneurship.

My hope is that after reading these pages your hope is renewed, your resolve strengthened and your dreams that much closer to being realized.

The Eureka! way is good for you. It works. So here we go. Get ready! Get set! Let's crank up your cranium!

Cheers,
Doug Hall
Springbrook, Prince Edward Island, Canada
Cincinnati, Ohio U.S.A.

INTRODUCTION

How Is This Book Organized?
And Who Is Doug Hall?

"Words may show a man's wit, but actions his meaning."
— **Ben Franklin**

"Jump Start Your Brain" Is Presented in Three Acts

I'll warn you up front: *Jump Start Your Brain* is not a scholarly work. It's sewn together with lots of grins, a few smirks, and all the stuff I know about inventing new-to-the-world ideas. My aim is to educate a little, entertain a little. My personal hero and America's first great inventor, Ben Franklin, had the same philosophy. In fact, some historical accounts suggest that the reason he wasn't asked to write the Declaration of Independence was for fear he'd slip a joke into it.

- **ACT I, BRAIN TRAINING:** SETTING YOUR MENTAL FOCUS TO NEW-TO-THE-WORLD IDEAS.

- **Act II, Jump Start Techniques:** 30 ways to reinvent your life and career, each explained step by step.

- **Act III, Go4It!:** Even the most glorious, magical idea won't do you much good if you can't make it real. Act III contains inspirational adrenaline to help you turn your dreams into reality.

Disclaimers, Warnings, and Other Minutiae

If you are allergic to data, you'll love this book. My apologies, data geeks. Though the book itself is based on hard data–from academic journals and original research–I've purposely kept technical discussions to a minimum. This book is designed to tell you in simple, action-oriented terms how to think smarter and more creatively about your life and career. Plain. Simple. Go.

If you like fun, you'll love this book. This book is written to provoke a sense of playfulness of mind and spirit. If you're a mature and proper RWA (Real World Adult), you might find the free-spirited nature of the writing, the use of **BOLD FACE** and lots of *!!!!!!'s* a bit annoying. But it's how I talk. It's who I am. The kindest thing said to me after my appearance on network television was that I was being myself. Besides, LIFE IS TO BE ENJOYED! There are too many BORING BOOKS ALREADY!

The Urgency for Thinking Smarter and More Creatively

In today's world, victory goes to those who have the most meaningful offering. This means those with the best ideas win. To paraphrase Emerson—"Build a better mousetrap, and the World Wide Web will open your door to success."

In the old days, you could build a business with a mediocre offering or with a lack of price competitiveness. In today's instant-connection world, this strategy is far less successful. The World Wide Web has created a true free market economy where meaningful ideas are the currency for success.

The consequences of not developing meaningful ideas are extreme. **If we don't think smarter and more creatively, we're all going to end up working for the folks in China and India.**

My Name Is Doug Hall

I've been called many things....

- "America's No. 1 New Product Idea Man" (*Inc. Magazine*)
- "America's No. 1 Idea Guru" (*A&E Top 10* and *CIO Magazine*)
- "Procter & Gamble Marketing Whiz" (*Wall Street Journal*)
- "An eccentric entrepreneur who just might have what we've all been looking for ... the happy secret to success." (*Dateline NBC*)
- "Counter-culture Entrepreneur" (*New York Magazine*)
- "Short, Balding Troll" (Comedy Central)
- "The Most Annoying Man in America" (Simon Cowell on *The Tonight Show*)
- Modern Day Ben Franklin (Joyce Wycoff)
- "Mr. Know-It-All" (ABC-TV's *American Inventor*)

And my personal favorite ...
- "Business Robin Hood" (Canadian Broadcasting Corporation)

That's the hype on me. The plain truth is, I'm a short balding guy with a taste for comfortable tropical shirts, comfortable jeans, and comfortable Birkenstock sandals. The difference is, I'm not afraid to think big, and I have sufficient supplies of energy and enthusiasm to turn my ideas into reality.

The Early Years—Real World Entrepreneur

I was born of a middle-class family in Portland, Maine, 253 years to the day after the birth of Ben Franklin, a circumstance that has tinted my outlook and influenced who I am.

At the age of 12, I started my first business performing as a magician and juggler and selling "learn to juggle kits", magic tricks, and balloon animal kits. I called myself Merwyn the Magician, after my dad, who was not a magician and who deeply regrets the fact that his first name sounds a lot like Merlin.

In college I formed Campus Promotions International, a little company that marketed beer mugs, T-shirts, and just about anything you could print a logo on to four different campuses. I published a vinyl phone book cover, the kind with the ads all over them. Money was tight, so I took lots of items in trade. I got a diamond ring from a jeweler that way. It was the ring I gave to Debbie, my high school sweetheart, when I proposed.

Twenty-something—Corporate Rebel

The University of Maine spat me into the world in 1981 with a degree in chemical engineering and a hankering to get into marketing. I'd worked as a summer engineer at Procter & Gamble's Mehoopany, Pennsylvania, paper plant in the pulp mill, where I learned that chemical engineering was not my life's mission.

Instead of taking the classic path for a chemical engineer, I applied to P&G's advertising department. At the interview, I performed a few magic tricks, figuring that any company that couldn't appreciate a trick or two was not a place where I wanted to work. I got an offer and was hired on with Coast soap, a fine deodorant bar.

> "Were there times I wanted to strangle Doug? Absolutely. He was what I call a 'high-maintenance subordinate.' You had to watch him like

crazy. He'd be nodding at what I was saying, but his mind would be somewhere else. Linear, he's not. His divergence paid off a number of times in the context of inventions that would not have been discovered simply by taking incremental steps forward from where we were."
– Barb Thomas, my first boss at P&G

In time, I became the company's first and only Master Marketing Inventor. The P&G Finance department calculated that my Invention Team could take a product to market with 10 percent of the staff, in 16 percent of the time and at 18 percent of the cost of a similar project in another part of the company. It wasn't that we were any smarter. It was that we had a different mindset; an entrepreneurial perspective I now call the Eureka! Way.

It was a wild time. We wore comfortable clothes, worked 16 to 20 hours a day and loved it. The company loved it, too.

"Doug brings an extraordinary degree of creativity, entrepreneurial instinct and energy to his work. He has brought eight product concepts from invention to shipping, all within the past year . . . with a ninth project soon to follow. This has to be something of a record."
– From my final personnel review at P&G

The corporation acknowledged and respected my efforts. But for all that, it's still a corporation. And as with all corporations, certain rules of protocol are to be followed. The review continued:

"Doug has just one key opportunity for improvement: he needs to treat the 'system' with more respect.... (He) takes almost malicious pleasure in 'beating the system' by developing new product concepts faster and cheaper than if work were done through traditional channels ... It

does not help to rub people's noses in their inef-
ficiencies, their cost of operation or their tor-
toise-like speed"
– More from my final personnel review at P&G

Guilty as charged.

One February morning, after about a decade at Procter, I
awoke and realized it was time to get on with the next phase of
my life's journey. A lot of people wait until they're 65 to retire
from the corporation and start living the good life. I retired in
my early 30s.

Thirty-something—Corporate Rebel For Hire

I borrowed Ben Franklin's pen name for my new company—
Franklin having published *Poor Richard's Almanac* under the name,
Richard Saunders. And that, in a nut, was the birth of Richard
Saunders International.

Ben is my spiritual mentor. He's the original American
inventor, as well as the original American entrepreneur. We share
the same birthday, January 17, a scant 253 years apart. We both
have receding hairlines and irreverent senses of humor. We both
have far-flung interests ranging from science to business to politics. Our profiles and physiques are strangely alike, although I
think Franklin may have had one or two more chins. The *Wall
Street Journal* noticed the similarities, too:

> (Hall and Franklin) "sort of look alike, especial-
> ly when the balding and bespectacled Mr. Hall
> wears colonial-style shirts with puffy sleeves."
> – The *Wall Street Journal*

The original vision was for Richard Saunders International
to pursue a combination of corporate innovation consulting and
independent inventing/licensing.

Inventing was fun and profitable; we sold or licensed a
number of board games and consumer electronic products.
However, the innovation consulting business quickly took off at a

level I never would have expected, and thus the inventing business was put on hold.

Our work for Pepsi-Cola, the Eveready Battery Company, AT&T, and Walt Disney generated a big buzz in the media world. In quick succession, we made multiple national appearances on Dateline NBC and CNN and were featured in *Inc. Magazine*, the *Wall Street Journal*, and others.

Lou Dobbs on CNN reported research that showed the average American home has, on average, 18 products that we've had a hand in jumpstarting. In some cases, it's been the invention of a new product or service. In other cases, it's been the invention or reinvention of a client's marketing methods. The number is not nearly as impressive as it sounds–when you realize that we work for clients like Walt Disney, American Express, Procter & Gamble, Johnson & Johnson, Nike, Kraft, Frito-Lay, Pepsi-Cola, and hundreds of others of the bestselling brands in the world.

As our work generated publicity, the name of our invention service, Eureka!, took over, and the name Richard Saunders International was assigned to the corporate holding company. With the construction of a custom-built creativity center just outside of Cincinnati we officially became known as the Eureka! Ranch. Franklin's spirit lives on in a display in the lobby and in the Eureka! Ranch logo, with its flying kite and rising sun

The official name is Eureka with an exclamation point. Eureka! recognizes that magical moment of creation, when the little hairs on the back of your neck stand up and you suddenly see with clarity the solution to a seemingly impossible challenge.

In the original Greek, "eureka" translates to "I have found it!" Legend has it that the Greek mathematician and physicist

Archimedes coined the term after being stimulated in a hot tub.

Settling in for a long soak one day around 250 BC, Archie was preoccupied with finding a way to determine the proportion of gold to ordinary metal in King Hieron's crown. Evidently, the king suspected he had been shorted by his royal crown supplier and was interested in ascertaining whether the crown on his head was mostly, if not all, gold or some cheap imitation. At the time, the weight of gold per unit volume was well known. But given the intricate nature of the crown's design, with all its curlicues and whatnot, it was impossible to measure its volume.

So as Archie lowered himself into the tub, he noticed his bath water rise. The lower he sank, the higher the water rose, until it overflowed. The stimulus of the overflowing hot tub gave Archie an epiphany. He suddenly realized he could measure the volume of the crown by simply dunking it in a tub filled to the brim, then measuring the water that overflowed.

Archie leaped from his tub and ran naked into the street hollering "eureka!" **Thus, in the grip of inspiration, he also invented streaking.** And it didn't end there–the hot tub revelation led him to the discovery of the law of specific gravity and the general science of hydrostatics.

Forty-something—From Idea Guru to Idea Factory Engineer

Eureka! success was tremendous. We had an industry-leading 88 percent repeat rate from some of the world's most demanding clients. However, much of our success came from my personal ability to think bold thoughts. Or as *Inc. Magazine* described it: "Most of the winning creative leaps, most of the marketplace-driven reshaping of raw ideas, took place in the caffeine-stoked furnace of Hall's own uniquely nimble mind, often at 2 or 3 a.m. during 72-hour sessions with clients. That's when the real rubber hit the road."

In the same article, writer John Grossmann described Eureka! as a professional practice not a reproducible business. "At the end of the day, Hall was no different from a doctor with a stethoscope around his neck or a wrench-twisting plumber. It all flowed through him. It worked because I ran around like the guy spinning plates on *The Ed Sullivan Show*," I told Grossmann.

Near this time, I traveled to the North Pole by dog sled. It was a brutal 200-mile trip at 40 below zero. During the trip I came to the realization that my "legacy" to date included the creation of new types of tortilla chips, candies, caskets, credit cards, and cars. And while it made me laugh—it was not exactly what I had dreamed my impact on the world would be.

On the way to 90 North a new vision was born: a dream to translate what I'd learned into a reliable and reproducible business; to make the creative impact I delivered to my small, select group of corporate clients available to the masses of Real World entrepreneurs and corporations around the world.

When I returned to the world of the warm, every Eureka! session became a laboratory experiment. I became fanatical about measurement. We measured client teams' states of mind before we worked with them. We measured them during the process of creating. We measured the end quality of all final ideas and their eventual impact on the world. We then did correlation and regression analysis to help us understand how to modify our actions to maximize client success.

The Eureka! method went through rapid transformations. As of this writing, we are at Eureka! 7.0—the seventh version in 21 years. Today's approach reliably helps companies develop measurably smarter choices for growth. To be specific—Eureka! 7.0 develops some 12 times more "big ideas" than Eureka! 1.0.

Most important of all, it's a reliable and reproducible system. This means that others can be trained to lead Eureka! Sessions with the same reliability as me. The chart below shows how even rookie facilitators generate results from each of the six cycles of a classic Eureka! Session that are nearly identical to those when I am in charge.

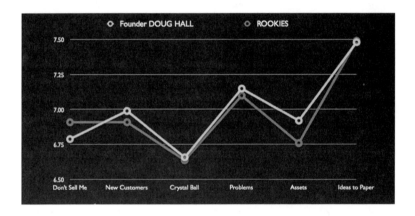

In effect, the system's research over the past 10 years has removed the greatest barrier to growth—ME. **I am fully replaceable.** Instead of building an empire of thousands of staff members— I chose to follow the path of Ben Franklin for expansion. Franklin expanded his print shop throughout the colonies through dozens of partnerships with local partners. In exchange for Franklin licensing his expertise and assistance he received a royalty. So too, we are following that same path as we partner with other companies to bring Eureka! to thousands of companies around the world.

The turn from guru to idea factory engineer resulted in a No. 1 national business best selling book *Jump Start Your Business Brain,* an honorary doctorate from the University of Prince Edward Island, as well as television and radio opportunities.

David Wecker and I hosted *Brain Brew*, a radio program of ideas and advice for entrepreneurs, for three years. Public Radio International distributed the show nationally. You can listen to the show at http://www.brainbrewradio.com. In Canada, I hosted CBC-TV Venture specials, where I was dubbed the "Business Robin Hood" for my efforts to help small-business owners.

Fifty-something—Real World Entrepreneur and Educator

As I embark on my fifth decade, in addition to our continuing work with corporate leaders, I'm returning to my entrepreneurial and inventor roots.

It's taken some time. Five years, in fact, of front-line testing and learning to help me regain my "feel" for the world of entrepreneurs (and detox myself from the corporate mindset). The result is a series of cost-efficient and effective programs called Eureka! Winning Ways.

We will soon have certified Eureka! Growth Coaches in all fifty U.S. states as well as dozens of countries around the world.

I recently had a wild ride as a judge on ABC-TV's *American Inventor* produced by Simon Cowell. The experience opened my eyes to the plight of independent inventors. Invention promotion firms steal thousands of dollars from tens of thousands of inventors. One company took money from 1,950 inventors, and only 5 made back more than they paid in.

Over the next 10 years it's my plan to create an HONEST and MEANINGFUL system for helping independent inventors clean, screen, and license their inventions to companies.

Lastly, it is my dream to create educational curriculum that can help students at universities, vocational schools and community colleges across the world "create and sell big ideas." **I believe that everyone, no matter what their profession, needs to understand how to create and sell their ideas for improving their company, community, or the planet.** The greatest waste of resources in any community are the ideas thought of but not acted on.

Translating what we've learned from "big companies" to "small companies" was difficult. However, initial indications are that translating our learning to the world of education is even more difficult. Companies are generally easier to work with as they have the simple and focused mission of making more money by serving customers. Educational institutions are more challenging as they often have multiple, conflicting missions.

The Trained Brains

Through these pages, you'll also meet my Trained Brains—the highest level of Eureka! Growth Coaches. They're a collection of bold and brave thinkers who have demonstrated a reproducible ability to invent fresh and feasible ideas for helping clients grow their businesses.

Just as our system has changed, so too has the role of the Trained Brain.

In the old days Trained Brains were my support team. Today, I support them as they lead some 90 percent of all Eureka! Sessions.

Yesterday's Trained Brains were entertaining performers. Style was more important than substance. Today's Trained Brains are experts at discovering big ideas and developing those ideas into persuasive written concepts.

Yesterday's Trained Brains were very imaginative. Today's Trained Brains are also practical and more successful. Today's Eureka! sessions result in ideas with a five times greater chance of marketplace success than those created by the average brainstorming session as practiced in most organizations.

While today's Trained Brains are significantly more effective, they haven't lost the spirit that is the heart of the Eureka! Way. Trained Brains laugh a lot. They're young for their ages. They long ago stopped heeding the advice of their elders to straighten up and fly right. Their eyes are wide open with wonder.

Trained Brains don't fit in, but they never feel left out. They avoid the beaten path and the well-worn rut as a point of pride. Somehow, they've been able to resist the corrosive forces of cynicism. They have a pure, simple way of seeing and an ability to extract the fresh from the mundane.

Most of all, Trained Brains have a gift for shaking it up,

twisting it around, and inspiring companies to make something new happen.

While this book is cast in the first person, it's an all-encompassing first person. It's not just me. It's the collective voice of the entire Eureka! Ranch team. The learning and wisdom of the full-time staff, the Trained Brains and the licensed Growth Coaches.

Friends have asked why I would give away my secrets . . .

My answer is, it's the right thing to do. It's an attitude I picked up while kicking around in juggling circles. The philosophy among jugglers is that if I can teach you a trick and you can teach me a trick in return, we're both enriched.

Then, too, there are these sentiments from two authorities for which I have the greatest respect:

> "He offered me a patent for the sole vending of them (Franklin stoves) for a term of years: but I declined it from a principle which has ever weighed with me on such occasions, that as we enjoy great advantages from the inventions of others, we should be glad of the opportunity to serve others by any invention of ours."
> – Ben Franklin

> "When you share ideas, you have more."
> – Kristyn Hall, my daughter, age 5

At the same time, I also respect trademarks, copyrights, and patents. Success today requires a blend of open and protected materials. That means that, by virtue of having purchased this book as opposed to shoplifting it, you are hereby granted a license to use its content to invent ideas for yourself or your company. All I ask is that you use the proper trademarks and acknowledge their daddy at the bottom of your work sheets thusly:

If you are an author, consultant, or trainer, remember, please, that it is neither nice nor right to steal, commercialize, plagiarize, or make money off this work without first asking permission. For permission call the Eureka! Ranch at (513) 271-9911 or e-mail me at DougHall@DougHall.com. Or else my wicked good lawyer, Patty Hogan, will call and have a chat with you.

NOTE: To date, I've never said no to anyone who has properly asked permission to use or reprint portions of my books, columns, or radio show segments.

FREE HELP: The Eureka! Ranch team offers a number of free services. Visit http://www.eurekaranch.com to learn how you can get free help with thinking smarter and more creatively about your challenge.

The Future Is Bright

The rising sun that is part of the Eureka! Ranch logo is a reference to Franklin's speech on the final day of the 1787 Constitutional Convention, as delegates were signing the document. Pointing to the carving of a partial sun at the halfway point on the horizon decorating the back of convention president George Washington's chair, Franklin said: "I have often ... in the course of the session ... looked at that sun behind the President without being able to tell whether it was rising or setting. But now at length I have the happiness to know it is a rising and not a setting sun."

So, too, do I have the happiness of knowing that the future of creativity is great. The sun is rising on a renaissance age of invention. The Internet, the global community and new technologies have made it possible for everyone—no matter who they are or where they are—to discover, develop, and sell big ideas.

Act 1

Brain Training

"When Doug meets Disney, creativity
ne'er wanes; our team explodes when he
jump starts our brains!"

– Ellen Guidera, Vice President, Walt Disney Company

INNOCENCE

"While we may not be able to control all that happens to us,
we can control what happens inside us."
— **Ben Franklin**

Creativity starts with the willingness to look at the world through innocent eyes. It involves shaking ourselves from our prejudices and established thinking patterns. Copthorne MacDonald, an expert on the cultivation of wisdom (http://www.cop.com), explains how innocence helps us discover new insights:

> "We find ourselves looking at the same old data, but we now see it in a dramatically different way. We experience another valid, and sometimes more significant way of understanding what is."

Sadly, the world grinds away at our trust and our innocence. Experience teaches us to doubt, to scoff and roll our eyes. **In no time at all, the world can turn a genuinely creative individual into a Real World Adult.** At that point, there's not much of the real you left—too often, just a job title on a business card, a nameplate on an office door, a number on a badge, a face in the crowd.

Think back. Remember when you were young and the world was a glittering place of limitless possibilities? Everywhere you looked, you found something new and different. Remember the magical feeling that you could do anything simply because nobody was telling you otherwise.

> A child's word is made of spirit and miracles. We sometimes think that children should follow us, listen to us, become like us. Follow a child closely for an hour. Not to teach or to discipline, but to learn, and to laugh.
> – SARK, "A Creative Companion"

Or to put it another way:

> "The secret of genius is to carry the spirit of the child into old age, which means never losing your enthusiasm."
> – Aldous Huxley

The key word is "spirit." **The goal is not to remain a child for the rest of your life, but to retain that childlike spirit of wonder**

and a willingness to innocently believe in possibilities.

As children we have a natural innocence. As we age we lose it. I believe that one of the greatest benefits of spending time with children and grandchildren is that they teach us the virtues of innocence—**IF we are aware and open to the learning.**

Three Quick Examples of Innocence

EXAMPLE NO. 1: TRUTH IS RELATIVE TO THE CUSTOMER'S VIEWPOINT

One day, I was reading Big Bird's Color Game to my then three-year-old daughter, Tori. On one page, Big Bird was shown thinking of something orange that's good to drink. "I bet you can't guess what it is," so said Big Bird in his word balloon.

On the next page, Tori had a choice of a half-dozen orange-colored items—a butterfly, a T-shirt, a jack-o-lantern, a toy boat, a tiger lily and a glass of orange juice.

Which one did you pick? Tori picked the tiger lily because of its long stem, which she took to be a straw. When you're three years old, "good" equals "fun." And it's a lot more fun to drink through a straw than from a plain old glass. The tiger lily might not have been the answer Big Bird had in mind, but it was a valid response to the question.

EXAMPLE 2: MORE THAN ONE RIGHT ANSWER

Children have an ability to see alternative answers as their brains have not become mentally constipated with the "one right answer." Consider an incident that occurred when my other daughter, Kristyn, was taking one of those pre-screening evaluations for kindergarten. The woman administering the test showed Kristyn a picture like this:

What does it look like to you? Kristyn decided it was a windmill. The nice lady explained that, no, it was an airplane propeller—at which point Kristyn launched a 10-minute counterclaim. She argued that, with all due respect, the picture she had been shown was most definitely and undeniably of a windmill.

Afterwards, the nice lady explained to my wife that, technically, she should have subtracted points from Kristyn's score for her answer.

"But she convinced me," the nice lady said. "I guess it is a windmill after all."

EXAMPLE NO. 3: WHO'S THE SMARTEST?

As an early post-toddler, my son, Brad,, was told that his clothes should match. He followed these directions explicitly. As a result, he often wore socks of two different colors. When it would be pointed out to him that his socks didn't match, Brad would argue they did. And he would be right, inasmuch as each sock would match a part of the rest of his outfit. After dressing himself with, say, a red shirt and a pair of blue pants, he would choose a red sock and a blue sock.

When you think about it, Brad actually might have a better idea. Just because his socks didn't match each other didn't mean that, in the larger sense, his whole getup wasn't color coordinated.

Grow Up but Don't Grow Down in Creativity

The whole point of growing up is to become a grown-up. It's too bad, really. What happens to us? In the transition from innocence to experience, why do so many circuits in our brains slam shut?

It's because, early on, we're told to stay inside the lines when we color. It's not a bad thing to learn how to color inside the lines, unless it's the only way we know how to color. In other words, **as our education increases, imagination often decreases. THAT IS IF WE LET IT.**

Think about what Marvin Camras of the Illinois Institute of Technology Research Institute, the inventor of magnetic recording and holder of more than 500 patents, said in an interview in *Inventors at Work*, by Kenneth A. Brown, published by Tempus Books of Microsoft Press:

> "I think little children tend to be creative, but the more education you get, the more the inventive spark is educated out of you. In our educational process, you have to conform. Educators don't like you to go off the beaten path. In math, for example, you have to follow the style that someone suggests. After you've gone through more and more education, you conform more and more. You might even say that you're discouraged from inventing. Of course, different people have different natures. Some people can invent in spite of their education."

As we march toward Real World Adulthood, we become increasingly categorized, polarized, and depersonalized. We learn to wear uncomfortable uniforms so we can be identified quickly and efficiently. We take the safe road—the one in the middle. We accept conventional wisdom and toe the company line.

We read from the same books, take the same exams, and drink from the same cup of knowledge. This cup has been passed around quite a bit. In the process, we inevitably consume a certain amount of backwash.

"Never let formal education get in the way of
your learning."
– Mark Twain

This is not to say there's no value to growing up. We need
Real World Adults to beat back the wilderness and keep the
wolves away. But we pay a price. To give our lives focus, we put
on blinders. We starve our imaginations. We fall out of sync with
our inborn ability to see what no one else can.

**Recapture the innocence of childhood, and you'll open
the windows in your brain.** Once the windows are open, you
can't keep imaginative ideas from entering—or, more important, from coming out.

Great ideas can come from childlike minds, the psyches
that are naive and unafraid. The essence of the Eureka! Way is
to rekindle that way of thinking, so that you see, hear, smell,
taste, and touch as if for the first time.

**Recapturing innocence and opening our minds is more
than just a means for getting greater pleasure out of life. It's a
method for capturing the spirit of entrepreneurial thinking
and enthusiasm that made this country great.**

It's also key to jump-starting your brain.

Consider your last five jobs or significant life roles. List
them on a piece of paper like this:

Job 1: _____

Job 2: _____

Job 3: _____

Job 4: _____

Job 5: _____

Think back to your first 30 days on each. Try to recall the
rush of ideas you had, the problems you saw, and the solutions

you imagined. If you're a parent, remember the thoughts you had before your child arrived. Remember how you were determined to be the perfect parent? Remember how you weren't going to make the same mistakes your parents made?

Chances are, you were a fountain of energy and enthusiasm, a veritable fireworks display of ideas. Why? Because you were new, naïve, and innocent.

Then one of two things happened. You ran with your ideas because you didn't know any better and you shined ... or your ideas flickered and died because you kept your mouth shut. And that was the end of that. Before long, you were "educated," as in "processed."

Where are those thoughts now? Whatever became of them? What do you wish you'd done with them?

> "You just open yourself up to become like a child. All of a sudden, the world is a wide-eyed experience again. You start feeling again, and you see the world through the eyes of a five-year-old. Once you get rid of preconceived notions, ideas can start to cross-pollinate."
> – Eric Schulz, Buena Vista Home Video,
>   the Walt Disney Company

Once, when my eldest, Kristyn, was small, she decided she would grow up to be an artist. The day before that, she was going to be a nurse. The day before that, she was going to be a ninja. Today she's studying engineering at Smith College and still dreaming. Last fall she wanted to solve the world's environmental challenges. This summer she wants to be a patent lawyer helping independent inventors.

To her, everything was possible—and happily, still is. It may not be the most practical point of view, but it beats being a Real World Adult.

The Power of Simple Things

Step outside yourself. **Are you the person you wanted to become? If not now, when will you get back on track?**

1. One of the great powers a child has is the ability to find joy in small, simple things. As adults, we have a love of complexity. To recapture that wonder of small, simple things, spend a day with a child. If you don't have a child of your own, borrow one: a child between the ages of four and seven, maybe a niece or a nephew, a neighbor's kids, or your grandchildren. You want a child with no grown-up tendencies whatsoever.

Go for a walk, take a ride, share a Special Day with a child. Special Days are big occasions at my house. On Special Days, the kid is boss. The kid decides what to do and where to go.

Be forewarned that you run a risk here. You risk floating a paper boat on a pond at the park, building a kite from scratch or maybe heading off to a second-hand thrift store and buying a bunch of dress-up clothes. You run the risk of lying on your back in a grassy meadow and imagining faces and horses galloping in the clouds overhead.

Whatever your child does, you do it, too. Don't just stand there like a bump on a kosher dill. Ask your child lots of questions. Find out everything you can about your child. Don't be afraid to ask silly questions. Have some laughs.

2. Read a book to a child. Find a book with no connection with reality, like one by the late Dr. Seuss, arguably one of the great creative minds of our time. His characters and stories will live forever because they aren't like anything anywhere anyhow.

Grab your coat, run to the library or nearest bookstore and pick up a pile of Dr. Seuss' greatest works. Here are a few suggestions. Note: these are also ideal books for your personal creativity library.

- *Did I Ever Tell You How Lucky You Are?* The old man in the Desert of Drize shows us how good we really have it.
- *Oh, the Places You'll Go!* The world is a big place,

filled with colors, shapes and possibilities. It's dangerous and scary, but you'll succeed if you only get going.

• *The Sneetches and Other Stories* This collection of stories exposes the silliness of prejudice and stubbornness and equips you to battle your fears.

• *Oh, the Thinks You Can Think!* The doctor prescribes methods for stretching the imagination, a la "Oh, the THINKS you can think up if only you try!"

• *The Lorax* An environmentally-conscious fable of high drama about the Oncle-ler and the damage he did to the Truffula Trees for the sake of his lousy Thneeds.

3. Another way to recapture innocence is to kick loose from your day-to-day modus operandi. Take a mental vacation, even if for only five minutes.

Sure you could hook yourself up to a biofeedback machine or go floating in a sensory-deprivation tank, but there are plenty of simpler, less expensive ways to kick loose, many of which are available at your local toy store.

Here are some of my favorite prescriptions for restoring the spirit and innocence of your once childlike mindset.

• **Get outside:** Take a hike, go for a bike ride, or take a flying leap into the nearest lake—feel the group hug of Mother Nature in the great outdoors.

• **Look closely:** Get out your digital camera and take 100 pictures of your backyard. Look at the grass, the fence, and the dog doo through new eyes.

• **Make music:** Get out your old trumpet, tuba, or fluegelhorn and reprise your high school fight song. At campfires, pull out a bandolier loaded with harmonicas, even if you can't play a lick. Take your tom-tom and beat it. Better yet, get some friends together and do your own version of a Stomp performance (for hints and inspiration, visit http://www.stomponline.com.)

• **Stretch yourself:** Buy a cookbook and force your-self to create dinner from scratch. Go to the local hobby store and buy a kit for making stained glass, painting, soap, candles, or whatever interests you.

As noted, most of these activities have some degree of risk, at least initially—there's a chance you'll feel a tad bit silly. Don't worry. It's just the Real World Adult in you rebelling.

Fight back. Seize control of your imagination. You can do it. After a while, you won't feel silly at all. You'll be on your way to the best of both worlds.

> "There is too much sadness to hold your mouth down. When I see people like that, they hold their lip just so, and I go up to them and just say, 'Boo!' People today are in a rut. They're afraid to think."
> – Hazel Louise Emerson Hall (my Grandmother)

To reconnect with innocence, ponder this essential Eureka! truth:

To thine own self, be the true you.

It's your call. It's your life, too. Totally and irrevocably.

MUSIC BONUS: The link below takes you to a Web page that with a song called **"The Problem with Grownups"** written and performed by Scott Johnson of Google Press. It captures in lyrics and music the essence of this chapter.

The Web page also has links to two Brain Brew radio segments that David and I did where we had middle school students answer the question: The problem with grown ups is...

Visit http://www.doughall.com/JSYB2

2

ADVENTUROUSNESS

Adventure drives the creative engine. Adventure awakens the imagination, fires the adrenalin, and ignites a willingness to try.

The spirit of adventure makes it possible for you to move forward, to take that leap of faith. Without it, life registers on an oscilloscope as a flat, horizontal line. Nothing adventured, nothing gained.

Adventures happen on many different, not necessarily grand, scales. You don't have to be Magellan, Freud, Einstein, or Lewis and Clark to blaze a trail. You might be an assistant manager negotiating a better idea through a maze of corporate bureaucracy, a soccer coach working to motivate 10-year-olds who have yet to win their first game, or a smitten young man trying to string together just the right words to ask the woman of his dreams to become his wife.

Entrepreneurs are the modern equivalent of the great adventurers of history. Entrepreneurs pledge their lives, their fortunes, and their sacred honor to create new products and services that make life better for some people in some meaningful way. They listen to the little voice inside them that says, "I can make a better product and find a better way to deliver that service in a smarter way," then they set forth to do it.

Personality Traits that Drive Creativity—Here's the Hard Data

As part of an ongoing Eureka! Ranch investigation into the invention process, we engage in lots of research. In one such effort, we pooled random groups of people and asked them to come up with new ideas for eyeglasses using a variety of Eureka! Stimulus methods.

Each group was given 45 minutes to complete the task. Afterwards they answered 100 questions designed to form profiles of their values, personalities, and attitudes. We then compared the quality and quantity of each person's creative output with his or her personal profile.

The overwhelming conclusion: **The power of creativity is tied most directly to an adventurous mindset.** The strongest correlation between quantity and quality of ideas turned out to be a person's sense of adventurousness. **Those tested who** thought of themselves as having a spirit of adventure aver-aged **72 percent more wicked good ideas in 45 minutes than those who saw themselves as more cautious.**

In other words, to leverage all the assets available to you in the process of jumpstarting your brain, **you have to embrace adventure.** And a tentative squeeze won't do it. I suggest a big-time bear hug.

An analysis of the profiles of those who saw themselves as being more adventurous found that they are much more likely to:

1. EXHIBIT HIGH LEVELS OF DISCONTENT WITH STATUS QUO

Adventurers ask themselves, "Is this all there is?" They see accomplishments as stepping stones, not resting places.

Their open-mindedness is tinged with pessimism, tem-pered with an edge of cynicism. Their discontent spurs innova-tion—and it is the individual, not the masses, who are respon-sible for innovation. Henry Ford gave us the mass-produced automobile. But it took Charles Kettering to invent the self-starter, thus making it possible for us to turn over our engines with an ignition key instead of a hand crank.

2. ACT SPONTANEOUSLY

Adventurers are willing and eager for new experiences, if for no other reason than the exhilaration of it. They have a lot in com-mon with the fool, whoever it was, who first climbed to the top of some craggy precipice, strapped bungee cords to his or her ankles, yelled "Geronimo!" and let it rip.

Those who have bungee-ed invariably tell me it was a huge rush. Still, the feeling that seized the heart of that first jumper when he or she went sailing into space that first time must have been monumental; everyone who jumped after that point was just following.

3. CALCULATE THE RISKS

Adventurers weigh the odds, contemplate obstacles and plan for contingencies. Adventurers are not daredevils.

Christopher Columbus had good reason to believe the planet was not flat when he set sail for the New World; he'd noticed that the masts of departing ships appeared to shorten as they approached the horizon, a phenomenon he took to mean that there was a curvature in the earth's plane.

4. HAVE LIBERAL ATTITUDES

I'm talking the literal definition, not the political one. Creative people embrace and encourage new views, fresh perspectives, and differences of all kinds.

The data indicates adventurers are significantly more forgiving, more adaptable, and more open to fresh ideas. They're comfortable in many different settings and able to function equally well under wildly extreme circumstances. Given the opportunity, a proper adventurer can get along with an aborigine on a desert island as easily as with a head of state at a rodeo.

Likewise, **adventurers don't require perfection.** They're absorbed with the process, as in what's happening at the moment. The sculptor Korczak Ziolkowski spent three and a half decades blasting away, ton by ton, on a granite mountain in the Black Hills of South Dakota, slowly shaping it into a colossal statue of the great Sioux chief Crazy Horse astride a mustang, his arm outstretched toward the horizon.

For sheer magnitude, Ziolkowski's project remains the most ambitious undertaking in the history of art. It's 641 feet long and 563 feet high. All four of the 60-foot high presidential heads of nearby Mt. Rushmore would fit easily under Crazy Horse's headdress.

At the time of Ziolkowski's death at the age of 74 in 1982, it was estimated the project would require another five to ten years of blasting before any actual carving could begin. As of this writing, the face of Crazy Horse has been finished and work now moves to the horse's head. For more details, visit http://www.crazyhorse.org.

Ziolkowski had a vision. He was not focused on the thought that, someday, he would actually behold the finished sculpture. He realized early in the project that he probably wouldn't live to see it completed. What drove him was the process, the knowledge that with each detonation, each ton of rubble, he was inching toward his destination.

5. POSSESS HIGH LEVELS OF SELF-ESTEEM

Adventurers are predisposed to saying "I can." Or to put it another way, "What, me worry?" They can't help it. Repeated failures fail to daunt true adventurers. They see setbacks as lessons and each lesson as another step forward.

Adventurers respect others' accomplishments, but aren't intimidated by them. They tend to think that, if they applied themselves with sufficient dedication, they could do the same thing. In fact, the accomplishments of others often inspire them to reach further. Paul McCartney was so impressed upon hearing Brian Wilson's landmark *Pet Sounds* album that he sat down and wrote most of the songs for the iconic *Sgt. Pepper's Lonely Hearts Club Band* album.

Even in the most regimented system, you can be a swashbuckler. I dedicated a decade of my life to Procter & Gamble, one of the most blue-blooded, buttoned-down corporations in the world. But I wore my colors proudly. I forsook ties and suits and declared a personal embargo on all nonproductive meetings and paperwork. My office was festooned with a six-foot Bugs Bunny, a humongous Kermit the Frog, two eight-foot cardboard palm trees, and several surfboards. I filled the air with Jimmy Buffett tunes, thought big thoughts, and made them real.

I hear you. You're saying, "Hey, that's fine for you. You're different."

So are you. You're different too. That's the point. Be yourself. Whoever you are.

As we grow up, we become progressively more cautious. We learn not to touch hot stoves and stick our tongues on monkey bars in winter, but we soon begin confusing hot stoves and frozen metal with potential adventures. We fall into deep, cavernous ruts.

We encourage children to reach out to new experiences. We arrange dance lessons, swimming classes, and soccer leagues for them. But we don't do as we preach. We're too quick to slap our own hands. As adults, we live predictable, restrictive lives.

ENOUGH! WAKE UP! DARE TO DARE! If you want to grow, force yourself out of your ruts.

If you want to Jump Start your imagination, you have to

feed it new stimuli, new people, new experiences. Choke off the stimuli, and you choke off your brain.

Take those first few tentative steps. Here are some suggestions for climbing out of ruts. But be careful—as simple as they are, they can lead to unsettling new levels of stimulation:

1. Be adventurous. Take a different route to work or school.
2. Be adventurous. Buy five magazines you've never read about subjects in which you know nothing about.
3. Be adventurous. Buy the No. 1 and number 10 paperbacks on the *New York Times* bestseller list and read them.
4. Be adventurous. Ask the seventh person you talk to at work to lunch.
5. Be adventurous. Write the numbers of the channels on your TV or cable system on little scraps of paper. Put the scraps in a hat. Pull out a scrap and turn to that channel. Set a timer for five minutes and watch. Pay attention. When the timer runs out, pull out another slip. Repeat until your eyes are bloodshot. Absorb each different world.
6. Be adventurous. Call the family member you have a grudge against—a really long-standing, hostile bout of bad blood—and say you're sorry and want to start over.
7. Be adventurous. Convince a Rolls Royce salesman that you're wealthy and take one for a test drive.

You'll surprise yourself. You'll discover you like things that you used to know you wouldn't. You'll tap into a whole new set of ideas, options, and perceptions. You'll be taking the critical first step to recapturing your lost spirit of adventure.

The key to becoming an adventurer is in learning to be at ease with two of the most central elements of life—CHAOS AND UNCERTAINTY.

Too many of us have decided we need a certain guarantee before we embark. Or we think we have to know the answer before we ask the question. So we never take the first step. Or the question never gets asked.

But no matter how many travel brochures you read, you won't know how it feels to stand with your feet planted

on the beaches of your destination until you get there. And you most assuredly will never get there until you take the first step. Granted, you'll be risking failure. At the same time, you'll be enhancing your odds from "impossible" to "possible." You'll also be running the risk of accomplishment.

HOLD IT RIGHT THERE!
You're not listening. You're nodding your head, but you're not internalizing. You know in your mind I'm right, but you don't know it in your heart, which is where all such knowledge has to be known before you'll act on it.

Put this book down right now and engage in some off-the-wall act of spontaneity—something that makes your toes tingle and the hairs on the back of your neck prickle. Something that makes your heart gallop and reminds you you're alive. Step outside yourself.

Can't Think of Anything?—Here's an Option

My informal survey indicates that virtually all adults at one time have tossed some tennis balls, apples, or rocks in the air and wondered what it would be like to juggle. However, few have actually learned how to make three objects dance in the air.

Myself I'm a big fan of juggling as a way to de-stress. Because it demands single-minded concentration, juggling is just the ticket for sweeping cobwebs from a tired brain. When you're juggling, you can't be thinking about anything else. If your mind wanders, you're liable to get beaned with a ball, ring, or club.

The purpose of learning to juggle here at this moment is to give you an adventure that feels a little scary but that in truth is not nearly as hard as it looks.

As a life member of the International Jugglers' Association, I'm sworn to pass the art along to as many non-jugglers as humanly possible. What follows is the method I used to teach it to thousands of folks of all ages while kicking around New England as a performer.

DOUG'S JUGGLING METHOD

(Read entire instructions before starting. If you're left-handed, I'm sorry, but you'll have to reverse these instructions.)

Step 1: Find three tennis balls. Better yet, get three bean bags. They don't roll as far. To minimize spinal stress from excessive bending over, practice over a bed. Or, to minimize runaway tennis balls, situate yourself in a sandbox, on a beach, or in the middle of the Sahara Desert.

Step 2: Hold one ball in your right hand with your arms bent at a 90-degree angle as if you're carrying a tray. Slide your right hand to the center of your body, right about where your bellybutton is. Open your hand and pop the ball up and across to your left, to a spot just above your left ear.

Step 3: Catch the ball in your left hand. Then slide your left hand to the center of your body and pop the ball up and across to your right, to a spot just above your right ear.

Step 4: Practice the slide, pop, and catch until you can do it without thinking. The ball should follow a sideways figure-eight trajectory. Pop the ball with your wrist up and across your body. Don't use your arm. Your elbows should not move. A common beginners' mistake is known in juggling circles as the "stiff-wristed roll-off." Instead of popping the ball across their body, they roll it off their fingertips causing it to go forward instead of across.

Step 5: Put a ball in each hand. With your right hand, slide and pop up and across. When the ball reaches its peak, slide and pop the ball in your left hand up, across and

under the ball in the air. Continue practicing: RIGHT - LEFT - STOP - RIGHT - LEFT - STOP. Now do it the other way: LEFT - RIGHT - STOP - LEFT - RIGHT - STOP. Remember this tempo. When you're juggling three balls, the rhythm is the same.

Step 6: Now it's time for partner juggling. Recruit an assistant, lovely or otherwise. Stand side-by-side. Put your adjacent, inside arms behind your backs or, if you and your assistant are on intimate terms, around each other.

- The person to the right puts two balls in his or her right hand and makes the first toss up and across to the left.
- As ball No. 1 reaches its peak, the person on the left tosses ball No. 2 up, across, and back to the right.
- As ball No. 2 ball reaches its peak, the person on the right tosses ball No. 3 across and back to the left … etc., etc., etc.
- Continue popping back and forth until you establish a rhythm.

Step 7: Juggle solo. Put two balls in your right hand and one in your left. Remember to pop each ball up, across, and underneath the ball that preceded it. Always use your wrists.

Relax. Don't watch one ball at a time. Concentrate on the three moving parts as a whole. Picture yourself as the nucleus of an atom, the balls orbiting around you like electrons. Don't rush—gravity controls the speed of the balls. Get a feeling for the speed of gravity. Once you understand the tempo, you'll have it made.

If you have problems with tossing balls forward instead of up and across, practice in front of a wall. The balls will hit the wall, then they'll hit you. After you've been clunked in the noggin a few dozen times, you'll learn to pop up and across.

The International Jugglers Association is a wicked good organization. To learn more visit http://www.juggle.org.

NOT INTO JUGGLING?—HERE'S A GROUP ADVENTURE TO TRY

Pick up the phone and call the couple you always get together with on Friday night. Invite them to a Friday Night Eureka!

Adventure. Tell them to expect a surprise. Do the Eureka! adventure as part of a group—there's safety in numbers. Doing a Eureka! adventure night with friends also makes it more fun.

Do the following:
• Have appetizers at the fifth restaurant listed in the yellow pages.
• Have your entree at the thirteenth restaurant listed in the yellow pages
• Have dessert at the twenty-third restaurant listed in the yellow pages.

If this is all a tad too random and free-spirited for you, then have each person in your party write the name of a restaurant that they want to try, but have never visited, on a slip of paper and put the slips in a hat. Pull them out and have drinks, appetizers, entrees, and desserts at the restaurants in the order they are pulled from the hat.

If time allows, go to the movie with the greatest number of letters in the title. In the event of a tie, flip a coin.

NOTE: A friend in New York City did this and e-mailed me that they also found some great new restaurants as a result. Sounds like they have a real appetite for adventure.

My wife, Debbie, once suggested we go to the movie with the greatest number of letters in the title—we ended up at *The Making Of An American Quilt*, a tear-jerking chick flick. I was the only guy at the show; I think it was a set up. However, the experience did inspire some fresh marketing ideas for a telephone company client a month later. You never know where adventures will lead or pay off.

WE INTERRUPT THIS BOOK UNTIL AFTER YOUR ADVENTURE. PLEASE PUT THE BOOK DOWN AND ENGAGE YOURSELF IN A SPONTANEOUS ADVENTURE. NO, REALLY. PLEASE.

E-mail your stories, digital photos, or videos of your adventure to DougHall@DougHall.com. I'll respond to every e-mail and post the most inspirational ones at http://www.EurekaRanch.com.

Imagine how it would feel to live out an adventure every day, all day long. Imagine being able to transform the obstacles that life dishes out into opportunities. Imagine taking control of your circumstances, rather than allowing your circumstances to control you.

Adventure is about thinking big and taking action on the thoughts. It's about having the courage to be bold and brave.

Adventure is not something you simply imagine—it's how you must live.

Good for you, traveler. You're on your way!

MUSIC BONUS: The link below takes you to a web page that with a song called **"Let Your Dreams Come True"** written and performed by Scott Johnson of Google Press. It captures in lyrics and music the essence of this chapter.

The web page also has a link to a *Brain Brew* segment where David and I did helped a caller quit her job and pursue her dream.

Visit http://www.doughall.com/JSYB2

WE HOLD THESE TRUTHS TO BE SELF-EVIDENT

The Eureka! Way of Life requires that you be EXCITED, AWARE, PASSIONATE, and ENTHUSIASTIC. It requires that you not be BRAIN DEAD!

Being brain dead is being dull and terminally serious. If you want to experience brain death, ask an insurance salesman to explain the difference between term and whole life insurance. Or make an appointment at a funeral parlor to discuss advance payment programs.

> "It's your brain. Use it or lose it."
> – Richard Saunders

Under the Eureka! Way of Life, it's advisable to avoid exposure to the brain dead. Here are 10 dead giveaways for identifying brain-dead individuals:

1. They don't observe the holidays of April 1 and Oct. 31.
2. Their fingers point in only one direction—away from themselves.
3. Their doors are closed, their shades are drawn, and they cast no reflections.
4. The family pictures on their desks are studio portraits, not snapshots.
5. They think Dr. Seuss is a pediatrician.
6. They're rude to waitresses and waiters.
7. They wish children would "just grow up."
8. They once had an original thought, but decided it was gas.
9. They have chapped lips from kissing the boss' butt.
10. They get wicked mad when you tickle them.

The brain-dead are everywhere. I once encountered one at an outdoor summer concert of the Cincinnati Pops Orchestra. It so happened I had a half dozen bottles of soap bubbles on my person. A handful of 10-year-olds nearby looked bored, so I gave each a bottle.

It was an enchanted evening. As the fireflies flickered and the orchestra played an arrangement of Tchaikovsky's Symphony No. 5 in E Minor Opus 64, those of us who were so equipped blew bubbles.

Then we noticed Brain Dead Man, sitting cross-legged on his blanket. As our bubbles floated by, he scowled and swatted at them.

My jaw fell open. The kids shrugged and took their bubbles elsewhere.

Those who embrace the Eureka! Way of Life are not big on rules. For the most part, we regard a rule as an item to break, bend, circumvent, spindle, fold, mutilate, vault over, limbo under, or otherwise grind into a fine powder.

But there are exceptions. And while the notions of innocence and a spirit of adventure are overall life goals, a number of more tactical precepts—call them rules if you must—are available to help you enhance your creativity.

So whereby we, the people, seek to recapture the hope, faith and innocence of childhood, and whereby we strive diligently for purity of thought and freshness of idea, we hereby hold the following truths to be self-evident—the first being:

Respect the Newborn!

Ideas, when they first occur, aren't full-blown finished products. They aren't born one second then standing up and walking the next. **Thomas Edison didn't conceive of the light bulb on Monday morning then flip the switch that afternoon.**

Newborn ideas are fragile, like babies. Most newborn ideas are ugly, wrinkly little wretches. If the newborn is your own, you're predisposed to think it's a thing of wonder and beauty. But it's going to need a whole lot of nurturing before anyone else will think so because it's not his or hers. They need nurturing, protecting, patience, loving, commitment. They require you to sit up with them at night, fret over their futures, watch them grow. And like babies, they can't be hurried. They grow and develop in time.

The "virtual no" kills 100 times more ideas than brain dead bosses ever will.

By virtual no I mean the internal sensor that judges, "It's not reasonable, it's not practical, the boss won't like it, it's not even possible."

With my clients it's common for project team members to say that management has rejected specific ideas. However, when I ask their management why it rejected the specific idea, I get a blank stare. What has happened is the project team has killed the idea through the "virtual no"—they've anticipated that the idea would be killed and thus never presented it to management.

Adults are so accustomed to censoring themselves that censoring a newborn idea is almost an involuntary action. In time the difference between a genuine and a virtual no becomes blurred.

Admittedly, like babies, newborn ideas are often ugly. They may appear to be wretched little mutants that ought to be hidden away.

Don't hide them.

Newborn ideas seldom arrive as completed entities. How many gawky Little Leaguers have grown up to hit home runs in

All-Star games? How many former finger painters have created works that hang in the world's great art museums?

> "You'll increase your creative potential once you begin to value your own thoughts."
> – Richard Saunders

Give Newborn Ideas a Safe Place to Grow

"I thought of that" doesn't count. It takes courage to bring a real new-to-the-world idea out into the light of day because you're going where no one else has been.

I can't tell you how many times I've heard this marketing expert or that claim that, at one time or another, they'd conceived of the very same idea that happened to be on the table at the moment.

I would ask them what happened to the idea. "Aaaahhhh," they'd say. They'd decided to put the brakes on it. They didn't trust it. It was too different, too impractical, too something. They filled in the adjectives of their choice.

But all they'd had was the illusion of an idea. A figment.

Ideas only become real when you invest your energy into making them happen.

Don't make the same mistake. Give your newborns a safe place where they can be protected from the whims of ruthless Real World Adults. If you, your team, your company or your family is too ready to kill a newborn idea, try this:

When an idea sprouts in your mind, write it down on a scrap of paper. Then put it in a newborn incubator. This can be a folder, a shoebox, or an empty mayonnaise jar—any quiet safe place where your idea can have a chance to grow straight and true. Add other newborns as they occur to you.

At the same time, tuck your ideas away for refinement in the soft, warm folds of your subconscious. Then, after a few days or maybe even a few weeks, go back to your newborn incubator and sort through the occupants.

Every idea that travels through your cranium has some merit, even those of a seemingly hopelessly hair-brained nature. But it often takes time to discern their value. If you give them room to incubate, you'll be amazed at their potential.

Which leads me to the next self-evident truth:

Breakthroughs Contradict History!

Great ideas shake things up. They deny precedent and redefine the world. An idea has to break rules to be wicked good. If it doesn't, chances are it's been done before.

When an idea is not new and different, it's just another face in the crowd. When a number of companies sell the same product or service, they're dealing in a commodity market. Commodities sell for commodity prices; that is, they don't sell for much. New and different ideas are where the money is.

The same principle applies when you are the product. When I was fresh from the University of Maine interviewing for jobs, I sought to stand out from the crowd. Where my classmates carried textbook-perfect one-page resumes, I presented a scrapbook of my business ventures and copies of press clippings. I performed a magic trick I called Merwyn's Magic Bunnies and gave the interviewer a set of sponge bunnies for his very own. Despite a C-plus academic record, I landed as many job offers as my blue chip classmates.

"Inventing is the great theatrical art of 'what if.'"
– Richard Saunders

A good example of a product that contradicts history is the classic board game Trivial Pursuit. Back in the day when it first surfaced, back in 1983, it broke a lot of rules and cut deeply against the conventional wisdom.

- It was a board game for adults, and "everyone knew" adults didn't buy board games.
- It sold for $25, and "everyone knew" board games had to sell for less than $10 to succeed.
- It was a trivia game, and "everyone knew" that trivia games didn't sell.

As it happened, one board game buyer, Bill Hill, vice president of research and development at Selchow and Righter, saw some magic in the game.

"I played it and found it fun," he told me. "It was a trivia game but you didn't need a huge amount of knowledge to play it. The packaging, the game play, the entire concept was fresh and original for the time."

> "In today's sailing races, they have all these rules that restrict you. They tell you how to set every one of your ropes. I think I should be able to do whatever I can to win, no matter how dumb it may seem to those young folks, as long as I don't have an engine or a larger boat or sail."
> – William H. Holder (my great grandfather)

It's human nature to discourage the new and the different. **Human nature weighs heavily toward history while neglecting to take into account history's lesson—namely, that breakthroughs—those things that contradict history—are what change the world.** I'm all for respecting history, but I also believe in creating it.

And with that, we've arrived at the next self-evident Eureka! Truth.

Reality Is Not Relevant!

When creating ideas, you're best served when you ignore reality—at least during the invention process. You'll have time enough for reality later. It has a way of imposing its values in self-fulfilling ways.

Reality is relative. Current reality rejects new ideas in favor of conventional wisdom. With original thinking, it's possible to define new realities, change entire systems, and create a new balance of constraints and opportunities.

> "Of course it's impossible. That's why you should do it, and that's why you'll make money."
> – Richard Saunders

What's relevant is perception. What counts is what people think it is, not what it in fact is. Perception is the only reality customers will spend their money on. It's the only reality that will compel them to break their existing routine and switch to your business or contribute money to your charity.

If you want to Jump Start your thinking, forget about truth, reality, and fact. Enter instead into the world of perception, feeling, and gut instinct.

The legend of Ben, the new Procter & Gamble brand manager, illustrates the power of perception.

Ben was getting ready to attend his first annual budget meeting. It didn't take much for these meetings to degenerate into public floggings as senior management types challenged brand managers to justify marketing budget requests for the upcoming year. It was sport for senior managers. Great fun.

Ben hatched a plan. Just before leaving for the meeting, a formal affair where jackets were required, he asked his assistant for 2,000 sheets of paper. He divided them into stacks of 20 to 30 sheets each, piled each stack crosswise, one atop the other. On top of this formidable stack, he placed a real business fact sheet. All the other sheets were blank.

Ben entered the meeting room with the biggest stack of paper in the history of budget meetings. The meeting went smoothly for Ben. He was not challenged once, in fact. While no one can say for sure, it's widely suspected that his paper tower created among management types the perception that he had the answer to any question they might ask.

Fresh college graduates can have a hard time adjusting to the perception rule. They're used to dealing with numeric test scores and specific letter grades. The Real World is filled with abstraction and built on shifting sands, with an entirely different set of priorities and measurements.

In the Real World, a fresh college grad cries foul if he or she is passed over for a promotion or a raise he or she thinks is deserved simply because he or she has fulfilled the requirements of his or her position. Their problem is that they don't know how to keep score in the Real World. They're under the impression that it's enough to do their job properly.

Truth is it's more important the boss *thinks* they're doing a good job. This is not a veiled endorsement for brown-nosing. Not at all. Brown-nosing, butt-kissing, or politic playing is best left to those who don't have the brainpower to accomplish something of substance.

> "It's not boasting when you deliver."
> – Richard Saunders

Perception is about marketing yourself. It's about selling your substance, skills, and abilities. Muhammad Ali was arguably the greatest sports promoter of all time. His mouth generated worldwide attention. But the bottom line was that he delivered on his boasts in the ring. You either loved him or you hated him. But in his prime, no one doubted his ability as a boxer.

In the Real World, one must always remember to deal with how one is perceived. Are you seen as industrious, committed, and passionate about your work? Do you show up early every day? Are your reports on time? Do you anticipate problems or react to them?

> "Life, like love, is not logical. Life is a three-dimensional sensory perception."
> – Richard Saunders

Franklin addresses the importance of perception in his

autobiography. When he was starting out in the newspaper business, he occasionally had to borrow money. To that end, he'd make a great show of hauling the metal type from his press back and forth from his home to his print shop in a rickety wheelbarrow, passing by the tavern, where he knew the bankers would be drinking and discussing the issues of the day.

The clanking, clattering wheelbarrow drew the bankers' attention night after night. Before long, they formed an impression. That young Franklin, they'd say, certainly is an industrious type. A real go-getter.

In fact, he was. But the bankers wouldn't have discovered it for themselves as quickly as they did had he not set the stage by creating the proper impression.

With that, we have arrived at the fifth Self-Evident Eureka! Truth, namely:

YOU HAVE TO SWING TO HIT HOME RUNS!

Remember Reggie Jackson, the baseball player? Man, that guy could hit home runs! He knocked 563 balls into the seats during his 21-year major league career, good for 11th place on the all-time home run hitter list.

Reggie Jackson is No. 1 on another all-time list: he struck out more times than anybody—2,597 times in all.

Indeed, the top 10 home run hitters in big league history took 54 swings for every homer they hit. But swinging involves more than just making the effort. It also involves risking and accepting failure. On average, the top home run hitters of all time made eleven outs for every home run they hit.

How would you deal with 11 failures for every success in your life? Would you keep swinging for the fence, or would you start declining your at-bats?

> "Being alive is about playing to win. Being brain dead is when you play not to lose."
> – Richard Saunders

In that sense, ideas are like home runs. It takes a lot of whiffs to knock one out of the park.

The June 28, 1993, issue of *Newsweek* reported these findings by Dean Keith Simonton of the University of California, Davis:

> "In a study of 2,036 scientists throughout history, Simonton found that the most respected produced not only more great works, but also more 'bad' ones. They produced. Period."

The same article spoke to the importance of trying:

> "The creative geniuses of art and science work obsessively. They do not lounge under apple trees waiting for fruit to fall or lightning to strike. 'When inspiration does not come to me,' Freud once said, 'I go halfway to meet it.' Bach wrote a cantata every week, even when he was sick or exhausted."

How hard you try is rooted to how often you try. I'm always hearing from this person or that who is looking for a job or has an idea to sell. The first question I ask is, how many doors have been slammed in their faces? If they haven't already succeeded, a dozen doors aren't nearly enough. Not if they believe in themselves or their ideas.

> "It's to be expected that you make mistakes when you're breaking new ground."
> – Jerry Greenfield, Co-founder Ben & Jerry's Ice Cream, *Rolling Stone*, July 9, 1992

> "Every shot you don't take is a guaranteed miss."
> – Richard Saunders

There's no way around it. You have to keep trying until you're convinced you're all tried out. And then you have to try some more. Because one more try is often all it takes. Look at it this way:

STANDARD	No. of Failures Before Giving Up
If you're as good as the top home run hitters	54
If you're half as good as the top home run hitters	108
If you're 10 percent as good as the top home run hitters	540

It's the same story with ideas—**the more ideas you generate, the more good ones you'll have. And your good ideas will be of a higher caliber. Quantity is the shortest possible distance to quality. And more quantity is a straight line to higher quality.**

This was the finding of a series of experiments conducted in the fairly sanitary confines of the Eureka! Ranch laboratories. We assembled groups of ordinary people and asked them to invent ideas for new products. Each group's ideas were typed and tabulated.

An independent panel then reviewed the ideas, rating each for how "wicked good" it was. Stat man Mike Kosinski advised me that he could say with 96 percent statistical confidence that the quantity of ideas is directly related to quality. Mike modeled the data and found the following relationship between quantity and quality.

No. of Raw Ideas	No. of Wicked Good Ideas
25	5
50	10
100	19

MORE CHOICES MEAN SMARTER DECISIONS

Research with owners of small and mid-sized companies found that those companies with more choices for growth in their development pipeline grew 1.5 to 5.8 times faster than those with fewer choices. Net: in the real world it appears that the more choices you have the smarter the decisions you make. This is why I **challenge clients to come up with at least 50 written choices for growth before making decisions on what action to take.**

Summary

So there you have our self-evident Eureka! Truths, in no particular order. One more time, in short form, the list looks like this:

- You Have to Swing to Hit Home Runs (go for quantity)
- Reality Is Not Relevant (think of perceptions, feelings, tastes, sights, sounds, smells)
- Breakthroughs Contradict History (forget conventional wisdom)
- Respect the Newborns (write down every idea, no matter how loony it might seem)

What's Missing?

In the first edition of this book there was a fifth truth: FUN IS FUNDAMENTAL. It pains me to remove it from this edition. However, no matter how hard I've tried, I've found no correlation between increasing levels of fun and the creation of more genuinely "big ideas" for growing a career or business.

There's plenty of evidence that fun matters in "theoretical academic research." However, when faced with real-life challenges, laughing is not a lubricant for productive creativity.

While fun doesn't help with the creative process. Fun does help with the development journey. To contradict history—and change the world—requires energy to overcome the inevitable challenges that you'll face during your adventure. Speaking from nearly 40 years of entrepreneurship experience I'll tell you nothing builds energy like a sense of humor. And nothing kills energy like taking yourself too seriously.

So chill out, kick back, and enjoy the journey.

MUSIC BONUS: Life is meant to be lived and enjoyed. To punctuate the point I've included a link to another Scott Johnson tune **"Lighten Up There Boy"**—it's a tune that will help you chill out and set your mind straight. Before moving on click on it and give it a listen.

Visit http://www.doughall.com/JSYB2

IDEAS—THE GOOD, THE BAD, AND THE UGLY

You've got your good ideas, your bad ideas and your mud ugly ideas. The question is, how do you tell them apart? How do you pick the nuggets from the gravel?

Let's be honest. Most newborn ideas are ugly, wrinkly little wretches. If the newborn is your own, you're liable to think it's a thing of wonder and beauty. But it's going to need a whole lotta nurturing before anyone else will think so. Because it's not theirs.

As you go through life, you will decide the fates of thousands of newborn ideas. You'll need to know which ideas are worth nurturing and which, frankly, aren't. Most challenging is tapping those ideas that are really great, or "wicked good" as we say in Maine.

> "Life is a bowl of cherries. It's full of pits. Whether you control your life or it controls you depends in large measure on your ability to spit out the pits."
> – Richard Saunders

FACT: Picking winners and losers becomes increasingly difficult the more unusual an idea is. **The further removed an idea is from the confines of precedent, the more likely it is either to light up the sky or explode in a blaze of failure.**

Greg, a successful inventor, wrote to me regarding his experiences with trying to separate the good from the bad and ugly of ideas.

> "To date, I have had 10 of my inventions go worldwide, several national and many just fail completely because of timing, because of markets or because they were just bad ideas and I was blinded by my convictions. Over the years, I have made millions of dollars ... and lost as much."

To those who wonder why Greg didn't just keep the millions and never risk again, he goes on to explain.

> "To me, money is just a tool to allow me to work on another invention. That's my motivator, not money."

Here's the data on good vs. bad. Each point on the chart represents customers' perceptions of how interested they would be in purchasing a new product or service concept and how new and different they perceive the idea to be.

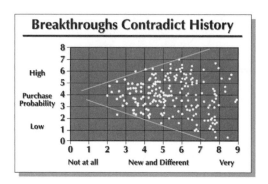

You can see that, with ideas that are seen as being really and truly new and different, they generate significantly greater and significantly lower purchase interest.

On the flip side, as an idea is less new and different, it moves more toward the essence of average. It becomes safe. Safe is fine for the brain dead; safe means they can't screw up. It also means they can't be great.

No Guts, No Glory!

Check out that chart again. It shows that when your idea is the same old same old, you have no chance. That's **NO CHANCE** of being great!

This is true for new product concepts. It's true for your career. And it's true for your life.

Minor differences have minor impact. Dramatic differences have the potential to be **GREAT, WORLD CLASS, *SPECTACULAR!!!***

The geniuses of creativity know this relationship.

Stephen Spielberg and George Lucas created two of the biggest box office hits of all time—*Star Wars* and *Raiders of the Lost Ark*. Both rated high on the scale of new and different. Both took risks.

Spielberg and Lucas also created *1941* and *Howard the Duck,* two of the most legendary stinkeroos of all time. Again, both movies were new and different. Twenty years hence, *Star Wars* and *Raiders of the Lost Ark* will be remembered. The other two will have been long forgotten.

NEW AND DIFFERENT GOOD VS. NEW AND DIFFERENT BAD

At the Eureka! Ranch, our focus is on the new and novel. As a result, we have a bi-polar research history. With most of our corporate clients, we've set records for both the best concept scores in their corporate histories and the worst.

You might suppose it would be easy to distinguish good from bad. The fact is, when you leave the world of the "known" and fully understood, it's quite difficult.

Even now, I chase lots of wild geese. Let me tell you about two of my most embarrassing failures.

The first is Stinky the Pig. I believed in Stinky. I could have sworn Stinky was destined to become the Barbie of kiddie games. Stinky was a plastic pig that "swallowed" numerous foul items. Using a pair of electronic tweezers, players removed plastic rotten eggs, sweat socks and overripe bananas from Stinky's innards before the timer ran out.

"But beware," so said the hype that accompanied Stinky. "If you're not careful, Stinky will let go a terrific 'bart.'"

A "bart" was the powerful aroma that would emerge from Stinky's backside. It's what made Stinky new and different. Inside every Stinky was a can of aerosol methane that would be triggered when the timer ran out or a player touched Stinky's sides when removing items from his digestive system. I spent thousands of dollars building models of Stinky and formulating various "bart" bouquets.

Your Mission, is to help "De-Stink" STINKY *the Pig*™

Stinky looked like this 👉

But as an idea, Stinky stunk. I pitched Stinky to one

toy company after another. No one would touch him. Indeed, Stinky and I were shown the door at Parker Brothers within seconds after the initial test blast from my prototype's porcine hindquarters.

Toy companies were concerned parents might be reluctant to embrace Stinky and bring him into their homes. The toy companies had a point. Parents often will look the other way at a toy that's gross or of questionable taste, but they draw the line at toys that smell up the house.

In an effort to soften the parental barrier, I tried a rosebud aroma. My hope was that parents would see Stinky as a new form of air freshener and that nine-year-old boys would consider a perfume smell equally distasteful and, ergo, appealing. My hope was dashed. In a research study, parents' ratings improved, but kids ratings took a sudden steep dive.

I still believe in Stinky. I do. But Stinky will never earn his keep. Still, I keep thinking of ways he might become a reality. That's how it is sometimes with newborn ideas. Your love blinds you to the realities of their market potential.

Then there was the time I aspired to revolutionize the hot dog business with an item I called the Sea Dog.

My premise was simple—consumers believe hot dogs are bad for them. They think fish is good for them. So they should love a fish tube steak. What a concept!

The ad copy put it this way: "New Sea Dogs are the ultimate in healthy hotdog-shaped products. They're made from fresh fish blended with low-fat tartar sauce for an absolutely delicious, absolutely different, absolutely healthy hot-dog-shaped taste sensation."

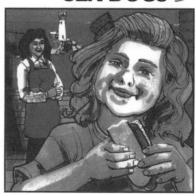

New and different, all the way. Sea Dogs contained no rat hairs or beef lips. But while the idea may have been good for a grin, it was bad on a bun. My dogs were revolting to consumers; the idea of a hot dog skin stuffed with fish held little public appeal.

The lesson I learned here was less costly than the one I learned from Stinky. This time, consumers tested the concept. And while Sea Dogs were being tested on the client's behalf, 24 other ideas were also being run past consumers. Of those, five ideas were identified as having serious market potential. The Sea Dog wasn't one of them.

WHAT SEPARATES NEW AND DIFFERENT GOOD FROM NEW AND DIFFERENT BAD?

So what went wrong with Stinky the Pig? What made the Sea Dog dead meat? Didn't both qualify as new and different? Didn't they satisfy the Eureka! rule calling for great ideas to contradict history?

Indeed, they did. Both ideas stretched boundaries of one sort or another. But the factors that made them stand out weren't meaningful to consumers. A wicked good idea needs to be *meaningfully* new and different!

"Hear reason, or she'll make you feel her."
– Ben Franklin

But how can you tell the difference? I continue to this day to search for an easy way. The best answer I have so far is the Merwyn Research system (named in honor of my dad—Merwyn Bradford Hall).

Merwyn is an idea-evaluation system created by the Eureka! Ranch team that evaluates how obvious and self-evident your idea is to potential customers. It accomplishes this by benchmarking the idea against some 50 success factors that were identified from an analysis of 4,000 ideas. The success factors were identified by reverse engineering what separated ideas that were successful in the marketplace from those that weren't.

Merwyn is a tough, disciplined tool. It doesn't take into account assumptions, implied understandings, or previous experiences in its assessment of the idea you're trying to sell.

The 50 success factors cluster into three overall "laws" that I've branded as the Three Laws of Marketing Physics. These are the three most important factors when evaluating the potential for success of your new idea.

Law No. 1: OVERT Benefit

Or as customers might put it, "What's in it for me?"

A benefit is what you promise that customers will receive, experience and enjoy in exchange for their commitment to your proposal, product or service. The customer in this case can be your boss when asking for a raise. It can be the father of your sweetheart you're seeking to marry.

Law No. 2: REAL Reason to Believe

Or as customers might put it, "Why should I believe you?"

What evidence is there to convince customers that the overt benefit you're promising will actually be delivered?

Law No. 3: DRAMATIC Difference

Or as customers might put it, "Why should I care?"

Is the combination of benefit and reason to believe something the customer cannot realize in any other way?

Each of these laws has a huge impact on success. Research indicates that all other factors being equal:

- **Having a clear Overt Benefit triples your odds of success.**
- **Having a real Reason to Believe doubles your odds of success.**
- **Having a Dramatic Difference triples your odds of success.**

Note: For an in-depth discussion of theses three laws—how to identify them, how to articulate them, and how to create them—read *Jump Start Your Business Brain.*

MERWYN IS TOUGH—VERY TOUGH—BECAUSE IT'S A TOUGH WORLD.

Because most ideas fail in the real world, most ideas fail in Merwyn as well.

Your life passes before your eyes as you wait for the scores of your precious newborns to arrive in your e-mail in box. It hurts to see many of your babies bite the dust. But that's how fragile newborns are. They can be eliminated with the press of a button. Still, it's a form of mercy killing. And it beats spending thousands, even millions of dollars preparing your product for test marketing, shooting advertising, designing packaging.

Merwyn itself is a wicked good idea. Tracking studies show it has one of the most accurate prediction records of any market research system ever tested. It's been shown to have an 88 percent accuracy predicting probability of success in the marketplace. It's been validated in the United States, Canada, and United Kingdom. It's been validated for written concepts, television commercials, radio commercials, direct mail advertisements, and e-mail campaigns.

Merwyn has increased our Eureka! Ranch success ratio considerably. But how do you evaluate ideas if you don't have Merwyn? And what if you have an idea that's not necessarily something to sell? The simple concept to keep in mind is WOW!

Wicked GREAT Ideas Make You Say WOW!

As a natural consequence of creating and testing thousands of ideas a year, I'm always learning about ideas—good, bad, and otherwise. The process, I hope, will continue as long as I live.

In my experience, I find that the most wicked, pure gold great, ideas satisfy a one-word criterion. They make you shout ...

Wicked good ideas make you catch your breath. A wicked good idea generates uncontrollable buzz, down the hall, around the corner, in the elevator, and throughout the building. The minute you tell it to someone, they shout *WOW!* And they tell it to someone else, who shouts *WOW!* It generates interest in the news media and the lunchroom. This doesn't do much for corporate security, but it's exciting.

There is no ONE way to WOW! In any given area of products, any given line, the number of WOW! opportunities is limitless.

You get WOW! when you bring together all elements of an idea to create a synergistic impact. It's like selecting individual notes to make a chord. The harmony is richer, more beautiful than any of the single notes alone. The harmony makes you gasp. It stirs you emotionally and rationally.

Ideas that generate a WOW! use beauty, simplicity, and elegance to appeal to the emotions.

Ideas that generate a WOW! offer logical, tangible superiority.

Just as the 12 notes of the chromatic scale can be arranged into an infinite number of melodies or the 26 letters of the alphabet can be combined to form an infinite number of books, so is there no limit to the WOWS! that can be extracted from any creative problem you may face.

The key is to stake your claim—define your area of excellence, then muster all your efforts into delivering that singular point of excellence.

WOW! ideas are the best at whatever it is they are. They identify a particular area of expertise and establish their entry as the ultimate in its class.

I SPELL WOW! LIKE THIS:
> Wicked easy to understand
> Original
> Whole Solution
> ! Be magic

WICKED EASY TO UNDERSTAND

Before we go anywhere with evaluating the idea—we need to understand what the idea is. Here are the facts…

> **FACT:** Eureka! Research on 4,000 innovations
> finds that ideas that are easy to understand are
> 70 percent more likely to survive and thrive in
> the marketplace.

> **FACT:** Eureka! Research on 4,000 innovations
> finds that ideas written at a fifth grade level, so
> that someone of about age 10 can understand it,
> have significantly higher odds of success.

"Wicked easy to understand" means that at first glance, you get it. If it takes more than 10 seconds to grasp or 10 words to explain an idea, it's probably not wicked good.

It doesn't matter if your challenge is a high-tech computer, a hydrocarbon chemical, a sugar-water soda pop or sliced bread. Complicated ideas never work. Complicated ideas are a sign of hazy thinking.

Nothing delivers the kiss of death more quickly than an idea that is unclear, complex or obtuse. If your customer or your boss or your banker doesn't understand, you lose. You are the only one who will give your idea the benefit of the doubt.

People need to get your ideas immediately, if not sooner. Unless you live in a bubble, any idea you want to develop has to be communicated to others.

The success of your idea will lean heavily on your ability to involve others in your mission. They can't wax enthusiastic about your vision if they don't know what it is. Martin Luther King Jr.'s vision, as he articulated it on August 28, 1963, was easy to understand.

> "I say to you today, my friends, so even though
> we face the difficulties of today and tomorrow, I
> still have a dream. It is a dream deeply rooted in
> the American dream.

> I have a dream that one day this nation will rise
> up and live out the true meaning of its creed:
> 'We hold these truths to be self-evident: that all
> men are created equal.'

I have a dream that one day on the red hills of Georgia, the sons of former slaves and the sons of former slave owners will be able to sit down together at the table of brotherhood.

I have a dream that one day even the state of Mississippi, a state sweltering with the heat of injustice, sweltering with the heat of oppression, will be transformed into an oasis of freedom and justice.

I have a dream that my four little children will one day live in a nation where they will not be judged by the color of their skin but by the content of their character.

I have a dream today.

I have a dream that one day, down in Alabama, with its vicious racists, with its governor having his lips dripping with the words of interposition and nullification; one day right there in Alabama, little black boys and black girls will be able to join hands with little white boys and white girls as sisters and brothers.

I have a dream today."

John F. Kennedy's vision on May 25, 1961, was likewise easy to understand:

I believe that this nation should commit itself to achieving the goal, before this decade is out, of landing a man on the Moon and returning him safely to the Earth.

Your idea needs to be self-evident. In the hyper-cluttered Information Age, there is no other kind. Self-evident products make you want to pick them up when you see the name and the front of the package. No additional communication is required.

Simplicity engenders impulse purchases. Complexity generates contemplation. You lose when your consumer has to contemplate your idea. In the process of all that contemplating, they begin to look at other options.

> "Simplicity is the essence of brilliance."
> – Richard Saunders

How to Know If Your Idea Is Wicked Easy to Understand

Write it down and read what you wrote, speaking the words out loud.

There is something about hearing your idea with your own ear that sparks fresh clarity. What seems easy to understand in your head may well be confusing when committed to paper.

Then e-mail your words to three friends. Ask each to write down any questions they might have about your idea. Process the feedback, make the changes, and send it out to three more friends.

As you clarify the idea, be very conscious about your changes. Sometimes as you bring clarity to an idea, you suddenly realize your idea is not worth any further effort. That's OK. Better to know sooner than later, after investing significant time and money on a mirage.

ORIGINALITY

Ideas must be original to be wicked good. Same old, same old doesn't cut it. You have to offer something that's original, new, and different to get consumers to change their buying patterns.

Wicked good ideas offer benefits that have yet to be experienced and appreciated. They chart new courses and explore new ground. Original ideas generate their own excitement and awareness. Everyone knows Neil Armstrong was the first man on the moon. But can you name two other Apollo astronauts who followed him? I doubt it, unless you're related to one.

Being the first, the original, sets you apart. Being the first is newsworthy. It makes people stop and take notice. It's the pioneers who reap the benefits of fame, publicity, and profits.

FACT: According to Eureka! Research on more than 4,000 innovations ideas with a dramatic difference are three times more likely to survive in the marketplace.

FACT: Research reported in the *Harvard Business Review* found that "extremely unique" products have a three times greater chance of profitable success.

"You double your odds of success when you stick out your neck and do something different."
– Richard Saunders

Look closely at your idea. Is it truly different? Originality leads. The same old stuff follows. It takes courage to lead. Franklin, Jefferson, Washington and Adams had it. The folks who stayed in England didn't. It's always much easier to stay in England. All you have to do is sit there.

How to Know If Your Idea Is a Grade-A Original!

Complete one or more of the following claims—adding appropriate qualifiers as necessary to make it a claim that is true and honest.

For the first time ...
The one and only ...
The first ...

Look at your claim. Is it exciting? Is it motivating? Is the idea something that breaks free from the same old, same old?

WHOLE SOLUTION

A wicked good idea is complete. It sweats the details. If it's a new product, it has a balance of marketing, packaging, and advertising that leaves you tingling with anticipation. And once you experience the product, it actually surpasses your expectations.

FACT: Ideas that have synergy between benefit promise and credibility are 74 percent more likely to survive and thrive in the marketplace according to research on 4,000 innovations.

Whole ideas fulfill all three of the Laws of Marketing Physics. They answer the three questions before a customer asks:

• What's in it for me? (Overt Benefit)
• Why should I believe you? (Real Reason to Believe)
• Why should I care? (Dramatic Difference)

Not much is worse than getting all worked up over a new product, service, restaurant, amusement park ride, or blind date only to have it fall short of expectations. You feel conned, like you might if you were to discover that you'd purchased swampland in Florida.

For what it's worth, your feelings of disappointment don't come close to the emotional upheaval of the folks who create these ideas. It pains me whenever I see certain products or services I helped create that, for whatever reason, lack completeness. Sometimes, we invent the product concept and leave the marketing to others. It's especially frustrating when the marketing falls short in telling the story of what makes a product or service worth having. Conversely, when we do the marketing and not the product, it's just as disappointing when the product doesn't live up to the expectations that the marketing is meant to promise.

Analysis of the Merwyn Research database and a range of academic studies show how important it is to have a whole idea; that is, both a superior product and a strong marketing plan. Products or marketing strategies that are significantly more appealing than what is currently available are registered as Outstanding. If they're significantly worse than what's already out there, they show up as Terrible.

SUCCESS RATE
Terrible Product + Outstanding Marketing Idea = 5 %
Outstanding Product + Terrible Marketing Idea = 10%
Outstanding Product + Outstanding Marketing Idea = 90%

How to Know When You Have a WHOLE IDEA?

Break your idea into its components. On index cards, list your idea's key elements—product, packaging, name, experience, feeling, and function, as well as any sensory sights, sounds, and smells it may offer. Sort your idea elements into Yes/No piles.

Does the element contribute to the whole idea? Does it reinforce and add to the customer's overall experience? Is the element generic, something that anyone could do, or is it exclusive to your idea? If it's the latter, put it in your Yes pile.

If it's not any of those, put it in the No pile. These are your Achilles' heels. These are places where your competition can take advantage of you. At the same time, they're places where you have opportunities to improve your idea.

Now, sort the cards from your Yes pile into Yes/No piles again, based on these criteria:

Is the element on each card feasible? Can it be researched, developed and executed? Can it be produced cost effectively? If so, it goes in the Yes pile.

Look at your no pile. These are your barriers to greatness—the hornets that will come back to sting you if you don't deal with them. These are the objections your boss, investors and/or teammates will raise when you're trying to sell your vision. Deal with these issues now. The more you anticipate their objections, the greater the chances they won't have any.

OK. If you've been through the piles and your newborn idea is still throbbing with excitement, party on. If not, then go back to Go and do not collect $200.

! (BE MAGIC)

This is the least tangible, most challenging element of the WOW! factor. It is also the most difficult to create. It's the spark that lights the fuse that sends ideas hurtling off into the strato-sphere. It's what makes people want to stand in line and pay prices that are so high it makes absolutely no sense at all.

It's a feeling you get when you see an idea for the first time. It's the kind of reaction that causes you to stop and take notice. It's a kind of pulse-quickening reaction that generates excitement.

Magic comes about from having the right mix of function, performance and spirit. I see it in Apple products, Swatch watch-es, L.L. Bean boots, and Ben & Jerry's Homemade Ice Cream. I also see it in the Real World Entrepreneurs and Inventors that I have the honor of working with.

How to Tell When Your Idea Has MAGIC!

Magic is the most difficult of all elements to measure. For the most part, it's more a function of emotion, art and feeling than it is of an engineered benefit.

I know of no way of knowing for sure if an idea is endowed with magic. But here are a few ways to tell if it might:

> • Your idea runs continuously through your
> head. You can't turn it off. It's all-consuming.
> • People try to steal it. Or take credit for it.
> • It has multiple dimensions. It has onion-peel-
> ing depth. When you describe it to someone
> else, they immediately have ideas and sug-
> gestions.

Write your core idea in the middle of a sheet of paper. Attach thoughts, associations and applications to it, like spokes from a hub. The more new thoughts and opportunities a core idea sparks, the greater the likelihood that you really do have magic on your hands.

If you don't think you have it, don't give up. But in those rare opportunities when magic strikes, grab it and hold tight.

When evaluating ideas, you have to be willing to walk away. There's a fundamental truth in the idea business: If you can create one, you can create many. On an average project for an average client, I find myself walking away from more than 100 ideas for every idea that I pursue. Of course, it's much easier to be selective when you have plenty of options. The point is, you need to know when to hold them, when to fold them and when to go on to something else altogether.

THE EUREKA! FORMULA
FOR CREATIVITY

Classic Brainstorming

The first edition of this book extolled the virtues of the Alex Osborn school of creativity. Osborn was the "O" in BBDO, one of the most influential advertising agencies on the planet.

Osborn invented brainstorming in 1938 as a way to generate ideas for advertising. The publication of his book, *Applied Imagination*, in 1953, and the subsequent founding the following year of the Creative Education Foundation at Buffalo State University in New York established brainstorming as the preeminent form of group creativity.

Osborn chose the term to denote the use of the brain to "storm" a problem. If you've ever been in a session with a moderator at a chart pad telling all in attendance that the rules for the day include ...

- No criticizing of ideas—defer judgment until later
- Quantity is good; the more ideas, the better
- Freewheeling is welcomed—the wilder the ideas the better
- When possible, build on the ideas of others ... then you've participated in an Osborn brainstorming session.

Osborn's *Applied Imagination* was the guiding force behind Eureka! 1.0, as well as the first generation of this book. Osborn's scriptures formed the core of my thinking —at the time, in the '80s and early '90s. Osborne's influence is so great that it's nearly impossible to find a book on creativity that isn't a variation on his work.

I summed up Osborn's work into a set of principles that I brazenly packaged into this equation:

$$\textbf{Eureka! = (Stimuli + Brain Operating System)}^{\textbf{Fun}}$$

Or in simple terms—the Eureka!, or the big idea, equals the combination of idea starters (stimuli) and the different groups of people (Brain Operating Systems) in your session, all magnified by how much fun you programmed into the session.

Data Discovers a Problem with the Equation

As I returned from the North Pole, I had the blessing of a booming business and a bundle of cash from the sale of AcuPOLL Research, another company I'd created. I decided to use those funds on research to prove that my original equation was actually true.

To validate the equation, we had to come up with a way to measure creativity during the process—not simply at the end of the process. My muse in this regard was Dr. W. Edwards Deming, a statistician sent to Japan to help our former enemy climb out of the post-World War II rubble.

If you were around from the late 1940s and into the late '50s, you'll remember that any product with a label that said "Made in Japan" was automatically considered to be a piece of junk. Today, of course, Japan is an economic super power—and Deming was key to helping Japan make that transition.

Note: the first company that Dr. Deming worked with when he returned to the United States was Nashua Corporation where my father was director of central engineering. It was through my father that I made the connection to Deming's work.

The core of Deming's philosophy was a focus on the system. He believed that 94 percent of failures were due to the system, 6 percent were caused by worker error. And to improve the system, one must have a process of measuring not just the final result, but also the process that leads to the final result.

> "In many fields of human endeavor, improved measurement has been a precursor and a necessary requirement for improved solutions."
> – Bob Goldstein, Procter & Gamble,
>   Vice President of Advertising

Using Deming as our guide we embarked on a series of studies to identify a mechanism for measurement. The Eureka!

Ranch provided the laboratory. Our "lab rats" were the executives from Fortune 500 companies who came to the Eureka! Ranch during the course of inventing sessions—real world projects convened for the express purpose of creating ideas for new products, services, or marketing ideas.

To help develop a system of measuring the creative process, I enlisted the services of Dr. Chris Stormann, a master researcher with an ability to think creatively as well as numerically. The research to follow was done with his expert assistance. To read an academic paper on the process we developed, visit the http://EurekaRanch.com Web site.

Study No. 1

In our typical inventing sessions, clients would be assigned randomly to one of four small groups, consisting usually of five to ten people each. At the end of each exercise, every 40 minutes or so, they would complete a quick survey indicating their perceptions of their respective group's dynamics, as well as the quality and quantity of ideas they were able to generate.

We experimented to find the question most predictive of the number of high quality ideas created.

Clients were asked to fill out a questionnaire detailing group effectiveness, how well they liked the exercises, how much fun the exercises were, how free they felt to speak their minds, and how diverse their groups were in terms of people adding different perspectives into the mix.

Once the surveys were completed, each team reported its ideas out loud to the larger group. I listened to each report and listed all the "big ideas" each team had created, not knowing how each team had rated its group via the survey.

Later, my tally of high quality ideas from each group was correlated against the teams' own appraisals of their outputs.

From this research, we found that the most valuable question to ask at the moment of creation in order to predict the number of quality ideas—and the question that correlated best with my count of the number of ideas created—was, "How effective was your group, as a whole, at creating big ideas?"

On our surveys, it looked like this:

"HOW EFFECTIVE WAS YOUR GROUP, AS A WHOLE, IN
GENERATING QUALITY IDEAS?

NOT AT ALL EFFECTIVE										VERY EFFECTIVE
0	1	2	3	4	5	6	7	8	9	1 0

For those interested in statistics the relationship was significant at the 98 percent confidence level [r = .296].

UGH!

To my dismay, we found no connection between the number of high-quality ideas and whether a participant *liked* the
exercise or how much *fun* it was. None whatsoever! That meant
that my creativity equation was wrong.

I had built my reputation—not to mention a toy-filled fun
house—on the virtues of fun. One of my refrains, in fact, had
been "fun is fundamental" to the creative process. I had
preached the virtue of fun up one coast and down the other.

The question facing me, then, was would I have to get rid
of my arcade games? What about the Nerf guns and my
Lawrence Welk bubble machine? If the IRS were to get wind of
this, would it invalidate some of my previous tax deductions?

The easy thing would have been to ignore the data, call it
a fluke, and pull the plug on the research. The alternative would
be self-destructive—something akin to running for city council
with a pledge that, if elected, I would increase taxes because
that was what was needed to pay for the necessary road and
school improvements.

To continue with the research, I would in more ways than
one be tearing down a house I had spent years building.

But it was the right thing to do. I had to push on and go
where the research would lead us. Besides, the engineer in me
was curious. I had to know what drove creativity.

Chris and I studied every variable: Numbers of people,

types of stimulus, individual thinking styles, the kinds of ideas that were created, groups' moods, and levels of optimism that a problem would be solved, or if a good answer to a challenge had been found, whether it would be put into play.

In the end, we discovered that the key variables for increasing the number of high-quality ideas created were:

- The quantity of high-quality stimulus
- The diversity of viewpoints explored

And we found one variable with a negative correlation. It centered on an intriguing point. On our survey, it looked like this:

"FOR WHATEVER REASON, I DIDN'T SAY ALL IDEAS THAT CAME TO MY MIND."

AGREE										DISAGREE
0	1	2	3	4	5	6	7	8	9	1 0

When the scores on this variable increased, the effective-ness ratings of the group—and the number of high-quality ideas that group came up with—went down.

Why?

Analysis on a group by group basis indicated that when the CEO or other high level boss came into a group, everyone else clammed up. No one wanted to risk looking like a fool in front of a superior.

After the sessions we asked some of the participants why certain exercises or groups were more or less effective for them. We didn't tell them why we were asking, we just asked. We knew the groups each person had been in so we could iden-tify particularly week groups.

The answer was another F word that we hadn't considered. *FEAR!!!!!!*

As in a case of the willies. In some group situations, they

had a greater fear of appearing boob-like. Or they were afraid of peers laughing at them. Whatever it was that people were afraid of, it was preventing them from sharing their ideas. They had a "virtual no" in their heads that was killing ideas before they even had a chance to breathe.

Study No. 2

With an understanding of the key variables we set up a more extensive study to track results. We explored group effectiveness, stimulus, diversity of viewpoints, and fear of stating all ideas that came to mind across 29 ideation sessions, and more than 2,000 client surveys.

First, we averaged the scores assigned to each exercise by each client for the entire day. Then we correlated the averages to the number of "big ideas" remaining two days after the session, after the raw ideas had been translated into written ideas, refined, edited, changed and eliminated by the client, myself and my team.

The relationship between group effectiveness and the number of high quality ideas was even stronger than in Study No. 1. The relationship was significant at the 99 percent confidence level (r = .61).

Birth of the Eureka! Formula for Creativity

With the new data we set out to articulate a new equation that explained in a simple form the relationships we'd found between stimulus, diversity and fear. Thus was born the Eureka! Formula For Creativity.

$$E = \frac{Stimulus^{\,Diversity}}{Fear}$$

BUT AS FAR AS I WAS CONCERNED …
EUREKA! AND HALLELUJAH!!! It was an equation that articulated for the first time what drives creativity.

Osborn had been right about the importance of stimulus and feeding the mind. His basic model that ideas are feats of association was indeed true: The more stimulus you have to work with, the greater your ability to make new connections and create new ideas.

But diversity was far more important than I had imagined. Far more important, in fact, than 5 + 5 + 5 = 15. It was more like 5^3 = 125. In other words, the impact of diversity was exponential. Being diverse was more than a proper, politically correct way to be. It was a Capitalist Business Building tool of huge proportions.

And fear was a direct negative. If you doubled your fear, you cut your output of ideas in half. It was that direct. Multiply fear by a factor of ten, and you have virtually no chance of creating a breakthrough idea.

My Thoughts Now

It's been six years since Chris and I defined the Eureka! Formula. He has since returned to the world of academia, where he exercises his PhD in criminal justice at the Institute for the Study and Prevention of Violence at Kent State University in Ohio.

Unlike the first equation which I created as a way to explain the creative process as I understood it at the time—the new one has stood the test of time. I've done dozens of experiments, and each one reinforces the fact that stimulus drives creativity, that embracing diversity adds an exponential kick, and that fear shuts down big ideas.

From a different perspective, the equation gave us a new way of thinking about the way we did business at the Eureka! Ranch.

To bring the Eureka! Formula to life—the next three chapters delve into each of the three key variables that control your creativity effectiveness.

What do you say? Let's get to it.

6
EXPLORE STIMULI

Creativity is about making 1 + 1 = 300. New ideas are feats of association between two or more old ideas. Just as water is a combination of one part oxygen and two parts hydrogen. Just as two parts nitrogen and one part oxygen produce laughing gas.

In real world situations, creativity is about making connections as quickly as you possibly can.

Cranium Connections

Think of your brain as an immense database of wisdom, experience, emotion, facts and solutions. When a creative challenge presents itself, your brain fires out data requests to the library of stuff inside your head, looking to make a connection and discover a solution.

With simple problems, the solutions often involve one-to-one connections. Simple problems lend themselves to ready-made solutions. Problem solved.

For example, you may find yourself sitting under a tree. Hypothetically speaking, something hits you on the head and bounces into your lap. You look down and, in your lap, you see an apple where, moments before, no apple had been.

Concluding that this apple is the same object you felt hit you on the head, you jump up to see who would have thrown an apple at you. You remember that you are on a deserted island and that there is no one around who could have thrown an apple at you. Then you look up and realize you have been sitting under an apple tree.

"Oh," you say. "I see what happened."

That's a simple case of deduction. It's almost like looking around the next corner to see what's waiting there. A leads to B leads to C, as far as the path may take you.

Another example of a problem requiring a simple one-to-one solution, although it certainly didn't seem so simple at the time, was discussed earlier in this book with the story of Archimedes' discovery of the law of specific gravity. Faced with the problem of determining the amount of gold in his king's crown, Archie noticed that, the more he lowered himself into his bathtub, the more water was displaced from the tub.

Applying his observation to the task at hand, Arch realized that if he were to place the king's crown in a vessel of water, capture the water that was displaced and weigh it, he would be able to solve the challenge at hand. Archimedes' discovery changed the world and it led to the general science of hydrostatics. At the time, it must have been mind-boggling. But with the benefit of hindsight, it was quite simple.

On the other hand, more complex problems, perhaps involving situations nearer and dearer to you, require multiple connections with stimuli to generate a solution.

For instance, you may find yourself arguing a case in a court of law involving a multi-million-dollar class action suit. Or you might be the director of a major motion picture. Or you might be a brain surgeon about to dig into someone's cranium. Or you might be about to start a business of your own.

In all of those cases, you'll face multiple contingencies in which numerous planets have to line up and all kinds of pieces have to fall precisely into place. Numerous twists and turns are involved and, at each juncture, you'll have to make the right choice to achieve overall success. That means you'll have to think on your feet. And that means thinking not just creatively, but quickly as well.

Speeding Up Your Brain's Database: There are two ways to speed up your general ability to make connections and be creative:

1. Add content to your cranium database: The more experiences and knowledge you have to connect with, the more creative you will be. In the academic world, this is referred to as "crystallized intelligence" and is defined as the knowledge base one acquires through educational and personal experiences.

2. Speed up your brain processing speed: Using the computer model, you can find ways to speed your mental stimuli processor. In the academic world, this is called "fluid intelligence" and is characterized as the ability to think with flexibility and to reason abstractly.

Research finds that for 98 percent of the population, the best way to increase creativity is to add content to your cranium—in effect, by reading, studying, traveling, tasting, touching, and experiencing, you can dramatically increase your ability to make connections and find solutions.

Research reported in the *Journal of Creative Behavior* (Volume 39, Number 2) found that crystallized intelligence was the most predictive factor when it came to increased creativity. These same researchers also found that "there is good evidence in the present study that for most people (i.e., those with average IQ), flexibility of thought and abstract reasonable ability has little to do with creativity."

PEOPLE WITH GENIUS IQS ARE DIFFERENT

The same study found that for those with IQ scores in the top 2 percent of the population (IQ scores over 120), the most powerful way to grow one's powers of creativity is to increase the ability to think with flexibility and to reason abstractly.

It appears that those with higher IQ have craniums crammed with more stimuli. For these people, the most effective way to increase creativity is to provide processes that enable the processing of the stimuli already in their heads.

WHY CLASSIC BRAINSTORMING DOESN'T WORK!

I've always maintained—and there's plenty of research that bear it out—that brainstorming, as classically preached and currently practiced, doesn't work. We asked business people how many classic brainstorming sessions they attend each year and how many "big ideas" they get by doing so. Dividing the number of sessions by the number of big ideas, we find it takes, on average, 7.3 brainstorming sessions to create one big idea. That's not much in return for all those bad buffets and long hours spent in windowless conference rooms.

If you invert the equation, **you have a 13 percent chance of coming up with a big idea at the average brainstorming session.**

The reason most brainstorming doesn't work is because it's focused on improving flexibility of thought—something that has no impact on 98 percent of the population.

The problem, then, is NOT the process of thinking. The problem is a lack of CONTENT with which to process. At the Ranch we constantly pour through academic journals, category research, and customer data looking for stimuli insights that can spark clients to create new ideas. The factual insights from the research are translated into teachings that are provided on a just-in-time basis, just as we're challenging managers to dream up new ideas.

Brain Draining

When you take the same old people and don't provide fresh stimulus the result is brain draining—comparable to the bloodletting they used to do in America's colonial days as an ill-conceived method of curing certain illnesses. **Instead of inspiring new ideas, brain draining inspires frustration and inferiority complexes.** People quickly conclude that they're incapable of creating new ideas. That belief becomes a self-fulfilling prophecy.

HOW STIMULUS WORKS

When a piece of stimulus enters your senses, it sets off a chain reaction, so that one thought provokes new thoughts, ideas, and inspirations. You experience a rush of new combinations of thoughts and ideas. Let's chew on a piece of stimulus right now.

Your brain immediately begins sparking connections. *Sweet, sticky, licking, on a stick, round, shiny, hard.* **As the seconds tick, more thoughts emerge:** *Wrapper, playground, friendship, mmm-good, smaller and smaller, tongue, Halloween, giving to the needy, food stamps, the time you found that half-licked sucker covered with hair in the cushions of your davenport. Boy, was that thing ever disgusting!*

A great thing about stimulus is its multiplicative impact. When the brain encounters new stimuli, they unfurl a new set of multiple thought patterns, like waves rolling across an ocean. As these waves of thought collide and pound into each other, more and more permutations are created. With the addition of even more stimuli, the beginnings of great ideas begin to gather momentum.

Stimulus can be considered anything outside your brain that you can see, feel, hear, smell, touch, taste, or otherwise sense or imagine. And the number of ways you can gather stimuli is unlimited. It can be a simple matter of leafing through a collection of books or magazines. Or walking through a mall with your eyes wide open. Or talking to the Good Humor man. Or putting yourself in an entirely alien environment for a few hours. The more varied the stimuli, the more rapidly your mind will click—but even a small dose can Jump Start your brain dramatically.

Throughout history, stimuli of one sort or another has led to all kinds of world-changing breakthroughs. A few examples from ye olden tymes:

• It was 1879. Harley Procter was stuck for a name for his firm's new soap, which was white and had the unique property of being able to float. At the time, his was one of dozens of companies selling soap that was white. He thumbed through his Webster's and his Roget's Thesaurus. He sifted through long lists of soaps made in other countries. Nothing seemed to help.

Then one Sunday morning at the Mount Auburn Episcopal church in Cincinnati, Ohio, Procter heard the minister read a verse from Psalms:

"All thy garments smell of myrrh and aloes and cassia, out of the ivory palaces whereby they have made thee glad."

Eureka! Thus came the inspiration for the name that would propel Procter's product to become America's No. 1 selling soap—pure, clean, fresh Ivory Soap.

• To perfect an invention he was calling the telegraph, Samuel Morse needed a way to keep his telegraph signal flowing strong over great distances. No matter how much power he pumped into the line, the signal faded in proportion to the distance it traveled.

One day while riding on a stagecoach from New York to Baltimore, Morse was struck by the stimulus of his mode of travel. His Brain Operating System related his problem with the fact that the stage company periodically harnessed new teams of horses to the coach to keep it running on schedule. In a like manner, he resolved to create relay stations to keep his telegraph signal running strong.

• Deep in the winter of 1873, Chester Greenwood was trying out a new pair of skates in Farmington, Maine. As you might imagine, the weather was quite blustery, so much so that poor Greenwood nearly froze off his ears.

Legend has it that, in an effort to reduce the likelihood of freezer burn, he held his mittens over his ears. "Hmmmmm," he thought, or something like it. "Mittens over my ears keep them warm, but it is rather inconvenient."

Chester asked his mother to sew pieces of fur to two ear-size loops of wire. Four years later Chester was granted U.S. Patent No. 188,292 for earmuffs.

• In 1887, when bicycles still had hard rubber tires, John Boyd Dunlop found it very uncomfortable to ride his bicycle over cobblestone streets, hemorrhoids notwithstanding. The stimulus of a garden hose pulsing with water gave him an idea. He wrapped a hollow rubber tube around the rims of his two-wheeler and pumped them full of air, inventing the pneumatic tire.

TRY IT YOURSELF

To help you better understand the power of stimuli, let's walk through an example.

Your task: To come up with ideas for an unforgettable, one-of-a-kind family vacation.

Brain draining: You take out a sheet of paper and begin listing all the ideas the come to you. These include where you've been, where you might like to go and places others have told you about. Before long, your stream of consciousness slows to a trickle and not long after, it's nothing but a dried-out creek bed.

The Eureka! Way: You array before you a gang of mental triggers—stimuli to lubricate the crankshaft of your cranium. These include:

- A map of the USA or a topographical globe
- Vacation brochures and travel magazines
- Articles about bicycling, waterskiing, art museums—stuff that interests you, as well as stuff that you don't think holds much interest
- Assorted New York Times travel sections
- A book on country inns
- A Robin Leach video of "Lifestyles of The Rich and Famous"
- Stepping outside the four walls of your normal environment, talking with other folks who will push and prod you with off-the-wall suggestions
- Going to a place that can stimulate the mind with vacation ideas—a zoo, a mall, a travel agency, a sporting goods store, a book store, a museum, a store that sells foods from around the world

It shouldn't take long before you feel the ideas for your next vacation welling up inside you. You've gone from 0 to 60 in no time at all.

Brain draining vs. the stimulus approach—which method do you think will lead to more ideas? Better ideas? Seems obvious, doesn't it? It is.

Some might complain that it's unfair to have all that stimuli to create ideas. These same people might consider it fun to push an elephant with diarrhea uphill.

Remember this: **You're rewarded for the quality of your ideas, not the pain it took to create them.** Sure, it's macho to tough it out. But why bother when you can think quicker, better, and faster with stimulus-activated thinking?

Stimulus works. It opens the mind and quickens the soul. And it's light years more fun than brain draining. More importantly, it consistently produces wicked good results. At the typical Eureka! session, ideas fly like bees to a hive. Like sparks from a grinding wheel. Like snowflakes in a blizzard.

Still not convinced? Try the following test.

TASK No. 1: A joy buzzer factory is for sale and you have the option to buy it, but you have to justify the purchase to your investors. You have 10 minutes to come up with ideas for maximizing the plant.

TASK No. 2: The largest whoopee cushion manufacturing facility in the world is for sale and you have the option to own it. Once again, you have to justify the purchase to your investors. You have 10 minutes to come up with ideas to maximize the factory capacity. Number your ideas as you go along. Use as much paper as you need. But this time, use any or all of the following words, selected at random from a recent issue of *USA Today*, to stimulate your thinking.

- Aladdin
- U.S. Postal Service
- Brewers
- Bully
- Weight Lifting
- Hospital
- Assault
- Kite
- Championship
- Sandwich
- Edison
- Beer
- Pillows
- Tennis
- Sailing
- Defense

- Harmony
- Sledgehammer
- Coffee
- Armageddon
- Cowboy
- Heritage
- Lobster
- Innocence
- Aviation
- Insects
- Packaging
- Montana
- Gossip
- Viper
- Candid
- Airbags

Ready? Count the ideas you created with either approach. When I do this exercise in a Jump Start Your Brain seminar setting, I usually collect at least twice as many ideas with stimuli versus without. If the allotted time is extended from 5 minutes to 30 minutes, to three hours and on to a full eight-hour day, the difference between brain draining and the use of stimuli becomes even greater.

The University of Oklahoma's Dr. Arthur Van Gundy, an internationally known authority in the field of creativity, compared the effectiveness of brain draining with the use of stimuli in a series of experiments early in 1993.

He randomly recruited college students, assembled them into sets of six groups of four and gave each group 45 minutes to invent ideas for new snack products. The participants in the six

Brain draining test groups were given no special guidance and no special direction. They were simply asked to come up with ideas for new salty snacks: chips, pretzels, that sort of thing.

After their brains were drained, Van Gundy counted an average of 29.7 ideas per group. That's a shade better than one idea every two minutes. At that rate, it would take more than 33 hours to come up with 1,000 ideas, not allowing for potty breaks.

Then Van Gundy let similar groups of college students work stimuli. Members of the Eureka! Ranch team helped them process stimuli such as product samples and magazines. These groups churned out, on an average, 310.8 snack food ideas in 45 minutes. That's better than 10 times what the groups using the traditional Brain draining method were able to muster.

More Wicked Good Ideas!

But the difference in quantity is only part of the story. Van Gundy collected all the ideas from all the groups he tested, then had them evaluated by a trio of real world new-product gurus — two from the Frito Lay company, which is, of course, in the salty snack business, and one outside new product expert. The ideas had been shuffled and scrambled, using a random number generator, so that the evaluators would be unable to identify the sources of the ideas.

The real world evaluators scored each idea on a scale of 1 to 5, based on the marketplace potential they saw in each idea. The lists were unscrambled and the votes tallied.

The results? The average group using the Stimulus approach generated 36.3 ideas with wicked good marketplace potential, while the average brain-draining group came up with 6.5.

To put it another way, the stimulus approach generated 558 percent more wicked good ideas than the creative method used by most people most of the time.

More ideas is a great result. More *GREAT IDEAS* is even better.

Greater Personal Satisfaction!

Another intriguing aspect of Van Gundy's study centers on how his test subjects felt after using the two approaches. He asked each the following questions to gauge their levels of satisfaction with whichever of the two processes they used.

1. To what extent did you feel free to participate and contribute your ideas?
2. How satisfied are you with the quantity of ideas generated by your group?
3. How satisfied are you with the quality of ideas generated by your group?
4. In general, how satisfied were you with the process used by your group?

The results were tabulated and added together on a 100-point scale, with 0 scraping bottom and 100 knocking on heaven's door.

Brain draining scored a 64.8. In school, that's worth an F on the report card. The use of Stimuli scored a 96.8—an easy A by anyone's standards.

Wow! **Not only does the use of stimuli generate more wicked good ideas. It also builds self-confidence, spirit and enthusiasm!**

The Same Principle at Work with Rats

The stimulus approach has proven itself in the academic community and with clients in the marketplace. Want more evidence? A landmark scientific study adds more weight to the argument that this method is in line with the way the soft tissue between your ears works.

Consider the humble rat. Consider, too, the rat's humble brain. In a famous study on the effects of stimuli with these creatures, University of California at Berkeley psychology professor Mark Rosenzweig put a dozen lab rats in a roomy, three-by-three-foot cage full of toys—ladders, running wheels, light bulbs, ping-pong balls, and an assortment of other bright, colorful items that he supposed might amuse a rat. This he called an "enriched environment."

Into smaller cages, about one foot wide by eight inches

deep, furnished only with a food dish and a water supply, Rosenzweig placed a single rat. He called this an "impoverished environment." You can find similar impoverished environments in most major American corporations, usually occupied by a mid-level manager.

From the late 1950s and into the early '70s, Rosenzweig compared the rats in either setting as to their abilities to solve problems.

The rats in the stimulus-enriched environment turned out to be a lot better at problem-solving—a result, Rosenzweig concluded, of a combination of social interaction with other rats and their ready access to objects d'fun, a.k.a. objects d'stimulus.

He also found that the brains of the rats in the enriched environment were more developed; indeed, that certain cognitive parts of their brains weighed up to 10 percent more than those of the lonesome rats in solitary confinement.

" … we took cross-sections from the brain and measured the thickness of the cerebral cortex, which controls memory storage and information processing. We found the cortex was thicker because, in the enriched environment, the nerve cells had branched out and made more connections. We concluded … that complex interaction

with the environment leads to a significant increase in the development of the brain and a significant improvement in the ability to solve problems."
– Dr. Mark Rosenzweig, University of California
   at Berkeley

In fact, Rosenzweig's rat studies are the reason why many of today's baby toys are so brightly colored. At the far end of the creative stimulus landscape are the Eureka! invention sessions we hold for clients looking for new products or services to sell to the world. These sessions are loaded with stimuli in the form of the exercises we lead. They stretch stimulus thinking to the extreme and, if the occasion calls for it, absurd lengths—my feeling being that more is better, unless you're on a diet.

"A little brain with imagination makes your brain bigger."
– Kristyn Hall, my daughter at age 7

Kristyn's comment is more insightful than it might at first seem. The number of brain cells is not the relevant factor when it comes to jump starting your brain. What counts is the number of connections between them. When your brain is exposed to a piece of stimulus, it creates new wiring connections. As more connections are completed, your brain becomes bigger, heavier, and smarter.

It's a short hop to the inevitable conclusion:

The more stimuli you use, the more powerful your brain becomes.

Think of your brain as a vast series of electrical circuits. Each of us is born with about a hundred billion brain cells, which is roughly equivalent to the number of stars in the Milky Way, according to the people in charge of keeping track of such things.

Each cell communicates with other cells at a rate of 100 million electrochemical impulses per second across a network of brain wiring. That may sound like a lot, but the total wattage of these impulses is barely powerful enough to light a nightlight. In that sense, even Einstein could be considered a dim bulb.

The more connections your brain cells share, the more efficiently and effectively your brain works. Scientific proof abounds. Brain scans of people with higher IQs indicate that less of their brain is active when they are solving a problem then those with lower IQs. Because their brains have built more connections, it takes less work for them to solve problems, draw associations, and invent new ideas. Their tachometers redline far less frequently.

As you exercise your brain with stimuli, you multiply the connections between brain cells. You become smarter.

Remember when you first learned to backhand a tennis ball, dribble a basketball, or maneuver on ice skates? You were aware of every little movement you made. With practice, you became more familiar with the process. As you became more and more skilled, you seemed to operate on automatic pilot.

Experience opened your mind to new plateaus of performance. You were able to think in terms of topspin, cutting to the basket or executing a triple axel. In the same way, brain workouts generate brain efficiency. The reason we can invent ideas as quickly as we do at the Eureka! Ranch is that we've already written oceans of ideas. Ideas beget more ideas. The more you invent, the better you get at inventing.

It's true with any pursuit. The more you do it, the better you get at it—as long as you're in a mind to get better. When my friend and co-author of this book, David Wecker, was a newspaper columnist writing three times a week, the question he was most often asked was: How do you keep coming up with ideas for stuff to write about?

In the early days, David says, it wasn't easy. But over time, he built a repertoire of ways to cull ideas—from scanning the AP wire to leafing through the Yellow Pages, from watching trends to realizing that the world around him was filled with stimuli for column ideas—which he could readily tap. Then, too, when you're in the habit of regularly cranking out 1,000 words about someone or something, you develop a discipline for it—a set of mental muscles that makes the task seem easier.

From time to time, I find myself suffering from inventor's block. In almost every case, the reason is that I've gotten lazy in the care and feeding of my mental food processor. I've drained my brain. What I need at such occasions is to refill, recharge, and refresh my cranium. I need to get up, move my feet, and feed my brain some stimuli.

> "Always taking out of the meal tub, and never
> putting in, soon comes to the bottom."
> – Ben Franklin

On a recent flight, I was trying to create names for a breakfast product. The hour was late, and I was beat—so much so that I fell into the trap of brain-draining, listing ideas on a sheet of paper. An hour later, I had nothing but a collection of doodles.

What I needed was stimuli. But how? Where? The airline magazines! I lunged for the pocket of Delta Travel Vacations, *Delta-Sky Magazine*, even the airline emergency card that tells you what to do when the yellow oxygen masks drop from the ceiling. The ideas began to flow—ideas for fun names, international names, funky names, sensory names, rational names, image-laden names. Within half an hour, I had three dozen viable alternatives. I faxed them to the client on arriving at my hotel. As this book was about to be released, a new breakfast product was being introduced with a name inspired from the pages of *Delta-Sky Magazine*. I wish I could tell you the name, but as of this writing, I am bound by my contract with the client to keep it a secret.

Gathering stimuli can be a simple matter of talking to other people about the challenge, strolling through a supermarket, watching MTV, leafing through the latest copy of Gourmet magazine, flipping on a Three Stooges video, watching Wile E. Coyote employ another Acme product in hopes of finally catching the Roadrunner, playing with a client's latest Thingamabob or violating the speed limit on the interstate with the stereo turned all the way up. Wherever you are, you can find stimuli.

"When I need to jump start my brain, I go to a baseball stadium with real grass, sit in the sun and let my mind wander. Or maybe I crank up some early Clash and drive at high speed. I recommend 'Clampdown' or 'Safe European Home.'"
– Page Thompson, Pepsi Cola Marketing Manager

An idea stimulus can be anything that takes you out of your normal frame of reference and, if only for a moment, opens your eyes a little wider.

THE BOTTOM LINE

Knowledge is key to creativity. And the key to gaining knowledge is to have a never-ending curiosity about life. When you read and study, you have more options with which to make connections. All of your education, your experiences, your successes and even your failures add to the storehouse of stimuli available for solving whatever problem presents itself.

LEVERAGE DIVERSITY

To get from zero ideas to something you can work out, you have to be willing to let go of where you are. That means you have to embrace diversity. You have to open yourself to exploring different opinions, alien viewpoints, and unlikely perspectives. Eureka! Ranch research says it works. Academic research confirms it. Harriet Zuckerman's study of 41 Nobel Laureates found that Nobel Prize winners collaborated with others significantly more often than a set of similarly experienced and educated scientists.

Diversity Is Not for Wimps

It takes courage to explore alternative perspectives. If you ask others' opinions, you might not like the answers.

If I'm working with a team of 20 corporate managers, I tell them that if they all agree, then 19 represent cost-savings opportunities. They usually laugh. Sometimes, I get the feeling they think I'm joking. I'm not.

Each person's responsibility in any situation is to speak his or her mind. To tell the truth and nothing but. Sadly, most adults gave up speaking truth years ago.

DIVERSITY EXPONENTIALLY MULTIPLIES YOUR BRAIN POWER

The power of seeking the ideas and advice of others is exponential. Remember the equation:

$$E = \frac{Stimulus}{Fear}^{Diversity}$$

What this means is that if you have 5 ideas and your friend has 5 ideas and another has 5 ideas, you don't end up with 15, as in ...

$$5 + 5 + 5 = 15$$

Instead, you end up with an exponential kick of 125 ideas

$$5^3 = 125$$

Why? Because the links between all of your pieces of stimuli, compounded by your accumulated knowledge and experiences, networks with your friend's knowledge and experiences to create an exponentially greater volume of possible thought combinations.

More Reasons Why Group Brainstorming Is Not the Best Solution

Group situations often give rise to social pressures, which in turn create artificial responses as a result of a variety of factors, among them:

> **Cultural Norms:** People filter their ideas based on what they think the boss wants to hear. Or what the organization expects them to say. Think of it this way: When you start a new job, you're likely to be a volcano of new ideas and fresh perspectives. Then when you've been on the job for a while and beaten down a few times, you learn about truth, reality and what the boss thinks. It's human nature to want to stop beating one's head against the wall, to stop fighting and give in to the brainwashing.

> **Self-protection:** Out of fear of looking foolish or being laughed at, people tend to stick to what they know for sure. But it's a gray world, it's not black or white. This is especially true when it comes to connecting stimuli from past education or experiences to new challenges.

> **Not Trusting Gut Instincts:** Asked our opinion on this or that, we rarely blurt out our thoughts, as most children are prone to do. Instead, we run our gut instincts past our rational brains for approval. Our rational brains flash a red light, and the gut instinct is stopped in its tracks. That is when we censor thoughts and ideas before they ever see the light of day. I call this the "Virtual No." The Virtual No is not conducive to creativity.

Person-to-Person Power

You don't need a group of folks to leverage diversity. You can just ask others for ideas and advice, one person at a time. It can be as simple as taking a walk and asking co-workers, family, or friends for ideas and advice. Or you can work digitally, using today's interconnected world. Among your options:

Dial an Expert: Connecting to others by phone is powerful because the person at the other end isn't swept up in all the background baggage that you might have in a given situation. In addition, the act of talking it out forces you to describe the challenge and possible solutions with clarity, which as often as not can add clarity and new ideas to your own thinking.

Instant Messaging: The IM format of typing short thoughts encourages fresh, honest and instinctive feedback. Having more than one IM conversation at a time can multiply the feedback, leading to lots of new ideas.

E-Mail: Requests for ideas and advice via e-mail allow for a more considered response then verbal or IM responses. They let you present your idea and gather ideas and advice against tightly directed questions.

Video Phone: AT&T created a stir at the 1964 Worlds Fair with its Picturephone with its football shaped screen. It's been a long time, but the dream is finally becoming reality. My MacBook Pro laptop has a video camera built into the case. Connecting with my office and home takes but a click. This technology will create a new world of possibilities. At my office, for instance, I recently had a three-way videoconference between people on three continents. In real time, problems were discussed, ideas were shared and solutions were discovered.

You Get What You Ask for

Whether seeking opinions or giving them, we have a responsibility to be brave and consciously state what is NOT the accepted, politically correct and expected response. Some of us have a real problem with this. Some of us don't.

Either way, one of the most effective ways to get diverse opinions is to ask for them directly. Research found that when test subjects were asked to come up with "creative" solutions, they did exactly as they were told. They created more solutions that were judged to be creative, far more so than when they were simply asked to solve problems without any prompting to be creative.

The conclusion: When asking others for their thoughts, be specific. State overtly that you understand the "proper action"—what you're asking for are fresh, even controversial insights.

So when probing for ideas and insights ask for what you need.

> **If you want *creative* ideas, ask for them.**
> **If you want *daring* ideas ask, for them.**
> **If you want *the safe solution*, ask for it.**
> **If you want *wild and wacky idea starters*, ask for them.**

Proof Positive of the Power of Diversity

To really understand the financial impact of diversity, read *The Rise of the Creative Class* by Richard Florida. He documents how tolerance of diversity is the singular greatest driver of economic success for cities and states.

> Embrace diversity. It gives birth to creativity, innovation, and positive economic impact. People of different backgrounds and experience contribute a diversity of ideas, expressions, talents and per-

spectives that enrich communities. This is how
ideas flourish and build vital communities.
– Richard Florida

IDEAS AND ADVICE FROM THOSE WHO DON'T KNOW JACK

The value of diversity is such that it extends to those who have
no specialized expertise in the task at hand. It's the value of
"fresh eyes."

I once made a point of asking dozens of adults what they
do when stuck for an idea. Their No. 1 response was that they
leave their offices and talk to someone who knows absolutely
nothing about their problem. Many spoke at length about the
value of talking to those who are not close to the problem, who
are detached from and ignorant of the situation.

**There is real value in having to explain a challenge to
those who have no prior knowledge of what you're talking
about.** That's because they're not locked into the "we can't" or
the "we'd better not" aspects of your situation.

Another advantage of talking to naives is that they tend to
give simple ideas and advice. They take what you say and simplify it. In the process, they can help bring clarity. They can help
burn off the fog.

Listen closely to those who know nothing, and you just
might hear something that sparks a breakthrough.

RECORD ALL IDEAS

Consider each piece of feedback and let your mind overflow
with ideas. Accept everything, regardless of how outlandish or
absurd it seems. Use a recorder, take notes, or save your instant
message exchanges.

Be open to even the worst of ideas. **A dangerously insane
idea that arises from one person may seem perfectly practical
when paired with another twisted notion from someone else.**

And remember to respect each newborn idea. Great
inventions are usually made up of several small ideas assembled together. Keep in mind that Toyota's rise from no place to
number one in the world is a result of thousands of continuous
improvements. Each individual change is small, but the cumulative impact in immense.

The pace of your diversity gathering, especially at the beginning, should be roughly equivalent to the frenzy that might occur, say, if the Hatfields and McCoys were trapped in the same elevator. You should have a runaway-train sense of being slightly out of control. If you're doing it properly, your heart will be pounding. You'll be breathing hard.

Talk to everyone you can find. Fill your cranium with new ideas and fresh insights on your own ideas.

Hints for Finding Great People to Connect With

When all you're looking for is ideas, it's easy to get people to help solve your problems. People are dying for other people to come along and ask their opinions. Asking someone for help is a sign of respect. All you have to do, most of the time, is ask. The opportunity to pull together is as American as the barn raising, the church supper, French fries and the Reuben sandwich.

Here are some quick hints of finding great people to learn from...

- People inside the company who don't conform. Like the guy at the end of the hall who wears bow ties and checkered pants. Or the woman on the second floor with the hand-painted neon-splatter sneakers.

- Former co-workers who have recently retired. When someone enters the hallowed realm of senior citizen, he or she often experiences an unfettering of previously pent-up thoughts and opinions.

- Newcomers to the company. The fresher, the better.

- People at your local YMCA, barbershop or coffee shop who are known for expressing opinions and favoring change. Your doctor, your tennis partner, your mailman, your neighborhood grouch. In short, anyone who has a mind and is willing to speak it.

• Folks who have left to start companies of their own. In general, I've found independent entrepreneurs provide some of the best perspectives. Even though their businesses are sometimes small, it takes a real spirit of adventure and heavy doses of courage to create a business of your own. Both qualities are important to the creative process.

• People with whom you violently disagree. You'll have to swallow some pride—but if you can find the strength, you are virtually guaranteed to learn a lot. Just remember to use your ears and not your mouth. You can't hear much when you're talking.

Most important of all, thank those who share their ideas with you. Thank them overtly and directly. When possible, make specific mention of what elements they offered that were helpful.

"It's not possible to thank people enough for all they're willing to do for you. And nothing motivates more effectively than the overt, emotional, unconditional feedback of an honest thank-you. Whether it's a child, a friend, an employee or a boss, a genuine heart-felt thank you works miracles."
– Richard Saunders

I.D.E.A.—A Simple Outline for Exploring Diversity
The mnemonic I.D.E.A. provides a place to start with your exploration of diversity of opinions, ideas and advice. In short, it stands for: Internet Dive, Do the Numbers, Experience First Hand and Ask Overtly.

INTERNET DIVE

The Internet should be your first method of exploring a diversity of ideas and advice. The volume of stimuli and diversity of thinking is nearly endless ...

- **Blogs** gives you opinions, opinions and more opinions. For every subject under the sun, you'll find a Web log.
- **Customer feedback postings** on competitors provide insights into the key positives and negatives with current products and services. Negatives in particular have value—mega-businesses have been built on problems in need of solutions.
- **News media sites** provide information on trends in whatever industry. The same sites are rich sources of stories from the past, just by looking into their archives.
- **International websites** can provide perspective on trends elsewhere that may be headed in your direction. What are they doing overseas that they aren't doing where you live?
- **A library card** from your local library can give you access to hundreds of commercial databases that cover academic research and news archives. My public library card has saved me tens of thousands of dollars in subscriptions and fees.

There are no excuses for not doing web searches. During the taping of *American Inventor* for ABC, I was amazed to discover how few of the inventors had done simple searches. It was not uncommon for me to find nearly identical products with two simple searches. Or to find background information on panelists inventions that brought into question the integrity of their claims.

DO THE NUMBERS

In looking for diversity of opinions, it is extremely helpful to ground your conversations in numbers. The more you can talk about specifics—and nothing is more specific than numbers—the more you will get ideas and advice you can actually use. Even approximate numbers can bring focus to the conversation.

- **Work the extremes of numerical options.** If you're working on a fundraising event for a non-profit or something as crass as a new product, talk what price you might charge. Then talk options. For example, if you charged $15 per ticket, what would/should the fundraiser look like? What if you charged $100 per ticket?
- **Get help estimating the numbers.** Ask others for ideas and advice as to how the costs might work out for whatever you're trying to build. For example, ask someone at the hardware store what it might cost to build a playhouse for your kids by yourself.
- **Ask about your odds of success.** Ask experts how they might rate your odds of success for various approaches to solving your challenge. Keep it simple. Would they guess the odds are 50 percent, 80 percent or 10 percent? This approach lets you distill a mass of pros and cons into a single forecast.

"The world isn't black and white. It's gray scale. As an inventor, you have to see things in gray scale. You need to be open. You have to live in the gray-scale world, not the black-and-white one, if you're going to come up with something no one has thought of before."
– Steve Wozniak, Co-founder of Apple Computer
From his book *IWoz*

EXPERIENCE FIRST HAND

I've said it before, and I'll say it again: Nothing beats seeing, feeling and experiencing first hand. **Get up, get out and experience your challenge for yourself.** Don't review it from afar—be fully engaged and hands-on.

- **Do the obvious.** Most people think they know how it feels to try something, use something or be involved with something. And while it's possible to glean a rational sense of any given situation from mere observation, you can't feel it in your heart, your gut or your bones without first person, hands-on experience.
- **Compare and contrast.** Having experienced whatever the "it" is, now experience the alternatives. If you're evaluating a food product, taste what the competition has to offer. If exploring software options take the time to download the demos and try a simple task with each. If you're a Porsche, test-drive a Ferrari and an Aston Martin.
- **Ask the front-line experts.** When you're engaged up to your elbows in the process, don't ignore the wisdom and experience of the front-line experts. Ask the person who brews the coffee, who cleans the room, who works the cash register what they think. When you gain their trust, you'll unlock a vault of wisdom that can only be gained from the folks in the trenches, the ones with the day-in-and-day-out experience.

And remember: During the experience process, maintain innocence. Avoid evaluation. The point is to gather information. Be open to all thoughts that fly across your radar screen. If you really look, you'll be amazed at how much information is out there. Before long, your brain will be a gurgling cauldron of ideas.

"A pair of good ears will drain dry a hundred tongues."
– Ben Franklin

I get a ginormous kick out of seeing, feeling and experiencing. As one of the four judges on ABC's *American Inventor*, I was always the first to volunteer to test the contestants' products. I wobbled across the set on oddball bicycles, allowed myself to be stretched in a human spider web, worked up a sweat with an exercise machine and smashed my thumb with a hammer while wearing a prototype hand protector.

It's just fun to do. It's one of my favorite ways to jump-start my brain. Here are some other examples of how I've used it:

- Assigned by Folgers to recruit a new generation of coffee drinkers from the ranks of college-age Americans, I arose at five o'clock for a month of mornings to interview Miami University students in Oxford, Ohio. It was the best way I could think of to gauge their feelings about coffee, how they felt before their first cup in the morning and how they felt immediately afterwards. In the first light of day, you don't get thought-out responses. You get blurted truth.
- When the Eureka! Ranch did a project for Avon, I hit the bricks as an Avon sales representative. Ding dong, Doug Hall calling!
- When the John Morrell Company hired me to create new meat products, I visited the world's largest hog slaughterhouse, located in Sioux Falls, South Dakota. It wasn't the most uplifting tour I've ever been on, but I learned what I needed to know to understand the company's manufacturing capabilities.
- And when it came time to dream up a new refrigerated food product, I spent a morning at the refrigerated food aisle of a grocery store, where I talked with the woman who stocked the shelves. She didn't have a high school diploma, but she knew her customers, and she was proud of her aisle. And she gave me more insight for areas of exploration than the 10 pounds of documents the client gave me.

WHEN I NEED TO JUMP START MY BRAIN ... "I sit in bus stations or college student unions or the McDonald's on the side of an Interstate. And I look at people and listen to what they say. All you

see at an airport or an upscale mall are people like yourself. All of us talk too much and listen too little. Or I create situations where I'm loose. Like Einstein said, 'It comes to you when you get out of your own way.' Or I teach Sunday school to third graders and sixth graders, and I listen to their problems. Or I read cultural anthropology, like letters from soldiers at war or non-famous people's diaries. Or I go to estate sales to see what was left behind from somebody's life. Or I drive through poor neighborhoods."
– Watts Wacker, Futurist,
  Yankelovich Partners, Inc.

ASK REAL EXPERTS
Ask real experts what they think. Use your Internet search to find the world's top experts and ask their opinions. You won't always get through to them—but when you do, you'll get the best thinking in the world.

- **Visit a college campus.** These are communities where tolerance and bold thinking is often accepted. College is a time in our lives where all things are still possible. By including a few college students or professors in your discussions, you're practically assured of getting fresh perspectives and perhaps even a little idealistic motivation.
- **Get two experts with opposing views to debate.** Bringing together two experts to discuss pros and cons can be hugely helpful. The convergence of two distinct perspectives can create tremendous synergy. The iPod is but one example.

"Apple's whole history is making both the hardware and the software, with the result that the two work better together. With the iPod, Apple made iTunes the software and iPod the hardware. They

work together as one. Amazing! It's only because Apple supplied both sides of the equation that it was able to create a product as great as this."
– Steve Wozniak, Co-founder of Apple Computer

• **Ask bohemians.** The Random House dictionary defines a bohemian as someone who lives and acts without regard for conventional rules and practices. These people are also experts who can help you, since they make their living breaking conventional rules. (I love bohemians) In his book, Rise of the Creative Class, Richard Florida created a Bohemian index for each major U.S. city based on the number of writers, designers, musicians, actors, directors, painters, sculptors, photographers and dancers living there. This index was found to correlate directly to growth of high technology and regional growth in each respective metropolis. A quick way to identify bohemians is through their clothes. The ones that don't wear the same old same old—are a likely bet as living and acting without regard for conventional rules and practices.

Don't be surprised when the experts don't agree—with each other, with what you might have found on the Internet or with what you might have dredged up from personal experience. That's the wonder of the world: It's all shades of grey. It's up to you to listen, learn, and, finally, take charge to push your idea forward.

Maximizing the Wisdom of the Masses

In his best-selling book, *The Wisdom of Crowds*, James Surowiecki outlines four conditions that, when met, dramatically increase the wisdom of feedback from the masses.

Diversity of opinion: Each person should have some private information, even if it's just an eccentric interpretation of the known facts.
Independence: People's opinions are not determined by the opin-

ions of those around them.
Decentralization: *People are able to specialize and draw on local knowledge.*
Aggregation: *Some mechanism exists for turning private judgments into a collection decision.*
　　　– James Surowiecki, *The Wisdom of Crowds*

　　You can be more effective in your search for ideas and advice from diverse groups of people if you maintain these same principles:

Diversity of Opinion: Seek out those who think differently and/or come from different backgrounds. Find butchers, bakers and candlestick makers.
Independence: Ask those from different geographical locations, different sides of the tracks, and different walks of life.
Decentralization: Seek out micro-experts—those with specialized knowledge about each element of the challenge. Hold it up to the light and look at it from all sides and angles.
Aggregation: As you gather insights, record them. Don't trust your memory.

If in Doubt, Do
Don't waste a lot of time thinking about whom to talk to. Just start talking. Gather each idea and insight, no matter how small. Write down the thoughts that you do understand as well as those that, at first, you don't. The answers to your creative challenge will soon reveal itself.
　　Finally, throw yourself into the challenge whole-heartedly and with energy. And remember these words:

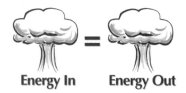

Energy In　　**Energy Out**

"Energy in = energy out."
– Richard Saunders

DRIVE OUT FEAR

Research finds that as fear increases, the number of big ideas generated decreases. It's a direct negative relationship, in fact. Double your fear, and you'll cut your creativity in half.

In his landmark book, *Out of the Crisis*, Dr. W. Edwards Deming wrote about the need to eliminate fear in order to achieve quality:

> "No one can put in his best performance unless he feels secure. *Se* comes from the Latin, meaning without, and *cure* means fear or care. 'Secure' means without fear, not afraid to express ideas, not afraid to ask questions."

Nice Theory, but What about Reality?

Right about now, you might be saying:

"Okay, Doug, let's see if I've got this straight—contradict history, be original, change the world, chase dreams. Easily said. It's tough out here, man! The economy is tight. The competition is brutal. Companies are laying off people left and right. Are you out of your mind?"

Well, yes, I suppose so. Guilty as charged, Your Honor.

But I can't help it. I love trampling on the established ways of doing things. I love to shake it up.

Then again, what choice is there? If you do something, anything, you stand a chance of failing. There's also a chance you'll succeed.

Most everyone wants to live on the edge—or wishes they would. Maybe the feeling is deep down, but it's there. Most everyone would like to be out front, the very best. The fact is the only way of knowing you're on the edge is by slipping over it from time to time. You can't inch your way to it and peek over. Nope. You have to step out front and fall a few times. Success doesn't happen without failure.

Maxime Faget, NASA's chief designer for more than 20 years, put it this way in an interview with Kenneth A. Brown, which he published in his book, Inventors at Work:

"No one felt like every test had to be a success, like it is now in NASA ... A test is supposed to find out if something works, not prove that it works ... We had something like 20 different tests of the Mercury capsule without men, and six or seven were failures ... We'd have a failure, and a few months later, we'd have a success. If we had a failure, we didn't shut everything down for a couple of years and put our tails between our legs and hide. We just kept going ... We learned what was wrong as well as what was right."

Don't labor under the assumption that the safe way is to do nothing. If you're not moving forward, the competition is passing you. Standing still is not a realistic option. You can't afford to maintain status quo.
Just accept it: There's no escaping change or risk.

"It's as risky to maintain the status quo as it is to reach for the new and bold. In the first case, you can get run over. In the second, you have a chance to swing for the fence."
– Richard Saunders

If you want to change your life, your job or your business, you'll have to change the way you do things. You can't wish your way there. You have to take action.

"The only way to get significantly different results is to do something significantly different."
– Richard Saunders

I see a lot of fear. I see it in clients at high levels and low levels of their oganizations. Maybe they fear for their jobs. Maybe they work for companies where reorganization is a seasonal event, where a lack of leadership at the top trickles down to pain and suffering in the ranks.
I've gotten so I can smell fear. In 10 minutes of entering a client's office, if it's there, I'll know it. It casts a pall over the con-

versation. The good thing is, most of these people aren't hopeless cases. Usually, all they need is a jolt of entrepreneurial enthusiasm.

The High five of Fears

Where does fear come from? What does it look like? On the theory that once we know where our fears come from, we can begin to deal with them, I've identified the High 5 of Fears. Here they are, along with the five best ways I know for finding the remedy—courage!

1. FEAR of being laughed at: It's one of our most basic of fears. It starts at an early age. When we are young, maybe we're insecure about our abilities. We're still learning what we can and cannot do, pull and/or get away with. The sad truth is, we often try to mask our insecurities by laughing at others.

The fear of ridicule causes us to build walls. It prevents us from asking questions. It keeps us from taking on new and different pursuits because we might fall on our faces. It discourages us from reaching out and revealing our true selves because we might be rejected. It ties our hands, clamps our mouths shut, and shuts down our minds.

The problem can be attributed to a phenomenon I call W.A.W.P.T., short for **Worrying About What People Think**.

W.A.W.P.T. saps our energy, drains our self-respect, and makes us choke up on our swing.

I sometimes get caught in this trap myself. When making presentations to corporations or giving lectures, I always wear jeans or shorts and sneakers or sandals. I believe in looking the part of the entrepreneur since that's what I'm selling. Besides, it's more comfortable.

That's not to say there haven't been occasions when my surroundings compel me to rethink that position.

Like the time I delivered a *Jump Start Your Brain* lecture to a group of company presidents and their spouses at a castle in The Hague, Netherlands. A cocktail reception was held beforehand. The ambience was a bit intimidating—waiters in black tie, a huge coat of arms hanging over the fireplace, upper-level executives in gowns and designer tuxes, each worth more than my entire wardrobe. Even the custodian wore a tux—no, really.

I was in my customary bare feet, jeans, T-shirt, and laced up in a straightjacket. In my bags, I had 120 whoopee cushions. I can't say for sure, but I bet it was the first time anyone had brought whoopee cushions to this place.

The stark contrast between my attire and demeanor and the general atmosphere of old-money formality had me rattled. I made a tentative start on the lecture. Instead of throwing myself into it, I pulled back on the jokes. Instead of playing to win, I played not to lose.

I was in the death grip of W.A.W.P.T. Ten minutes into my talk, it became painfully evident that it wasn't going at all well. Soon, I would arrive at the point in my presentation when I would distribute the whoopee cushions, with instructions to my audience to inflate them, then sit on them, the idea being to expel a roomful of "hot air" and have a laugh. I could feel the flop sweat rolling down my back.

Just then, I looked at Liam Killeen, an Irish friend who had arranged my series of lectures that day. Liam is a dream to work with. He works and plays hard, like few clients I've known.

In the haze of my panic, I saw Liam hoist his beer glass in my direction, his grin as wide as his face. In an instant, I regained my composure, turned on the jets and let the enthusiasm fly. Some of my points seemed to hit, others didn't. But the energy in the room increased a couple notches. My formal audience actually laughed out loud at the whoopee cushion gag.

To my surprise, I was mobbed at the end of the presentation. An animated ring formed around me. They told me they needed to hear more messages like mine, that they needed to learn how to open their minds, have fun, kick back, and relax. "To be more like you wild Americans!"

Since the Holland trip, I've made it a point to crank up the energy for every lecture. At the first hint of W.A.W.P.T., I think of Holland and of Liam raising his glass, grinning at me like a skunk.

If you're not careful, you can let a lot of energy evaporate by looking over your shoulder. Don't think about W.A.W.P.T. Put it out of your head. Instead, concentrate on swinging through the ball and giving it your best shot.

> "Being laughed at is a sign of potential genius.
> Think of Franklin in a thunderstorm, the Wright
> Brothers on the beach at Kitty Hawk, Edison with
> his light bulbs, Ted Turner with his crazy all-news
> cable network."
> – Richard Saunders

My great-grandfather, William Holder, didn't suffer from W.A.W.P.T. His father, George, ran a sail-making shop in the New Brunswick harbor town of Saint John. It was one of a number of shops on the bay in those days that manufactured handcrafted sails for the tall ships. The process was an arduous one, and my great-grandfather decided there had to be a better way.

He talked his father into buying a couple sewing machines as an experiment. It was the first time anyone had ever seen sewing machines in a Canadian sail loft, and the men who

worked with him didn't take kindly to them. Young Will Holder came to be known as the Petticoat Sailmaker. He was the laughing stock of the harbor.

Instead of caving in, great-grandpa paid extra to any man

willing to work with his machines. And while the old-timers laughed, he began taking their business. More than a century has passed since then. Today, the George E. Holder & Son is the only sail-maker sign still hanging over the bay in Saint John. That is because it's the only one still in business.

2. FEAR of losing what you have: I built my reputation at Procter & Gamble on solving the unsolvable. From Spic and Span to Folgers coffee, I developed solutions to seemingly hopeless challenges. I thrived on it. In fact, it's almost easier to solve the insolvable. When a problem has the appearance of being insolvable, people are more likely to muster the courage for bold and sometimes bizarre solutions, which is usually just what such situations require.

The fear of change—or of losing what one has—is at its most damaging in the middle when you are neither succeeding nor failing dramatically. Highly successful people often think they're bulletproof. They believe they have the Midas touch. Fear is hard for them to fathom. At the other end of the scale, when people have hit rock bottom, when they have nothing to lose, they have nothing to fear. And they are more willing to accept significant change.

But the people in the middle are comfortable with coasting. They often play not to lose instead of playing to win. They're the ostriches of the human race. They create elaborate justifications for their lack of action and forward motion.

The result is disillusionment. Which leads to twisting in the wind, which in turn leads to death.

"If you hang on too long, and that is all you do,
you are most assuredly going to get hanged."
– Richard Saunders

3. FEAR of rejection: This fear can be pretty intense in high school. You can stew for months over a certain dreamy and unapproachable someone, wondering how to break the ice in just such a way to ensure the two of you live happily ever after in Tahiti. But you never find the right words. Or if you do, you bite your tongue when the moment arrives because you couldn't bear what you're sure would be a withering glare. So you never do get to Tahiti.

The fear of rejection grows stronger as we become adults. Instead of speaking our minds, we become conditioned to sit on them. After a while, we stop trying because whatever it is we're trying just seems *TOO DANGED HARD*.

> "Unless you try to do something beyond what you have already mastered, you will never grow."
> – Ralph Waldo Emerson

Separate the "it" from "you." Recognize that when one of your ideas fails, it's not a reflection on you. It's a reflection on it. Failure is part of the process of learning. Your best teachers are your mistakes.

Consider the baby learning to walk. The baby gets up, the baby falls, the baby gets up, the baby falls, the baby gets up again. The baby learns without realizing it. And one day, the baby is able to walk because it never occurs to the baby to give up.

Hold your focus on your goal. Think of the bumps in the road—you can count on there being bumps in the road—as milestones that mean you're getting closer to success.

> "Finding courage requires believing in what you're doing and being secure in your ability to go do something else. It requires that you not be afraid to take it to the monster. Find the courage means you're not afraid of getting kicked out—and know that if you did, you'd land on your feet."
> – Dave Howe, AcuPoll Research

4. FEAR of the unknown: Many of us lack courage because we think we need to choreograph every step before we embark on the adventure. We want a detailed roadmap with a clearly focused beginning, middle and final destination—along with a synopsis of all the roadside rests and comfort stations between here and there.

Sorry. It doesn't work that way. Consider America's westward migration. The trail to California wasn't paved. There were no HoJos with HBO and heated pools. The pioneers in their covered wagons had to learn to deal with contingencies—rattlesnakes, wolves, bears, the Rocky Mountains, flaming arrows fired from the bows of war-painted locals atop galloping appaloosas. And you think you have problems.

"It takes ignorance to do new-to-the-world ideas. Ignorance is as big a factor as courage—ignorance of how hard whatever it is you're trying to do is to do. If someone had sat me down and said, 'Guy, let me tell you how hard it is to evangelize a new computer. Everybody's going to tell you they don't want to risk it. It's never been done in the history of man,' I never would have done it."
– Guy Kawasaki, Macintosh Software Evangelist

When I first tried to sell "ONCE," my storytelling board game, ignorance was in my corner. I didn't know you weren't supposed to sell games to big companies.

So I flew to New York for the International Toy Fair, an annual event where the toy industry showcases its wares to retailers, and checked into a reasonably priced hotel that might best be described as a bag of fleas.

I was turned down more times than a wino at a debutante ball. I felt like an onion bagel in a doughnut factory. All I needed was one person in a position of power to say yes. Or at least say something nice. I just had to keep looking until I found that person.

That person turned out to be Bill Hill, then vice president of product development for Selchow & Righter. Bill had made his mark in the business as the man who purchased Trivial Pursuit while all the other big game companies were passing on it. He took a look at my game. He didn't buy it, but his insights and encouragement gave me the courage to carry on and, as it happened, ultimately sell the game to Western Publishing.

"Doug's game had the same magical ingredient as Trivial Pursuit; it started conversations. Doug thought logically and sometimes illogically, but he thought. He didn't copy. Most inventors take something that exists and give it a twist. All Doug's stuff was original. And he believed in it."
– Bill Hill

If you want to be great, you have to learn to live with uncertainty—and to have faith in your ability to adapt and react. Ignorance of the future is not a sign of stupidity; it's part of the human condition.

5. FEAR of exposure: This is one of the more crippling forms of dread; the fear that a deep-seated insecurity will be dragged out into the light of day. We accumulate variations on this fear all our lives—as in, "I'm not (smart, creative, tall, good-looking, fill in the blank) enough."

These fears comprise your most formidable barriers to success. They build up over time, like soap scum in a shower. You have to scour them away. You do this by facing them head on, ignoring the warnings and moving forward.

Granted, some warnings are for our own good. Like, "Don't touch that hot stove, you idiot!" The warnings you have to watch out for are the ones designed to inhibit you for no good reason. Like, "Go ahead, if you want everyone to see what an idiot you are." You have to ignore this second kind of warning, no matter how authoritative the source.

Think back. What tasks or activities have you never believed you could perform? In what ways have you allowed yourself to be limited or stereotyped?

Stop and think of five stereotypes you've been saddled with at various times in your life. Which ones made sense? Which ones heightened your fears? Which ones caused you to change plans?

If you're having trouble here, close your eyes. Review your life in *Reader's Digest* terms. Recollect your years in elementary school, junior high, high school, and college; your first girl or boyfriends; your first jobs and first bosses.

How did these settings and personalities dictate your expectations? How did they whittle down your perspective and carve in your brain ways of seeing things that shackled your thoughts?

Identifying your fears is the first step to freeing yourself from them. Once you've seen them for what they are, once you've hung signs around their scrawny necks, you can turn your mind to full power.

The High-Five of Courage

Now that we've identified the five fears, let's kick their boo-tays.

First, you must absolutely, positively, unqualifiedly be committed to your idea—and to the notion that you can make your idea happen. You have to commit yourself with abandon.

> "If you don't believe, you won't achieve."
> – Richard Saunders

To help you on your way, here's a list of the High 5 Sources of Courage. I dip into each of these wells to generate, nurture and maintain courage in my own life.

1. Look to teammates: Pioneers need partners. Great adventures are team efforts, and big ideas need big teams to make them a reality.

The band of folks you assemble is your greatest source of courage. They understand the mission. When the forces of the real world are pressing down, you can find support and strength from your teammates.

They might be folks you work with at Giant American Conglomerates Unlimited. Or they might be fellow members of the cast of your junior class play. Or the architect who's designing your home and the contractor who's building it.

Or you might have just one teammate. Like, say, your spouse—your dearly beloved, the one who promised to love and obey you until death do you part. Mine is named Debbie, and I'd never launch a venture without her total support.

If you don't have a mutually supportive relationship, get the relationship fixed. Never, ever set sail on a grand adventure without the support of your spouse. This person must be the personification of faith and support. If you have that, you're blessed indeed. Anything short of it will deflate your oomph, drain your energy, and puncture your balloon.

> "A good wife and health, is a man's best wealth."
> – Ben Franklin

> "That goes for good husbands and health, too."
> – Richard Saunders

When I launched my company, my financing took the form of a most excellent set of MasterCard's. It was expensive, but it worked. In this regard, as in so many others, Debbie was the Queen of Supportiveness.

> "Starting the business meant working extra hours. When we got our MasterCard bill, I'd sign up for extra shifts at the hospital. I was working nights at the time. At one point, I worked 18 nights in a row at two different hospitals."
> – Debbie Hall, R.N., my wife

Children are powerful little courage generators. They have the ability to put your life into perspective, a gift for stripping away the peripherals and getting to the heart of a situation.

If you're really scared, try talking to a child about fear. Ask what scares her and how she deals with her fears. In just such a conversation when my daughter was five years old she shared a revelation with me that put into perspective how large children's fears must seem relative to adult fears ...

> "Dragons and monsters are what scare me most. When I get really scared, I count to 10 and that takes my mind off it."
> – Kristyn Hall, my daughter

Wow! I may have fears in my day-to-day business life. But I never have come face to face with dragons and monsters.

Talking with a child has a way of making your fears seem not so big. Most adult fears melt away under the scrutiny of a five-year-old. One of the wonderful things about kids is that no matter how great your success or dismal your failure, they'll love you just the same. Your children have total faith in you. Believe in that. Use it to believe in yourself.

Over breakfast, a friend of mine passed this same bit of advice to a major league baseball pitcher who was going through a slump, a guy who was growing numb to the sound of tens of thousands of people booing. His confidence was shot. But when he considered that no matter what happened at the ball yard, his three-year-old wouldn't care, he began regaining his faith in his abilities. Once he turned that corner in his mind, he beat the slump.

2. Taking Action: Think of yourself as a deer on a highway. If you freeze in the headlights of an oncoming 18-wheeler, you're road kill. When fear hits you, it's time to move your hooves. Move them, and your body and mind will follow. You may fall on your face, but at least you'll be moving forward.

Fear is a mirage arising from your own uncertainties. Take action, any action. It's better than standing still. In most cases, if you challenge your fear through action, you'll find it's not nearly as formidable as you thought.

> "I am in the midst of learning to face my fears. It seems that fears are all based on these things: illusion and future thinking, with a side order of 'what if.'"
> – SARK, Inspiration Sandwich

Think of a group of explorers at the base of a mountain

range. They can sit and ponder the fearful vagaries of fate or they can start climbing. As they make their way up the slope and toward the peak, they'll find many opportunities and alternative routes they never could have seen from the base of the mountain.

> "You can't think and hit at the same time. To really hit, you have to just get out there."
> – Yogi Berra

It's hard to find opportunities if you stay put. If you get moving, new opportunities will present themselves. Besides, once you're moving, you're building momentum. To paraphrase Dr. Franklin, an ounce of momentum is worth a pound of courage.

Another way to build momentum is to break your fear into pieces. Then act on each piece, one at a time. Celebrate small victories. **Realize that each small victory represents another step up the mountain.** Manhattan wasn't built in a minute. Small successes add up to increased confidence and positive momentum.

I once led a creativity seminar for 100 executives at a leading corporation. At the end of the session, I gave each executive a paper airplane and asked that they write any suggestions for improving the seminar on the wings. The idea was to get them to scribble a comment and let the their plane fly, then grab any planes that came their way and expand on the thoughts already there.

I got lots of good suggestions from them. But one plane in particular gave me an insight into the different perspectives on my message. I think Person No. 3 got the picture.

> Person No. 1: You're not in touch with the real world.
> Person No. 2: Can you help us translate learning to the real world?
> Person No. 3: JUST DO IT!

3. Covering Your Bets: Contrary to popular belief, most entrepreneurs—and certainly 99 percent of all successful veteran entrepreneurs I've ever come across—are extremely conservative. Entrepreneurs are not daredevils. They don't take long shots. Instead, they reduce fear by covering their bets. They use a number of tricks to minimize risk and increase their courage, including:

- **Under-estimating expectations**. A classic rule of thumb is to round all costs up and all revenue estimates downward. Then cut all assumptions by 30 percent to 70 percent. If you find your plan will work even when cut to a fraction of its regular size, your courage will grow.

- **Building back doors.** Figure out fallback positions in the event your initial plan falls flat. The more options you have today, the more courage you'll have tomorrow.

- **Be the best.** When you take the high ground and create something of genuine value, you'll be strengthened. If an idea is true, if it's not of dubious value, you'll be more apt to have the courage to see it through. The best ideas are the ones that bring out the idealist in you.

- **Have non-negotiable ethics and a low overhead.** The following story regarding Ben Franklin tells it well.

"Soon after the establishment of his paper, a person brought him a piece, which he requested him to publish in the *Pennsylvania Gazette*. Franklin desired that the piece might be left for his consideration until next day, when he would give an answer. The person returned at the time appointed and received from Franklin his communication, "I have perused your piece, and find it to be scurrilous and defamatory. To determine whether I should publish it, I went home in the evening, purchased a two-

penny loaf at the baker's, and, with water from the pump made my supper; I then wrapped myself up in my great coat, and laid down on the floor and slept till morning, when on another loaf and a mug of water, I made my breakfast. From this regimen, I feel no inconvenience whatever. Finding I can live in this manner, I have formed a determination never to prostitute my press to the purposes of corruption, and abuse of this kind, for the sake of gaining a more comfortable subsistence."
– Isaiah Thomas, History of Printing In America

4. Replaying Success: Another way to heighten your G.Q. (Guts Quotient) is to visualize success.

- **Visualize previous wins.** Think back to a moment when, by some sudden serendipity, you created a solution, found a shortcut, or concocted a new way to reach a goal. Recall a moment of revelation in which the curtain pulled back and you were given an answer from somewhere outside yourself. Hey, you did it once—you can do it again.

- **Recall the great ones**. What would your hero do in this situation? If you don't have a hero now, who was your hero when you were small? How would John Wayne, Amelia Earhart, Zorro, Betty Crocker, Jesus, Sam Snead, Eleanor Roosevelt, Conan the Barbarian, or Ben Franklin proceed under these circumstances? One of the reasons fear paralyzes is that it befuddles. Often, a fearful person's biggest problem is simply in knowing which way to turn. By stepping out of yourself and letting a hero be your guide, you can find that direction.

5. Bursting the Worst: What is the worst that can happen?

Think about it. Write it down. Articulate it. How bad could it get? Now deal with it.

Is the worst case really all that bad? The specifics of the worst case are often much less than your vague imaginings of it.

Then consider that it's not likely you'll let things get to a worst-case scenario. Take heart in that.

> "When I'm not feeling creative, I turn off the word processor, sit back, take a sip of coffee and say to myself, 'Hey, I can ALWAYS get another job, such as coal miner.' And then I turn the old word processor right back on and become AMAZINGLY creative."
> – Dave Barry, humor columnist, author

During my stretch at Procter & Gamble, I was responsible for the national introduction of Spic and Span Pine Cleaner. So I wanted to kick up a ruckus that would have the competition trembling with fear.

Through a happy coincidence, it turned out that Spic and Span was about to celebrate its 75th birthday, an occasion that translated into a Diamond Anniversary. About that same time, I happened to hear from a friend about a new type of man-made diamonds called cubic zirconium's. These separate pieces of information came together into an idea for a promotion where a diamond—some of them real, most of them man-made—would be placed in every box and bottle of Spic and Span.

The idea was not without its risks. Given the huge scope of the line, it was decided we'd have to corner the world market on cubic zirconiums for four months. Additionally, there were concerns about getting the stones in the boxes and what to do to keep unscrupulous consumers from opening the boxes in the store to get to the rocks.

Procter & Gamble's legal, manufacturing and public relations departments strongly recommended against the promotion—at least until it could be tested.

The Vice President of my department Ross Love asked if I had another option. I told him our traditional plan had been to offer a 25¢ coupon and a 35¢-off price pack, which is P&G-ese

for a coupon that's printed on the package itself. The results were predictable enough, seeing as how sales had declined each year for the past five years we'd taken this route. How much did it cost to stage this traditional marketing event? About $2 million per year.

I told him the diamond promotion would come in at $1.3 million.

Ross knew there was some uncertainty with my diamond campaign. He also understood there was little uncertainty about the coupon promotion; it was virtually guaranteed to be a waste of $2 million.

"Let's do the diamonds," he said.

With his support the idea grew in dimensions. With the help of my direct boss, Kip Knight, we gained the support of the Jewelers Association of America, which agreed to place signs in the windows of its stores identifying them as "Spic and Span Diamond Validation Centers." These were places where you could have your diamond checked to see if you had a cubic zirconium worth $ 5.00 or a real one-third carat diamond worth $600.

Finally, the program was launched in February, around Valentine's Day, The whole shebang linked Spic and Span's 75th anniversary, Valentine's Day and diamonds. In my mind, the slogan "Buy your honey a box of Spic and Span for Valentines" was a wicked neat twist on an old theme.

I was promoted shortly after creating the idea and setting it in motion. The marketing event garnered millions of dollars' worth of free exposure — from "Good Morning America" to The Wall Street Journal. More importantly, it generated record sales for Spic and Span and helped Spic and Span Pine set a P&G record for exceeding it's first year volume objective.

> "Corporate Americans have a fear of doing anything new. They're comfortable doing the same thing over and over again. You know, 'We ran that promotion last year. Let's run it again this year!'"
> – Eric Schulz, Walt Disney Video Marketing

We've established that you're not a machine. You're a

human being. Otherwise, fear wouldn't be a factor. You'll need courage to get started, and you'll need grit-your-teeth, clench-your-fist perseverance to keep going when war-painted locals atop galloping appaloosas start firing flaming arrows at you.

But don't fear fear. Make it your friend. Use it to fuel your energy. It prevents complacency. It will make you reach inside yourself and stretch your potential.

> "Years ago, when Ken Stabler was a quarter-back for the Raiders, a newspaperman said, 'Ken, I want to read you something Jack London wrote: "I would rather be ashes than dust. I would rather that my spark burn out in a brilliant blaze than be stifled by dry rot. I would rather be a superb meteor, every atom of me a magnificent glow, than a sleepy crumbling planet. For the proper function of man is to live, not exist. I shall not waste my days in trying to prolong them. I shall use my time." And the reporter then asked Stabler: 'What does that mean to you, Kenny? Without hesitating, Stabler said: 'Throw deep!'"
> – Michael Wagman, *Advertising Age*

One reason I left P&G was that I no longer had any fear. My work there was no longer new. The edge was gone. It seemed too easy. Opportunities to throw deep were gone.

For all its allure, stability can be too comfortable. Stability taken too far leads to stagnancy. Stability is the absence of change. Dead people are stable.

You'll get your chance to be brave. Remember what the wizard told the lion:

> "As for you, my fine friend, you're a victim of dis-organized thinking. You are under the unfortunate delusion that simply because you run away from danger, you have no courage. You're confusing courage with wisdom. Back where I come from, we have men who are called heroes. Once a year,

they take their fortitude out of mothballs and parade it down the main street of the city. And they have no more courage than you. But they have one thing that you haven't got—a medal."
– The Wizard of Oz

It was true then, and it's true now. In keeping with this sentiment, I hereby present you this medal of valor.

The hardest part is taking the first step. Once you get your feet moving, opportunities will reveal themselves.

WELCOME TO
THE RANCH

The proper setting can be a tremendous asset when inventing big ideas. The proper place inspires, excites and, at the same time, offers the comfort of a lakeside cabin in New England, the sun coming up, an old pair of jeans and your favorite sweatshirt.

I've worked hard to make the Eureka! Ranch a haven for free and original thought. It's a cozy place in a rural spot just outside the gravitational pull of Cincinnati, Ohio, a place where even the stiffest, staunchest, starchiest RWA can uncoil without suffering withdrawal symptoms.

My clients have come to think of it as a corporate detox center. That's what I've tried to make it.

Quick History of Eureka! Spaces

The first Eureka! office was the basement of our home in Cincinnati, Ohio. The second and third were converted office park spaces. The fourth was an 1830's Greek Revival home listed on the National Historic Register we dubbed the Eureka! Mansion.

As we outgrew that space, the mansion became my family home. On the same property, some 140 paces away, we built the world's first 100 percent customized creativity space. Because we were building it from scratch, instead of converting another space we were able to turn the best of our previous four spaces into an idealistic creativity nirvana like no other on earth.

We call it the Eureka! Ranch. The name is meant to evoke

the spirit of the pioneers and adventurers who left the comfortable confines of the East for the great American West.

Yesterday we ran most of projects at the Eureka! Ranch. Today, 90 percent+ of our projects are run at client offices and at other facilities across the globe.

The Ranch is stocked with wall-to-wall arcade games, fine art, great food and plenty of everything to drink. It's a spot out in the country, just outside Cincinnati where CEO's, vice presidents, directors, market researchers, and assorted other RWA executives can draw a deep breath, heave a sigh and regain the courage to re-embrace the Eureka! Way as they did when they first began their careers.

You Need Your Own Special Place

The Eureka! Ranch is like that special place you had as a kid, where you could say whatever swirled into your mind and not worry what anyone thought. Maybe it was on top of the monkey bars, out behind the barn or in a private corner of the attic where you and your imagination could explore the farthest reaches of your universe.

When you went there, any fears you might have had couldn't find you. Try to remember the worlds you created there. Try to recall the heroic roles you invented for yourself, the demons that fell before you and the villains you vanquished.

Today, your enemy is sameness. The villain is Real World Status Quo. You need to rediscover that special place. **You need a Eureka! space of your own.**

> "The first step for me is to get into an environment where creativity can take place. It doesn't happen in an office, behind a desk with phone calls coming in from a billion different people. I have to break away and get back to being me. I have a room in my house that is my 'Sports Central.' It's got a cardboard Michael Jordan in a corner with Bugs Bunny from the Nike commercial. It's got basketball pictures everywhere, memorabilia stuff from my college days and a lot of historical

stuff to remind me of where I've been. Most of my
great ideas come to me in that room ..."
– Eric Schulz, Walt Disney Company

This chapter is a suggested blueprint for creating a special place for you. In many cases, I have scientific evidence to support my suggestions. In others, the lack of scientific evidence in no way hinders me from drawing conclusions. In those instances, I draw on experience and opinions—my own and those of my companions in creativity, the Eureka! Ranch Trained Brains.

My blueprint may not be your ideal. Tastes differ. For instance, you might be allergic to Prince Edward Island mussels or oysters. You'll probably have ideas of your own. That's fine.

The point is that every element in your special place is, in one way or another, a potential stimulus for ideas. This is just how I've done it. And I've had happy results using the environmental elements cited below with companies both large and small.

FOOD & DRINK

At the Ranch we take food and drink very seriously. That said, the role of food and drink in the creative process is a controversial one. I find two polar points of view—among the Ranch Staff, at least. I can see advantages to both sides:

Lean Mean Wellians: Their bodies are temples, not to be sullied with calories, fat, cholesterol or artificial sugars. In terms of liquid refreshment, their preferences run to spring water and fruit juices. Given a choice between a sticky bun and a carrot stick, they'll behave like a wild hare.

They believe the fuel provided by high-fat, sugar-caked foods burns out quickly and leads to premature crashing. And to the extent that scientific studies show that animals on low-cal diets live longer and healthier, they make good sense.

As a long-time junk-food aficionado, I find this position

more than a bit disconcerting. But I can testify to the impact of a reduced caloric intake. When I eat light, my energy level is generally greater. In the process of writing this book, I found that my pages-per-hour output increased by nearly a third when I ate lighter meals. When the belly is glutted with heavy grub, it seems the body spends so much energy processing the food that the brain is short-changed.

> "If thou art dull and heavy after a meal, it's a sign thou has exceeded the due Measure; for meat and drink ought to refresh the body, and make it cheerful, and not to dull and oppress it."
> – Ben Franklin

Lean mean wellians eschew fat in particular, leaning instead toward chicken and shellfish. The connection between creativity and ultra low-fat, high-protein foods has some basis in scientific fact. Indeed, numerous scientific studies indicate shellfish is the highest of all high-octane brain foods.

> "Shellfish, low in fat and carbohydrates, and almost pure protein, delivers large supplies of an amino acid called tyrosine to the brain, which then converts into the two mentally energizing brain chemicals, dopamine and norepinephrine ... Extensive research with both animals and humans proves that when the brain produces (these chemicals), mood and energy pick up. You tend to think and react more quickly, be more attentive, motivated and mentally energetic."
> – Jean Carper, The Food Pharmacy

One point to keep in mind when ripping into your shellfish: avoid butter, bread, potatoes, and deep-frying. Researchers tell us that loading up on fat or carbohydrates can dull the mind.

Of course, oysters, clams, crabs, and shrimp are fine. But in my totally biased opinion, the best brain foods in the world include: Prince Edward Island mussels, Malpeque oysters, and Prince Edward Island lobsters. The fact that I have a home on

PEI not far from Malpeque Bay is coincidental. And never mind that my neighbor, Kent Mackay, is a lobsterman and mussel farmer. Or that Carr's Oyster Bar is just around the corner.

Fat Sassy Hedonists: From a perspective of physical health, their bodies are temples of doom. They like their food rich, exotic, and in steaming heaps. Like Jimmy Buffett and my son, Brad, fat sassy hedonists believe the first item on the menu in paradise is a cheeseburger.

My co-author, David Wecker, professes not to share my affection for the music and spirit of Jimmy Buffett. And it's true I've never seen him in a tropical shirt. But he has always been willing to accept a free beer and a free lunch—in fact, just about anything that's free, Dave is up for it. On a diving trip to Key West, I bought him a lunch at Buffet's place there, on the condition that he order the menu's lead item—Cheeseburg-er in Paradise. This he did, feigning reluctance, at least until the waitress brought his burger. He consumed it with gusto. My conclusion: He's a closet Parrot Head.

Fat sassy hedonists argue that the supreme fluid for jump-starting a brain is coffee. While the debate over coffee's benefits has raged for centuries, I stand firmly behind the brown bean. Here's why:

- Coffee is 100 percent natural, with no chemicals or preservatives
- Coffee contains no calories
- A cup of joe costs less than a nickel a cup when you brew it fresh
- Ounce for ounce, a cup of brewed coffee contains five times the caffeine of colas

Throughout history, such illustrious figures as Franklin, Voltaire, Twain, Bach, Beethoven and Brahms have heaped praise on coffee. The brew itself is dark, but its power is clear.

"Caffeine results in a clearer and more rapid flow of thought (and an) allaying of drowsiness and fatigue. After taking caffeine, one is capable of a greater sustained intellectual effort and a more perfect association of ideas. There is also a keener appreciation of sensory stimuli, and reaction time is appreciably diminishedt ... In addition, motor activity is increased: typists, for example, work faster and with fewer errors."
– The Pharmacological Basis of Therapeutics

"Caffeine boosted (test subjects') performances on every single one of the mental tests ... (it) stirred the brain to improve mental functioning, reaction speed, concentration and accuracy."
– Jean Carper, The Food Pharmacy

More than 200 years ago in parts of Europe, distribution of coffee beans were restricted because the brew was thought to stir thoughts of rebellion among the masses. And indeed, the coffee houses of the day were forums for hothead radicals spouting doctrines of revolution.

"One of the most interesting facts in the history of coffee is that wherever it has been introduced, it has spelled revolution. It has been the world's most radical drink in that its function has always been to make people think. And when the people began to think, they became dangerous to tyrants and to foes of liberty, of thoughts and of action."
– William Ukers, *All About Coffee*

Medical opinions vary on the benefits and risks of consuming coffee by the bucketful. For every coffee-related study citing a potential negative health effect on the human physiology, you can find another to the contrary.

"The mystical, magical properties, of the wondrous, marvelous bean, will get you rolling in

the morning, and thinking swift and clean. The
power of this incredi-brew is almost too great to
conceive. Through morning, noon & night, it
will help you to achieve."
– Richard Saunders

So strong is my faith in the brew that I've developed a cus-
tom blend called Brain Brew, a mix of some of the world's greatest coffees—java from Java, pure Colombian, Hawaiian Kona
and exotic Tanzanian Peaberry—that can Jump Start brain cells
morning, noon and night.

For me, there's no finer moment in the day than when I
take my first sip of Brain Brew. The taste is great—in one taste
test, it beat Starbucks' house blend 2 to 1. It's so powerful that,
in another test versus a decaf control, participants invented 41
percent more ideas after chugging three mugs of Brain Brew.
This book was fueled with Brain Brew; during the writing of it,
Dave and I consumed nearly 5,000 cups.

"With coffee, all things are possible. Coffee
enables us to endure the hardships and weather
the tempests of life. Coffee helps us rise to challenges, overcome hurdles and, at the end of the
day, it's there to help us savor our victories."
– Richard Saunders

Fat and Sassy Hedonists avail themselves of any opportunity to indulge in sweets and ingest high-calorie foods. At our
Eureka! sessions, we find afternoon tea is helpful in overcoming
the inevitable post-lunch slump. I recommend a delicately flavored Darjeeling, but only if it carries the Darjeeling certifica-
tion symbol indicating it's the real thing. Today, my favorite tea
is a First Flush (first picked) Darjeeling from Harrods in London.
If Brain Brew delivers the Mac Truck of caffeine, First Flush is
the Ferrari.

For those who don't care for tea a suitable substitute is a
fine Margarita made the classic Eureka! Ranch way.

Eureka! Ranch Margarita Recipe
- 3 parts tequila (look for one labeled 100 percent Blue Agave - Reposado Age)
- 2 parts cointreau (don't think about using imposters)
- 1 part lime juice

Shake with ice and served with salt on the rim.

My favorite hedonists like to supplement afternoon tea with strawberries dipped in bittersweet chocolate, petit fours, fruit tarts, lemon mousse puffs, finger sandwiches, and rich, buttery scones with cream and strawberries. Admittedly, it's a little formal. But there is something refreshingly irreverent about having formal tea while attired in jeans.

In my experience, hedonistic inventing achieved its pinnacle during a Eureka! session convened to develop a new breakfast cereal for children. For an entire day, Trained Brains and clients alike gobbled fistfuls of sugarcoated flakes and fruity nuggets while guzzling urns of Brain Brew.

That session is a legend in Eureka! lore. On that day, ideas for new cereals flowed like lava from Vesuvius. In fact, when two or more of those who attended that session gather together, talk often returns to the Day of Sugar and Caffeine—sort of like what it must be like whenever veterans get together to discuss the Bataan Death March.

TOYS
The world wants to separate the men from the boys. I'm more interested in separating the child from the grownup.

> "Old boys have their playthings as well as young ones, the difference is only in the price."
> – Ben Franklin

We started out as children. All of us have children inside us. It's just that sometimes, it's hard to get the child to come out and play. That's why toys are important.

At the Eureka! Ranch, we take play seriously. That means toys, lots and lots of toys. In the great room, where the inventing takes place, we have Pinball Alley, a Skee Ball Alley, Professional Air Hockey, a pool table and a half-dozen other full-scale arcade classics. Outside we have a white-sand volleyball court, a basketball court, a horseshoe pit, a bocce ball court and a 65-acre lake stocked with kayaks, canoes, a ski boat, and any kind of freshwater fishing gear you might want.

When we're inventing, the toys are put aside. But during breaks, we throw on the switch and let the clients have at it. The toys help folks relax and connect to a fun-loving, playful spirit. We use play as a way to generate excitement and competition, as well as to reduce stress. I've seen studies that show these elements ignite more positive results in terms of stimulating creativity than more frivolous (as in silly and childlike) playfulness.

> "Believe none of what you hear and half of what you see."
> – Ben Franklin.

SWEATING THE BIG IDEAS

A 2005 study published in the *Creativity Research Journal* found that after 30 minutes of exercise, test subjects' ability to think creatively was much higher than that of a control group that didn't exercise. Significant improvements were seen up to two hours after exercising.

This means that boosting one's creative ability may not be as hard as we think. Stuck on an issue you can't seem to resolve? Have a problem with no solution? Need material for your next event? Put on those running shoes, go for a jog and wait for the answer to come to you.

THE POWER OF SUNLIGHT

Let there be light! You want plenty of windows that open easily. In the best of all possible worlds, for me at least, the view looks out across a range of purple mountains or a white-capped seascape. Short of those alternatives, I'm fond of views that bring in sunshine.

New scientific research confirms it to be a fact: Working and thinking in full-spectrum sunlight kick-starts your brain.

The study was monstrous, involving 750 classrooms and

more than 21,000 students. It found that children in classrooms with the most daylight learned 20 to 26 percent faster than students with the least daylight. The same study showed dramatic increases in standardized math and reading test results.

Walt Disney's belief in the ability of natural light to enhance the creative process was such that he designed his animation studios to let in as much sunshine as possible. Likewise, the inventing room at the Eureka! Ranch lets the sun shine in.

Unfortunately, too many of us spend too much of our working lives in dark caves. So open the curtains and pull up the shades. Get up, get out and let in the sun!

> "Psychologist Rachel Kaplin of the University of Michigan told the American Psychological Society in Chicago … Workers stuck in windowless rooms, even if they are well lit and modern, are more easily distracted, less flexible in their thinking, more impulsive, less able to solve problems and more irritable."
> – *USA Today*, June 28, 1993

If you're in an urban environment or lack windows altogether, you have other options. In my early days at Procter & Gamble, I had an inner office without a window. All it had window-wise was an indentation in the wall, with a curtain, where a window had been at one time before an office addition was built. It was a good spot for a travel poster. I was able, if so inclined, to change my view on a daily basis—from the beach on the Riviera to the Arctic tundra to a heathery Irish countryside.

Finally, a decent Eureka! room ought to have high ceilings to accommodate lofty thoughts. And a fireplace or woodstove of any sort is a desirable option, except perhaps in the Sunbelt, where you may wish to substitute a slow-moving ceiling fan.

MUSIC

The judicious use of music wreaks great works. It's a potent tool for setting tempos and getting the brain pumping.

We have two sound tracks of music on our iPods. The first is a classical track that's scientifically best for creativity, set at the proper tempo, with no lyrics to distract. The second track is a scientifically incorrect but emotionally awesome classic rock 'n roll track that clearly shows my age.

Both have power to excite and inspire. My personal favorites are B, B & B—Jimmy Buffett, the rock group Boston, and a great bagpipe tune by my friends at the College of Piping and Celtic Performing Arts of Canada in the city of Summerside on Prince Edward Island.

PROPER ATTIRE

We are quite strict about standards of proper attire. It might be easier to say what's not proper. No suits, no wingtip shoes, no silk stockings. No worsted wool, no high heels, no buttoned collars. No pants with creases or cuffs, no seersucker and no polo shirts with emblems unless they're funny. No power colors, no preppie pinks, no lime greens. *And no business casual, OK?!?!?!?*

Wear what you'd wear to the beach or the carwash or exercise class or bicycling or for chopping wood or to the drive-in movie or out to get the mail. Wear your lucky socks or don't wear any socks at all. Wear stuff that doesn't itch. Wear baggy duds that won't encumber you if you decide to do a somersault. Wear a giant Mickey Mouse head if you like the way it makes you look.

I have a preference for jeans, a comfortable shirt of the tropical variety, and Birkenstocks. My point is, I take a strong stand on clothes. If you want to make things happen, you have to be comfortable. It's part of the heritage from my forefathers, who helped fight for freedom from England. During the Revolutionary War, the British troops wore proper bright red coats, with heavy starch. For their part, the colonials wore working class clothes, replete with muted colors that helped them blend in with their surroundings.

And while the Redcoats did battle in the conventional manner, lining up on the village green in straight rows, the rebels approached their task in a more entrepreneurial way, fighting from behind trees and rocks, using their surroundings to maximum effect. It didn't matter what they wore. What counted was what they were able to accomplish.

As today's corporations have grown fat and rich, they often take on the style of the Redcoats. They need to realize that, in today's marketplace, what their customers want is substance—not form and style.

Speaking of form and style, the absolute worst fashion accessories you can wear to one of my inventing sessions is a necktie or a pair of pantyhose.

Wearing a tie to the Ranch is a hanging offense—and by that, I mean that it's an offensive thing hanging around your neck, not that we would actually execute anyone for wearing one. We're more forgiving about pantyhose, but only slightly. Both are completely nefarious. Both are the natural enemies of creativity.

But the necktie is especially insidious. Cravats of all sorts are thinly disguised neck tourniquets that block the flow of blood to the brain and cause a buildup of hot air that, if unchecked, can turn a person into a Fathead.

> "What would you think of that prince, or that government, who should issue an edict forbidding you to dress in a certain fashion on pain of imprisonment? Would you not say, that you are free, have a right to dress as you please, and that such an edict would be a breach of your privileges, and such an edict tyrannical?"
> – Ben Franklin

My gripe with ties is no mere publicity stunt. It's backed by scientific fact. I was once interviewed on the subject by the *Wall Street Journal*.

> "Some people in the medical field agree with Mr. Hall that neckties can be harmful to your health … Examination of patients who complained of dizziness and headaches … showed snug ties were the culprits in the cases of an estimated 25 to 50 white collar males—A study at Cornell

University arrived at a similar conclusion ...
wearing tight ties causes eyestrain."
– The *Wall Street Journal*

Dr. Bruce Yaffe, a Manhattan internist and gastroenterologist, adds his voice to the anti-necktie chorus. There is some evidence, he says, that when you wear a tight collar or a tie, the veins in your neck can be compressed, leading to pressure in the brain, leading in turn to lightheadedness and headaches:

> "You won't cut off the arterial flow by wearing a tight collar or a necktie, because blood is pushed through the arteries with some force. But you can slow the flow of blood in the veins, which can result in an accumulation of blood in the brain, resulting in pressure in the brain."

For all that, ties do have worthwhile applications. Here's a top 10 list for your consideration:

No. 10: Comes in handy if your rope ladder of success (or escape) is missing a rung.

No. 9: Useful as a narrow bib when eating barbecued ribs or spaghetti. Better if you have 10 or 12 of them to make a fuller bib.

No. 8: Can be used in a pinch if you're trying to run an idea up the flagpole to see who salutes and the rope is broken.

No. 7: Can be used as a crying towel during IRS audits.

No. 6: Makes a good headband when suddenly surrounded by a hostile street gang.

No. 5: With proper adjustments to accommodate eyeholes, can be used in lieu of ski mask when holding up neighborhood convenience store.

No. 4: Black ones make good armbands when mourning deceased heads of corporate state.

No. 3: Can double as blindfold when playing classic corporate game of pin-the-tail-on-the-scapegoat.

No. 2: Helpful when lashing down trunk filled with personal effects following corporate takeover.

No. 1: (drum roll, Maestro!) ... Works nicely as a bridle when playing giddyup-horsey with the kids after dinner.

DETAILED EUREKA! RANCH TOUR

The Ranch itself is a rambling, sprawling russet-stained complex that is a cross between a western bunkhouse and a Southwestern ranch. A wooden porch with all kinds of rocking chairs and hammocks to sit on, decorated with brightly colored flags and banners, wraps around the front. You walk through the front door into the Brain Brew Saloon, named after our coffee brand. For this, I imported a century-old tavern bar from Maryland and had it restored to its original glory. The bar is, of course, fully stocked with our favorite libations, including an extensive collection of coffee drinks, single-malt Scotch whiskies, and aged tequila. If you're in the mood for some honky-tonk, we'll flip on the player piano. Or you can sit down at the poker table and open a new deck of cards. On the walls is a collection of Ben Franklin memorabilia and photos of the Trained Brains.

To the left of the Brain Brew Saloon is the office space where my staff folks busy themselves all day long like the diligent honeybees they are. It's an Apple shop, filled with the latest generations of Macs. A school of ceramic fish swims over the doorway.

To the right is a hallway leading to the Ranch R&D team's Party Room, as they call it. The hallway itself is lined with autographed photos of various luminaries who sent good wishes when my various books have been published. They include Frank Sinatra, Cher, Peewee Herman, Michele Pfeiffer, Dr. Ruth, Ed Asner, Lucille Ball and dozens of others. The photos are interesting as they give you a peek at how celebrities visualize themself.

Proceeding past the Brain Brew Saloon, you enter the

Eureka! room where the inventing happens. At the head of the room is a giant stone fireplace. The room itself is about the size of a basketball court, with exposed beams a vaulted ceiling some 30 feet tall, with skylights to let the sun shine in. Around the walls are the arcade games I described earlier. In one corner is an M&M dispenser about the size of two refrigerators, stocked with about 50 zillion M&M's in gravity-fed dispensers, arranged by color, with nearly 30 different colors, way more than you can buy in the store. What can I say? I've done work for the Mars family, which owns M&Ms.

Hanging in the Eureka! room and around the Ranch you'll find original artwork. The Ranch is stocked with oil paintings, bronze sculpture, mobiles, and tapestries. Original art has a special energy that inspires original thinking.

In a space of prominence hangs a stadium-size banner commemorating the University of Maine's two NCAA championships in ice hockey, in 1993 and 1999—the U of M being my alma mater. Displayed on shelves throughout are gewgaws, trinkets and oddball items I've collected on my travels, all at the ready to be used as stimuli.

If you face straight ahead, to the south, the view through the giant wall of windows—for natural light—is our lake. The primary furnishings in the great room are mission-style couches and chairs by Stickley. The furniture reinforces our ranch motif, and the craftsmanship makes the furniture pieces of art.

Most newcomers spend the first 15 minutes or so looking around, saying

"Wow!" They then settle in with a feeling of comfort. A feeling that this is a safe place to take your shoes off, relax, and think bold thoughts.

*To view 360 degree movies of the Ranch, visit
http://www.EurekaRanch.com/Tour.*

Act 2

Jump Starts

Act II is a toolbox. You'll find herein the Top 30 Idea Igniters for making The Eureka! Way work for you, each loaded with examples so you can see exactly how to apply it.

This is my vintage collection. Each technique has been tested, sharpened and fire-refined over the years to bring out the ultimate in its elegance, efficiency and function. Like a bottle of fine Highland Park Scotch Whisky that's transformed in the journey from 12 to 18 years from merely extraordinary to defying spectacular (A shameless endorsement of Doug and Dave's favorite spirit. And a client, no less). So, too, these 30 Jump Start techniques are the best of the best.

- Chapter 10 details 10 sure fire ways to leverage stimuli.
- Chapter 11 documents 10 industrial-strength methods.
- Chapter 12 describes 10 of the best methods for group creativity.

Note—while most of these Jump Starts are described for individual use, most of them can be easily adapted for use by groups. And, the group Jump Starts can be easily adapted to individual use—or individual use with a partner via e-mail or instant messaging.

To heap it on just a bit higher, each of these techniques has proven itself repeatedly. These are sure bets. Dr. Franklin declared "nothing was certain but death and taxes" Well in my experience, to that list, I would now add these Jump Starts.

> "Well done is better than well said."
> – Ben Franklin

★ ★ ★ ★ ★ ★ ★ ★ ★ ★ ★ ★ ★ ★ ★ ★ ★

TOP 10 STIMULI
JUMP STARTS

★ ★ ★ ★ ★ ★ ★ ★ ★ ★ ★ ★ ★ ★ ★ ★ ★

Stimu-lee, stimu-la, stimu-lye. However you say it, nothing makes a brain function more productively or creatively.

As I have explained previously, you do have a choice. You can choose to brainstorm and simply suck ideas from your head—or you can use your brain as a computer and process stimuli into ideas.

"The biggest bonfire starts from the smallest spark."
– Richard Saunders

In the old days, back in the previous century, I encouraged toys and foolishness. Today, I've found a much shorter distance between a challenge and success. Today, I focus more directly on translating stimuli into insights and ideas. For example, if I'm working on "selling" a thing—whether it's a new product or service, a new sales message, or a nonprofit fundraiser—I encourage a focus on the Three Laws of Marketing Physics:

- **Overt Benefit**: What PROMISE are we making to the customer? Or as a customer might put it, "What's in it for me?"
- **Real Reason to Believe**: Why should the customer TRUST we'll deliver the Overt Benefit promised? Or in the words of the customer, "Why should I believe you?"
- **Dramatic Difference**: What makes our Overt Benefit and/or Real Reason to Believe dramatically different from what other companies offer? Again, in the words of the customer, "Why should I care?"

A stimulus is a fuse for lighting ideas. It can be anything you can use to prod and poke your mind, to make your mind react. Stimuli can include stuff that is related and/or unrelated to your task. A piece of stimulus can be as simple an item as today's newspaper, a rubber ball, a couple dozen cable TV stations, chocolate pudding, a paint chip, a song, or a banana peel. In other words, it can be anything that makes you think of something else.

The five senses are extraordinary collectors of information. Most of us trust them, but we barely use them.

Here's what I mean: An idea that backs up a claim of greatness with sensory support makes it easier for people to believe that claim and, as a result, makes it more likely they'll give it a try.

Three shining examples are Glad Bag's blue-and-yellow-make-green seal, the Ziploc "zipper" sound and the Oral-B Indicator toothbrush, with bristles that change color when it's time to replace your brush. In the first case, a visual indicator tells the consumer the product is working—that the bag is sealed tight. In the second, the consumer can hear the product working. In the third, the consumer gets a visual cue that the product should be replaced.

Likewise, natural foods draw more consumer interest when they look natural. An "ugly" breakfast cereal with odd-size chunks and imperfect clumps is more credible than processed pellets of perfection. And the label on Newman's Own salad dressing advises that the bottle be shaken to mix natural ingredients before opening. The message is that natural stuff separates, artificial stuff doesn't.

As you set off to explore stimuli, understand that the gathering process will provide half the solution you want; don't outsource the gathering. The process of sifting through the data, the comments and the observations offer a depth of understanding that you won't get from a distance or through second-hand experience. You have to go there.

So what are you waiting for? Let's get up, get out, and get going!

STIMULI MINING JUMP START NO. 1

The Three Dimensions of Stimuli

The Three Dimensions of Stimuli form the foundation on which your ideas will be built. The process requires you to gather up steaming heaps of stimuli, insights and information to bolster your creativity. The stimuli can be factual, perceptual, sensual, emotional and/or experiential. Think of this stage as tilling the ground before planting the seeds.

Objective: To gather information about the target of your creative desire, as well as to find areas of opportunity where a wicked good idea can grow.

Stimuli are like fish. They're brain food. The gathering of stimuli is as important to your creative efforts as Laurel was to Hardy, as Abbott was to Costello, and as Curly was to Moe and Larry.

How to do it: Snarf up every scrap of information you can find related to your task. It's up to you, Tonto, to scout out the situation and bring back a reconnaissance report.

Stimuli Mining is more than simply going to the library and looking up facts. It's a matter of personally wrapping your hands around your challenge. You have to experience it, or you'll never understand what it's all about. Whether you're looking for a new job or looking to invent a new product from the crimson creases of your imagination, you have to hone in on your area of exploration and greedily immerse yourself in it in order to gather pieces and parts of stimuli that can prompt your imagination.

You can't hire someone to immerse himself in your place. Baptism is not transferable. Take the approach of the artist. Artists learn by doing. Painters become painters by painting. Musicians learn by playing. Sculptors develop by plying hammer and chisel or welding torch. To accomplish any great creative act, you must develop an intimacy between yourself and the essence of the challenge.

There are three basic types of stimuli mining. It doesn't matter what form your stimuli takes—your collection can range from photos, samples, perspectives, and opinions to contact lists, sights, sounds, and smells.

Historical Stimuli or How We Got Here in the First Place

The focus is on learning from the past to avoid repeating mistakes. Historical data can come from such hard sources as library reference books and news articles or from soft sources, such as interviews with people experienced in the arena where you're working. When reviewing the history of a problem, the answer to the future often presents itself.

Factual Stimuli or the World as It Is

What's the current situation—the economics, the practical considerations, and the resources available to you? How big of a problem do you really face? What are its limitations, where are its boundaries? What are your advantages and disadvantages versus other people, other organizations, and other companies? Ask questions of current customers—work to understand why they love or hate the existing options. Push for an understanding of problems large and small.

Experiential Stimuli or Putting the Senses to Work

The emphasis here is on your personal experience. The human senses comprise the finest data-collection system ever devised. But as we grow into adulthood, we learn to rely less on our senses and more on logic. When I'm dealing with a problem, I have to feel it, see it, sniff it out. I get as up close and personal as I can with the subject of inquiry.

Three Dimensions of Stimuli in Action

Here's how I used the Three Dimensions of Stimuli when asked to invent a second generation of ready-to-drink iced tea products for the Pepsi/Lipton joint venture team. The project, which was featured in a story on *Dateline NBC*, was a follow-up to a successful Eureka! project that helped create Lipton Originals ready-to-drink iced tea.

Historical Stimuli:
- • I read a dozen books about the history of tea, the fine art of afternoon tea, and various collections of tea recipes.
- • I reviewed all beverage testing that AcuPOLL had done previously for potential Pepsi and or Lipton product ideas.
- • I conducted on-line database searches of every new tea product introduced globally over the past five years.

Factual Stimuli:
- • I met with experts from the Lipton Kitchens who provided volumes of information about tea and its uses.
- • I interviewed Pepsi/Lipton sales and marketing managers for their perspectives on the competition and the market in general.
- • I read pounds of market research data on the category, consumer perceptions, attitudes, and opinions toward ready-to-drink iced tea.

Experiential Stimuli:
- • I went to the lab to create new flavors, formulating 45 different iced tea products.
- • I gathered 120 aroma samples to spur images for new beverages.
- • I tasted tea products with Pete Goggi, president of Lipton's Royal Estates tea purchasing company. Pete is a gentleman with a fine appreciation

for the subtle nuances of tea. He gave me insight into the poetry of the brew and exotic tea varietals.

- I gathered samples of competitors' teas— mainstream products as well as more exotic "New Age" specialty brands, prevailing on a friend to ship samples from San Francisco.
- Having learned how important color is in the beverage world, I gathered a collection of hues, tints, and shades. These included paint chips from the local paint store along with vividly colored photos.

In all likelihood, your goal isn't to create a wicked good ready-to-drink iced tea for Lipton. Your task may be connected more to your life than to a client. Let's say you're a college senior looking for your first real job. How might you use the process to help you get started in a career?

Historical Stimuli:
- List every job you have ever had, either as a paid employee or a volunteer.
- List every boss you've ever had. Ask them to describe to you your strengths and your weaknesses. Have you addressed any weaknesses? Built on any strengths?
- Call three dozen students you admire who graduated the year before and ask what they did to find their jobs.

Factual Stimuli:
- Scan help-wanted ads from Sunday newspapers in cities where you would like to live.
- Take tests from books or career counseling centers to gauge your aptitudes.
- Visit your local library and review recent articles on job trends. Look for articles about companies that are expanding their job forces.

- Review your checkbook to figure out how desperate you really are.
- List the top 10 places where you think you'd like to launch a career. Find out everything you can about them. Talk to people who work there now or have worked there in the past. Get their annual reports, if they have them.

Experiential Stimuli:
- Find folks in fields related to your interests who will meet with you over coffee or for lunch. Ask them what it takes, aside from academic credentials, to function in their world.
- Contact professionals established in the field related to your interests and ask if they would allow you to shadow them for a day or a week. Or call the human resources department of a company you admire and see if a similar arrangement can be made.
- Subscribe to professional journals or trade publications related to your field.

To get the most from the Three Dimensions of Stimuli process, keep prodding, pushing, and poking. Keep reading, moving, and asking questions. The more questions you ask, the more opportunities will suggest themselves. Done properly, the process will ignite dozens if not hundreds of ideas for solving your creative challenge.

The process of digging deep takes work. In those times when you might think of quitting, remember these words.

"No pains, no gains."
– Ben Franklin

STIMULI MINING JUMP START NO. 2

Stimuli One-Step

You've pursued the Three Dimensions of Stimuli—you have scads of insights, examples and thoughts. During the gathering process, potential solutions to your challenge undoubtedly revealed themselves.

The next two techniques will help you process the stimuli into ideas. This can be done in one of two ways—the One-step and the Two-step. With the first, you make a direct connection from a piece of stimulus to an idea in a single leap of imagination. With the second, you identify attributes of various pieces of stimulus and apply those traits to your task.

We'll deal with the Stimuli One-step first.

Objective: To transform physical stimuli into thoughts and ideas. When Alexander Graham Bell was designing a receiver for his telephone, he used a Stimuli One Step to find a simple solution, if not a somewhat grisly one. He asked a doctor pal of his for an ear from a cadaver. Ear in hand, literally, he designed an earpiece to match.

How to do it: Look, smell, feel, touch, and listen to as much stimuli as possible. Move quickly. Tear through it like a lawyer lunging for loopholes. With the One Step, you're looking for first-glance ideas. You look, and a thought occurs.

As you rifle through the stimuli, keep sight of your task. If you don't, your mind may wander off into the stimuli itself, and you'll lose sight of the problem.

I find it helpful to have a stack of index cards on hand while going over stimuli. When I see a piece of an idea that might possibly become a piece of the puzzle, I scribble it on a card. This keeps me moving, so that I don't get hung up on any single piece of stimuli. Be very conscious about recording ideas and then sloughing them off, getting them out of your mind, so your brain is free and receptive to the next idea that might come along.

I also find it helpful to go through the stimuli two or three times—in different orders. I often make new connections on that second and third go-round because my head is already filled with the overall content of the stimuli.

One-step in Action

Before Debbie and I moved into our new home, we wanted to finish the basement and turn it into an office for my creative and development efforts. It was also to become the first Eureka! room.

The ceiling was a problem. Drop ceilings make me claustrophobic. Drywall was out because I would need access to the wiring and plumbing.

So I reached for some stimuli. A sequence of home design books and magazines didn't prompt anything. One of my favorite sources for idea starters, the Sears catalog, offered nothing for this challenge, either. Finally, having despaired of finding a solution in a dozen volumes on home improvement, I found balm for my basement woes in *Vogue* magazine—specifically, a photo of a Soho clothing loft with exposed rafters and track lighting, all painted the same color.

The answer was simple—spray-paint the entire basement white, from top to bottom, then hang halogen track lights from the rafters. I decided the best way to address the ceiling issue was not to put in any ceiling at all.

The result was better than I'd hoped for. It gave the room a much more spacious feel. Despite the exposed rafters, the consensus was that it didn't look like a basement.

In any case, the idea for the no-ceiling basement ceiling wouldn't have occurred to me had I simply sat and engaged in brain draining. It took a spark to light the fuse.

One note on the Stimuli One-Step: It may not seem especially sophisticated or complicated. It may appear too ridiculously simple to yield worthwhile results. You'll change your mind once you try it. It's not necessary to go through a series of complex machinations to find the best ideas. The simplest, straightest paths are often the most effective.

STIMULI MINING JUMP START NO. 3

Stimuli Two-Step

This approach is slower and more deliberate. It uses analogy to create. Instead of the direct associations made with the Stimuli One-step, here you break each piece of stimulus into its components and apply those traits to your task.

Objective: To identify the characteristics of stimuli and mold them to your task. To concentrate not on the stimuli, but on the elements that make it what it is.

How to do it: Using either a related or unrelated stimulus, list all the features, traits, and elements you can find in it. Look at it up close, from afar, and from different angles. List emotional, physical, or interactive elements. What features, elements, or mechanisms make your stimulus move, act, or deliver excitement? What suggests itself? Is the piece of stimulus scary, hot, slippery, fun, bright yellow, prickly, shiny, daring, explosive, musical, or odiferous?

Consider how each of these elements might apply to your task. Locating abstract elements in stimuli and reassembling them in different configurations can be akin to strapping jet engines to your thinking machine.

You can do the Two-step with virtually any piece of stimulus. But when you're first getting started, you'll probably find it's best to use stimuli that are somehow similar or related to your challenge.

For example, you might find a book about animal habitats helpful in prompting ideas for new construction methods. A study of the hundreds of ways different species of birds build their nests, for instance, is likely to suggest to you new ways to assemble your factory, clubhouse, or backyard deck.

Let's take another task. Let's say your challenge is to come up with ideas to amuse your five-year-old nephew, Arnold, on a rainy Sunday afternoon. All you have is the Toys "R" Us advertising supplement from the newspaper.

You don't need the actual toys that the supplement advertises. What you need are their operational elements. Look at the toys. What do they do? How are they used? What makes them fun?

Once you have the answers, you can make it happen for Arnold with everyday stuff.

The supplement is advertising a sale on Nerf products. What is Nerf? Well, it's soft stuff you can toss around, fling, and shoot indoors. So how might you duplicate the Nerf experience without the actual Nerf stuff?

How about using rolled-up socks as shot puts? Or couch pillows for Frisbees? Or a rubber band and tongs as a slingshot, using paper wad ammo?

Involve little Arnold. He doesn't need the toys—he needs the analogies. A squeeze bottle makes a perfectly good squirt gun. Pots and pans make for a perfectly good drum set. And when Arnold's sister, Iodine, comes over, you can cut out paper dolls from fashion magazines and glue them onto cardboard.

Two-step in Action: Once, when I was with a team assigned to develop new recipes for a cookbook, we decided to use a bottle of high-end vodka as a stimulus. We listed its basic elements; it was clear, it came in a glass bottle with its name painted on the surface, it had a healthy feel and it was expensive.

One of the team members mentioned that she was surprised it had such a strong taste.

Building that thought into a launching pad, the team quickly developed dozens of new bakery products around the theme of surprise. We did muffins and cookies crammed with jelly and chocolate-chip surprises on the inside. We did inside-out cakes with the frosting in the center, the cake outside. We did peanut butter éclairs, with chunky peanut butter.

The simplest impression opened a rich vein of ideas—rich in multiple ways. But the links we made were courtesy of a single characteristic of the stimulus.

All kinds of ignition systems are readily available for sparking original thoughts for icons, images, and names. The Internet is one giant stimuli-generating machine. In terms of tactile and sensory stimuli, here's a list of idea grenades to bombard your thinking:

Stimuli Prospecting

Chips ahoy: If the task requires an extraordinary hue, raid the paint-chip display at your neighborhood paint store, where you'll find an array of carefully considered names for every tint and shade on the color wheel.

Paint chips can be an almost bottomless source of stimuli for names, icons, and images. There's a whole world beyond red, white and blue—such hues as Glidden's chocolate kiss, for-get-me-not, gold coast, eggplant, flamenco, scrimshaw, orchid puff, smoked pearl, and fjord seem a bit more vivid. Each conjures images, moods, and emotions.

Greeting cards: Speaking of images, moods, and emotions, a good place to go prospecting is your local card shop. The Valentine's Day section, for instance, can be helpful if you're looking for ways to put love into words, even if you don't care enough to send the very best.

Video rental stores: When Ben Franklin founded America's first public library, I doubt he realized the culture's most popular libraries would one day be oriented more toward flickering images than words printed on paper. Aside from providing escapes from reality, movies are a great way to teleport yourself to any locale in the galaxy, from travel videos to *Jurassic Park* to *2001: A Space Odyssey.*

Rocky gave me the inspiration for a new make-it-at-home beverage combination. Remember the scene where Rocky gets out of bed, opens the fridge, cracks half a dozen raw eggs into a glass and chugs it down? I later developed a number of new beverages where the client's product is mixed with everyday fruits and juices. And it goes down a lot easier than raw eggs.

Specialty catalogs: There's a catalog for everything. Catalogs are a rich, often untapped source of stimuli for ideas. I especially appreciate the way the copy and visuals in catalogs are so tightly focused. In the mail-order business, either you get the idea in a hurry or they don't get the sale.

Wallpaper sample books: This is a resource most never think of using. A good wallpaper sample book can be a rich source of styles, moods, textures, images, and icons.

Coffee table books: You know the type—big, fat, awkward, won't fit in your bookshelves. Name a subject, and you can find a book of photos it inspired. Such books are abundant sources of material for idea stimuli. Best of all, they're usually marked down.

Music: Fast music, slow music, up music, down music, loud music, and soft music—it all has tremendous thought-provoker value. Whatever mood you want to be in, whatever attitude you're trying to develop, there's a piece of music to take you there.

Cookbooks: Tomes d'cuisine can be a handy resource if your task has any connection with food. Here you can find names and combinations of ingredients to provide insights into anything of an edible persuasion. Of particular value are cookbooks with personality that offer variations on common themes.

Cable/satellite TV: Take the classic man-of-the-house approach with the remote control. Flip through the channels at a minimal rate of one per second. No slower. Bombard your brain with images, scanning up and down through the channels like a person possessed. Don't just stare at the screen—absorb the images. Let them light fuses in your brain.

Dr. Seuss library: As I mentioned earlier, Dr. Seuss is a higher being on the creativity scale. At the Ranch, we're the proud owners of a complete Dr. Seuss collection. When a team is mired in reality, I pass out Dr. Seuss books to all concerned and invite them to invent a la Seuss. The beauty of Dr. Seuss' work is that very little is tied to the real world. Instead of People, Places and Things, he writes of Wockets, Solla Ollew, Thidwick, and the River Wah-Hoo. When I'm working on children's products, the doctor is a sure cure for Real World Adultitis.

Puppets: It's often easier to get people to verbalize their thoughts if they're not the ones doing the talking. A collection of puppets can be useful in articulating ideas and developing unusual personalities or proprietary characters for new products. When working with children, I ask them to make puppets from brown paper sacks. It helps kids give form to their imaginations and develop greater depth and personality to their ideas. It can do the same for grownups, too.

STIMULI MINING JUMP START NO. 4

To Market, to Market

The world is filled with thoughts. Ideas fill the air we breathe. To Market, to Market is designed to take advantage of the environment around us, wherever we happen to be at the moment.

> "Take a walk and look at the world around you. It doesn't matter if you are in a large city or the country. Look at nature, what is it doing? How is it responding to the wind, animals, cars, whatever? One of my most memorable discoveries came from watching how leaves dried and curled, and how that related to a problem I was having in obtaining curvature in a snack product. The answers to our problems often are as close as outside our windows."
> – Jeffrey A. Stamp, Principal scientist,
>   Frito-Lay Inc.

To Market, to Market is aimed at borrowing brilliance from examples that people bump up against every day.

Objective: To get up, get out and experience the stimuli around us—to go someplace, any place and mine it for visual stimuli.

177

How to do it: Head on out. Just get in your car and drive to Main Street, the park, or a part of town where you don't normally go. Or take a walk through a shopping mall. These monuments to conspicuous consumption are terrific places to watch people and fill the mind with multi-hued thought bubbles. As you wander, make a mental note of anything that strikes your fancy. You probably do this all the time anyway, don't you?

Take a digital camera to capture ideas. Stay focused on your object of inquiry. Keep repeating your challenge.

Do a Stimuli One-step as you walk. Force-associate that which you see with that which you need to solve.

Then do a Stimuli Two-step. Identify the underlying traits of what you see, feel, and experience and apply these traits to your challenge. Ask questions. Why does each experience or product you observe work? What does it do right? Where is its focus? What makes it different?

Don't limit your market walking to the upscale. Seek out the down-scale, too. Be an equal opportunity idea hunter. Check out the ghetto, the flea markets, your local St. Vincent DePaul store. One man's trash is another's treasure, don't you know.

To Market, to Market in Action

My clients have used To Market, to Market in expeditions for all manner of ideas. Once when searching for ideas for new types of merchandising displays for grocery stores, we sent teams to department stores with Polaroid cameras. The teams stalked aisles of perfume counters, hardware stores, sporting goods displays, bookstores, and, yes, even the lingerie cases at Victoria's Secret. They returned with a stash of photos that stimulated fresh, original thoughts, at least in the context of your typical grocery store. But do be subtle with your camera— a lot of businesspeople don't take kindly to people coming in off the street snapping pictures of how they do this or that.

I used the formula of To Market, to Market in junior high school when I was embarking on a career as Merwyn the Magician. I didn't have any money for fancy equipment, so I'd head to the local Goodwill store and the flea market looking for new props and ideas I could add to the act.

One weekend, I picked up a matched set of plumber's helpers (plungers) that were just right for juggling. Another weekend, I bought a 25-cent toilet seat. It was an impulse purchase, one that felt right, but for no apparent reason. But my brother, Bruce, turned it into one of the funniest elements of the show. The idea was a twist on the old Rocky and Bullwinkle gag, where Bullwinkle kept trying to pull a rabbit out of his hat and kept failing.

Dressed as BooBoo the clown, Bruce would appear onstage with the magician—yours truly—and say, "Hey, Merwyn! Watch me pull a rabbit out of my toilet seat." Then he'd hand me the seat, lift the lid, reach through the hole into his jacket, in full view of our audience, and pull out a rubber snake. Or a roll of toilet paper. Or a bowling pin. After two or three of BooBoo's failures, I'd pull a rabbit from a hat.

The gag became a staple of the act. The prop cost a quarter.

If your mission is to dig up an idea for a school project, a plan for redecorating your family room, or a costume for Halloween, take your pick and shovel to your local markets.

STIMULI MINING JUMP START NO. 5

Newsstand

Newspapers, magazines, radio, and TV news outlets are largely dedicated to reporting trends. These same information mongers are also slaves to public interest.

To varying degrees, the news media conduct research to identify subjects of interest to the public. So if you want to sort of learn about what tickles America's fancy, stop by a newsstand. I say "sort of" because the media occasionally attempts go beyond simply reporting trends to predicting them.

Hardly a subject exists that hasn't inspired a magazine, from *Soldier of Fortune* to *Self* to *Boy's Life* to *Plywood Today*. Collect them, trade them with your friends, use them as stairways to idea heaven. Need ideas for fund raising? Look to women's magazines for crafts you can make and sell. Need a theme for your party this weekend? Peruse the headlines for the controversy of the day.

Objective: To open your mind through current events and trends, as measured by the media. To leverage the hours of research bought and paid for by news outlets to your advantage. You never know when an idea will pop out at you from the cover of a magazine or a front-page photograph.

How to do it: Let your fingers stroll through a pile of magazines and newspapers. The randomness of this process is in and of itself a cattle prod to new thoughts. As your mind fills with images and statements from the publications, they become jumbled and connected in new ways.

A number of Jump Start techniques can be executed with news media images and icons, among them:

- Captions–You'll need magazines with lots of photos. Use magazines or photos with at least a tenuous tie to the task. If you're working on ideas for children, use magazines with lots of kids in the pictures. If you're trying to launch an aerobics class, use a fitness magazine.

  Write captions, titles, names, and/or brief descriptions that relate your task with your selection of photos on Post-It Notes and plaster them on the various images. If you're working on a new sports beverage, for example, you might mix images of waterfalls, rainstorms, and seascapes with photographs of athletes, cowboys, ballerinas, and middle-aged men mowing the lawn, or anyone else who is in any way exerting him or herself.
  Work quickly and instinctively, with no regard to the practical and feasible. Let the images provoke thought patterns. After having covered the

pages with yellow flaps, spread the images across the floor and begin to develop full-blown solutions, borrowing and swapping ideas from the images and your own scribbled thoughts.

I believe so much in this exercise that I've amassed a humongous library of photographs, picture postcards, and illustrations clipped from hundreds of books and magazines over the years. They're filed under such linear headings as "KIDS," "COUPLES," "SPORTS," "WET," and "MORNING," along with such abstract headings as "SPEEDY," "POWERFUL," "WARM," and "WOW!"

• Trend Scan–This approach is for those who can't live without numbers. At the Eureka! Ranch, we subscribe to slews of magazines in a flood of categories. The covers and tables of contents are copied and filed in a reference library under the heading: "Thought Stimulators."

To get a fix on trends, we sometimes track and tabulate magazine articles into what we call the Eureka! Index. It's not as well known as the Dow Jones Index, but it's more valuable for inventing ideas. If you want to know what's hot, a quick glance at the covers will tell you. My research company conducts testing for magazines looking to capitalize on subjects and celebrities that have the greatest potential to generate newsstand sales. So what you see is what consumers say they want.

All publications have something to offer when you're looking for ideas. My favorites include:

• Tabloids–These oft-shunted pieces of journalism represent America better than any glossy, big money periodical packed with Ralph Lauren ads. I find them a valuable source of creative inspiration, especially *Weekly World News*, which is the only source I know of for such headlines as

"Alien Mummy Goes on Rampage," "Infant Accidentally Packaged as Doll," "Batboy Sighted in NYC Subway," and "Obesity on the Rise among Telekinetics." While other members of the media report facts no matter how boring, the tabloids always deliver excitement— IN SCREAMING HEADLINES WITH PLENTY OF EXCLAMATION POINTS!!!!!!!!!!!!!!!!!

- *The Smithsonian* and *National Geographic*- Either one is just the ticket if you're looking for inspiration for an exotic or historical context. Nowhere else can you learn so much about the Arctic Circle, the stone crab and the Wildmen of Lower Umbroglio. I once bought a steamer trunk filled with *National Geographic* magazines at a library book sale for a nickel apiece. That afternoon, I mined them for dozens of wicked good ideas. The result was three winning concepts for new soft drinks.

- *USA Today*–It's the trendiest of the trendy. While roundly criticized in journalism circles as the publication for those who don't have time for television's fuller coverage, the nation's daily delivers facts, figures, surveys, and information in snapshot form.

Newsstand in Action

While developing a new bottled water, I gathered every picture of natural water I could find—including shots of oceans, waterfalls, rivers, lakes, drinking glasses, open sewers and so on. I laid out the images, stepped back, and drank in the view.

I arranged them in three sets, depending on whether they

made me believe the water would taste terrific, okay or horrible. As my mind processed the images, I saw patterns in the terrific images than were missing from the horrible images. Such factors as movement, coldness, clarity, and lack of a human presence were far more common in the terrific images. From this, I whipped up a list of package design traits. Later testing showed that applying these factors to the package design made a major difference in the way consumers reacted to the product. The actual traits and principles are, alas, a zealously protected client secret. But they work.

STIMULI MINING JUMP START NO. 6
Hello, Mr. Webster

Name a thing, and you make it real.

Whether it's the name of a product or a process or a color or a type or a formula or a three-legged dog, people will not take it seriously until they know what to call it.

Would a rose by any other name smell so sweet? Maybe so. But how would you know what to ask for at the flower shop?

Names have a broader application than products and services. Names also can be applied to promotions, parties, teams, and events, among other name-ables. A good name tells the world what you stand for and whether you're worth checking out. If you don't name it, the masses will. Or worse, they'll brand your product GENERIC. Like commodities, generic products always sell for less.

When you have a wicked good name for an idea, even the dullest idea comes alive. When a name isn't there, the idea is too easily lost in the explanation.

Focusing on the name of your object of inquiry has advantages beyond the acquisition of a trademark. Focusing on developing a name forces you to articulate your thinking with a brevity and simplicity that helps to deliver success.

During the summer of 1902, Willis Haviland Carrier was working for a New York publishing company that was struggling with its inks. Day-to-day fluctuations in humidity changed the way the ink looked on the paper.

Carrier realized he could stabilize the moisture if he chilled the air. So he designed a system for blowing air over cooled pipes. It worked. Eureka! He called it "Apparatus For Treating Air." Shama-lama-ding-dong.

About the same time, a textile engineer named Stuart Cramer had an opposite problem. He realized he had to add humidity to his factory to condition yarn. He called his system "Air Conditioning." The term caught on. Carrier liked it so much that he adopted it for his equipment and dumped "Apparatus For Treating Air" altogether. The air conditioner may well have become a success had it been marketed as Apparatus for Treating Air. But somehow, I don't think it would have caught on quite as quickly.

Objective: To identify and create names for ideas. Giving an idea a name, a handle, a point of proper noun reference makes it easier to describe, tout, and ballyhoo.

How to do it: In my search for names, I've discovered a remarkable secret: Most dictionaries are packed with words from beginning to end, many of which are perfectly suitable to use as names.

Tom Attea, a wizard of a copywriter, taught me how to find a name in a dictionary. The process is simple. Read the dictionary. Write down every name, word or word bit that relates to your task. In a day or so, you'll have amassed an amazing list of words while dramatically enhancing your vocabulary. Now mix and match the words on your list until the right name jumps off the page, grabs you by the throat, and hollers, "Where've *YOU* been all my life?"

A less extreme approach is to review a thesaurus, the *New Comprehensive American Rhyming Dictionary* and Richard Bayan's *Words that Sell*. The *World Atlas* is also helpful if you're trying to establish a connection with a far-flung locale, as in, say, the halls of Montezuma or the shores of Tripoli.

Hello, Mr. Webster in Action

The assignment is to name a new metric for determining the likelihood that any given manufacturing firm would achieve success, based on tightly honed projections that the company would show a profit in five years' time. The metric had been discussed in corporate hallways as the "death measurement." We needed something less dark, something a bit more clinical or scientific, but something that retained a sense of urgency. It had to have a ready-made official sound—like "wind-chill factor," "Internet performance rating," and "box office gross."

Looking up "death" in the dictionary, I found "bereavement," "loss," "demise," "decease," "expiry," "ruin," "collapse," "fatality," and more. I settled on "mortality," because the word could go either way on the scale of positive to negative. It could be a measure of life as well as a measure of death. From there, it was a hop, skip, and a jump to the simple, descriptive yet official-sounding "Business Mortality Index."

STIMULI MINING JUMP START NO. 7

Candid Comments

When exploring new territory, it helps to get the lay of the  land. Before the old wagon train headed out across the prairie in the Westward expansion, a scout was sent ahead to learn what dangers and opportunities lay ahead. That's the idea of Candid Comments.

This exercise is also handy if rigor mortis is beginning to set in where your task is concerned. It can help you see your task through new eyes.

Objective: To be your own Gallup pollster, gathering information, opinions, and insights you can use to build ideas.

How to do it: Take a walk. If you don't have a video camera, take a tape recorder or a notebook. Go to the scene of the challenge, where people are involved with your area of inquiry.

Go to recess at your PTA school where you're working to raise money. Go where people are using your product or the competition's product. Ask questions. Spend the day interviewing as many people as you can.

Catch people on location, while they're involved with your area of inquiry. How do they feel? What are their moods? What kind of day are they having? What's good, what's bad? What advice do they have? What would make it better? Less of a pain in the neck? More memorable? More fun? More of an experience?

With every answer you get, follow up with the standard 3-year-old child's favorite series of questions—Why? Why? Why? Why?

Who, what, where, when, and how are good, too.

Lap up everything surrounding your situation. See it, feel it, touch it.

Sharpen your sense of the attitudes, emotions, and motivations swirling around your task. Candid Comments can help you understand what people really think and feel, as opposed to what they say they are.

"Candid Comments is one of my faves. I'm a very visual person, and this exercise helps me see things, as opposed to just looking at them. It's the voyeur in me. I've always liked watching people, studying people. When I worked at Drackett, I took a video camera into people's homes and watched them clean house. They'll tell you one thing, but they'll do something else. You can get

a wealth of ideas by watching people."
– Diane Iseman, Marketing Consultant

Review your tapes or notes, then review them again. If you have them on tape, play the tape over and over and over, as if it were background music. Brainwash yourself. If you have it on videotape, look into the people's eyes and listen to their voices as they answer your questions. What do their non-verbal responses tell you that their verbal responses don't?

Around the 10th viewing, I stop hearing the words and start seeing pure reactions. I develop a reading of people's real inner feelings.

Candid Comments is not easy or quick. But it works. There is no better way to get a fix on what people want and what they don't want. Often enough, it turns out to be an express lane to the Mother of All Ideas.

Candid Comments in Action

When I'm hired to work on a new category of products I don't know much about, the first thing I do is hit the streets.

Hired to grow Duncan Hines cake mixes, I visited grocery stores and watched shoppers at the in-store bakery and the baking supplies aisle. It quickly became apparent they wanted stuff that was, in baking parlance, "decorated," turning up their noses at the unadorned cakes and cookies.

This observation led to the invention of Duncan Hines Pantastic Party Cakes, a line of cake mixes that come with their own molded pans and decorations so that people can make bakery-style cakes that look like Garfield the Cat, Kermit the Frog, Miss Piggy or a major league baseball stadium all in their own kitchens.

My co-author, David Wecker, swears by Candid Comments. Any decent journalist does. He has used the approach in newspaper stories that tied a Clark County, Ohio, sheriff to a stolen car ring; led to federal fines against the Frigidaire plant in Moraine, Ohio, for ignoring repeated safety warnings about a 10,000-pound punch press on which an underage female employee lost an arm, and beat the police to a city commission candidate in Covington, Kentucky, who was eventually convicted of murder.

Once, he was working a Saturday shift at the *Kentucky Post* when a report came over the police radio that a woman had been found decapitated in her apartment. The competing news media waited for the police report and did the basic who-what-why-where-when crime story, the kind that ends with the phrase "Police have no suspects."

David and another reporter, Gary Webb, went to the scene. They knocked on doors, talked to neighbors, found out who the woman's friends were and talked to them. Before the morning was out, the two learned that the dead woman had been dating the city commission candidate, that she had become pregnant, and that the candidate had been unable to persuade her to have an abortion.

David and Gary went to the candidate's house and talked to him. Where had he spent the night? When was the last time he had seen the dead woman? Did he kill her? The candidate was flustered, to the point that his denials began to contradict each other. He wove a tangled web, and he didn't notice that the reporters were taping the conversation.

They thanked him for his time and went on their way. As the day wore on, they called the candidate two more times, asking his help in clearing up certain confusing issues and taping his responses.

The more the candidate talked, the more his story unraveled. Along the way, David and Gary found two people who had seen the candidate climbing the stairs to the dead woman's apartment late the previous night.

The next edition of the *Kentucky Post* carried a banner story establishing that the candidate was the one of the last people to see the woman alive and that he was unable to account for his whereabouts on the night she was murdered. When police caught up with the candidate, he denied ever talking to Gary and David, unaware that they had his voice on tape. Their subsequent stories implicated him even deeper.

The candidate didn't get elected. He got convicted and sentenced. As of this writing, he's still in prison. David doesn't regard the case as an example of great investigative journalism. It wasn't a difficult story, he says. It was a simple matter of hitting the streets, asking questions, and listening.

STIMULI MINING JUMP START NO. 8

Magic Moments

We measure our lives in moments of experience. Our first step, our first kiss, the first time we got behind the wheel of the

"First words"

family car and backed it out the driveway—these are the moments enshrined in our personal halls of fame.

They're Magic Moments. We spend our lives in search of them. The more we collect, the better we feel about ourselves.

Magic Moments reach into the far corners of our lives. They can play a key role in determining what choices we make, how we cast our votes, what products we'll buy. Consider the following:

Pretend the boy on the box is your son. Why would you buy this item? Would you be buying a rocket? Or would you be buying the look on your son's face at the moment of lift-off, with the rocket you'd made trailing a plume of smoke as it disappears in the clouds? Would you be buying a thing, or would you be buying an experience?

If you're like me, you pay for

flying model rocket starter set

189

the rocket. But you buy the moment. Such shimmering spaces in time have an immensely powerful allure.

If you can isolate the Magic Moments associated with a task, if you can use them to create scenarios where people can project themselves into the picture, where they can see or feel or touch or anticipate the moment, you'll be able to squeeze off all sorts of wicked good ideas.

Objective: To cut to the core of your creative challenge. To identify areas of opportunity for creative exploration and find the critical moments that motivate, excite and thrill.

How to do it: Gather any props you'll need to role-play the experience.

If you're working on a new bread product, you should have a toaster, butter, jam, a knife, a plate, a loaf of something— the works.

Or if you're trying to land a job, you should have an interviewer, a resume, and the clothes you would wear to an interview.

Let's say your task is to build a better cat food. In this case, you'll need a bowl, a supply of cat food, and something approximating a cat. I lean toward the stuffed variety because they're less finicky and won't wet on you.

Use whatever you have to capture your Magic Moments— a note pad, a videocam or a digital camera will do nicely.

The object is to role-play whatever situation is involved in your challenge. Act out each role that comes into play. If you're inventing a better mousetrap, consider the challenge from the points of view of the mouse, the harried homemaker, the man of the house, the bait. What happens when the trap is baited? When it snaps shut? When it's time to get rid of the evidence? Take notes or photographs of each step as you go, as if you were creating a storyboard for a TV commercial.

Or using cat food as an example, your first Magic Moment might be when your cat wakes you in the morning as a prelude to the daily feeding ritual. Your second Magic Moment might occur when you reach for the cat's food in the cupboard; you shake the box, the cat comes running. Maybe your third Magic Moment happens when the cat chows down, and you stand back to bask in the warm glow of pet-owner accomplishment.

Take it back further if you like, all the way to the store shelf. Stretch it into the future. In each case, set the scene and photograph it. Play with it. Have fun. Find and photograph as many as you can.

After you've gathered your pictures, ask questions.

- Which moments could be more satisfying? How?
- Which moments haven't been fully tapped?
- Which are the best, most exciting, most intriguing moments?
- Which are the worst, most annoying, most aggravating moments?
- Which moment should be the focus?
- What are your feelings during the various moments?
- Where is the most magic?
- What is the defining moment?

Having defined the Magic Moments and the elements of each, take another look. Think of each moment as an area of opportunity. Look at each moment as a stepping-stone to a great new idea.

As you search for Magic Moments, think about how each awakens one sense or another. Regard the task in terms of the way it feels, smells, sounds, tastes and looks.

Isolate the Pavlovian responses—the psssst when you open a cold can of cola; the rich, dark aroma of fresh-brewed coffee first thing in the morning; the squeezable softness of Charmin; the snap, crackle, pop of Rice Krispies; the whiter whites of Tide.

Think about the feelings those responses elicit. Do they make you feel cooler? Ready to start the day? Pampered? Hungry? Clean? None of the above?

Great ideas have been built with sensory Magic Moments. Seeing is only part believing. There's also touching, smelling, tasting, and hearing.

Magic Moments in action

One of the magic moments in my life was when I proposed to Debbie. Like any other guy who has ever proposed marriage, I was looking for an idea to make the moment ultra-memorable. I thought about hiring a skywriter, mailing myself to her, and plastering my proposal across a billboard on an interstate highway. But those ideas didn't feel sufficiently romantic.

I began thinking of the act of proposing in terms of a Magic Moment; specifically, the moment when the diamond would for the first time be reflected in Debbie's eyes. I could produce the ring through sleight-of-hand, but that's the kind of thing she'd expect of me.

I zeroed in on the diamond, on how light glinted from it. Diamonds have facets, facets create sparkle, sparkle is magic. What else sparkles? Diamond, glass, crystal. *Voila!* I had my idea.

I asked Debbie to a play at a summer theater. On the way to the theater, I stopped at Greeley Park on the premise that we'd share a picnic under our favorite tree before the show. I spread a blanket out on the ground, uncorked a bottle of champagne, and poured some into a pair of long-stemmed Waterford crystal glasses. I turned my back briefly and dropped the engagement ring into one of the glasses. Then I handed Debbie the spiked drink.

She was impressed at the service. Then she looked into her glass. At first, she thought it was scratched. She swirled her glass, then she saw the ring. I blurted out my proposal. She accepted, pulled out the ring, dropped the crystal glass, and started crying. For an awkward moment, I confused her tears for despair. She quickly assured me I was wrong.

I took a picture of Debbie with her ring and the champagne glass under that big old tree. Of all the photographs in all our photo albums, it's the most magical.

Here's another example of Magic Moments in action. The elementary school my elder daughter attended was looking for room mothers to help out in classrooms. The leaflet the school sent home was a masterful piece of Magic Moment leveraging. It included clip-art illustrations to not-so-subtly remind moms of the big three school events they would be involved in should they choose to be room mothers. Placed strategically in the copy were images of a Halloween witch, a Christmas tree, and a Valentine.

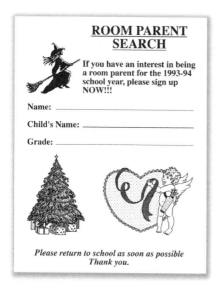

ROOM PARENT SEARCH

If you have an interest in being a room parent for the 1993-94 school year, please sign up NOW!!!

Name: _____

Child's Name: _____

Grade: _____

Please return to school as soon as possible
Thank you.

Talk about your gut punches. The message was clear: If you want to attend the three best parties of the year, you'd better sign up to be a room mother. The school quickly filled its vacancies.

STIMULI MINING JUMP START NO. 9

Kitchen Chemistry

Play with your problem. Spill it out on the table and put your fingers in it. Bake it, shape it, bend it, spin it over your head like a lariat. Do it once following the directions and do it again without them. Add ingredients. Take away ingredients. Be a mad scientist.

Once you've given your task three dimensions and have seen it from the north, south, east and west, you'll have a better idea which direction to take it.

Objective: To invent ideas based on interaction with your subject of inquiry. Kitchen Chemistry involves playing, prototyping, and modeling alternative solutions. It's a tinkerer's dream.

How to do it: When I'm called upon to create new food or beverage products, I routinely knead, scald, freeze, whip, shake, boil, mix, fry, and bake the client's products and competitive products. This is especially valuable if you're not a technical or product development person. If you're working in a corporate setting, ask your product development people to set up a "play" session for you.

As you approach your task, try building it in miniature. If you're looking for a marketing idea, frame it inside a commercial. If you're working on a Boy Scout fundraiser, frame it inside a brochure or a poster. Consider what you'd call your idea. What claims will you make? What makes it the best? How would you explain it to interest your target market?

When you play with your ideas and visualize your thoughts in 3-D, you can see what works and what doesn't. You find ways to make it the best it can be.

Kitchen Chemistry in Action

When I was on the Safeguard soap detail, I developed a fork demonstration. This was something I learned while playing with the product. You probably didn't realize it, but if you stick a fork in a bar of Safeguard, it goes in smoothly. If you stick a fork in a bar of Dial, the bar splinters.

So what? Well, at the time, I was looking for a way to establish Safeguard as a deodorant soap that was also soft on your skin—not harsh like (*ahem!*) Dial. My fork demonstration would have been a good way to make that point visually. But I was naive in the ways of corporate salesmanship and was unable to get management to buy the idea.

Too bad. A few years later, Lever Brothers introduced

Lever 2000, a bar soap that featured a similar combination of deodorant and skin conditioner that generated record sales.

Kitchen Chemistry proved that Soft Scrub liquid cleanser, while generally thought to be safer for delicate surfaces than Spic and Span powder, was in fact far from it. This was a major point of distinction. The result was an advertising campaign that showed Soft Scrub leaving gouges on one lens of a pair of plastic sunglasses, while the Spic and Span lens remained as smooth as, well, glass.

My father used a parallel process to create designs for our home. Before he committed hammer to nail, he would build miniature models. He drew the plans to scale and cut tiny furniture templates from graph paper. He spread the whole thing across the dining room table and walked around it, inspecting it from this angle and that. He looked at his model as if he were already living in it.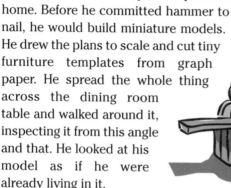

Once his mind's eye could see it, he could build it. A blueprint wasn't enough. I've taken the same approach in designing modifications to our home and the Eureka! Ranch. The only difference is that I build my home improvement models on a Macintosh computer.

"But take the problem and reduce it down to visual analogy. Go collect how much fat is in a product and see it for yourself! If you're writing ad copy, get the product and don't just use it, play with it. This is where you can really let your child come out.

"One of my trademarks at Frito-Lay was that you could usually find me playing with ingredients. But it works. For example, we determined how to redesign a prototype snack's shape to make it stronger by learning how it broke by playing horseshoes with it. We noticed that the pieces always landed a certain way under force and, sure enough, the same phenomenon was

happening during mechanical transfer at the packaging machine."
– Jeffrey A Stamp, Ph.D., Principle Scientist Frito-Lay Inc.

STIMULI MINING JUMP START NO. 10

Chilling Out

The last method for processing stimuli is the easiest.

A study reported in the *Journal of Creative Behavior* found that when students came to an absolute blockage on a problem-solving task, a 15-minute break dramatically recharged their creative abilities.

It doesn't take much to clog up the mental food processor with emulsified thoughts. When it happens, it helps to walk away from the problem and let your subconscious mind find the solution. We've all had the experience of having a name or a thought on the tips of our tongues. The more you consciously try to dislodge it, the deeper it becomes imbedded, only to have it come to you once you stop chasing it. What happens is that your subconscious mind continues to process the data request even though your consciousness has let go.

"I back away from conscious thought and turn the problem over to my unconscious mind. It will scan a broader array of patterns and find some new close-fits from other information stored in my brain."
– Art Fry, 3M Scientist, Co-Creator of Post-it Notes

Objective: To recharge your creative brain when working through piles of stimuli.

How to do it: Put away your stimuli and index cards. Empty your mind. Different people have different ways of doing this. Some meditate, some put on biofeedback headsets. My favorite ways of emptying my mind include juggling, jogging, putting my BMW through its paces on a backcountry road, and playing a high-intensity game of anything competitive. To free your mind of your challenge, engage in a different activity that totally occupies it.

After an hour or so, come back for one more go-round. Push yourself to think of an audacious idea that sweeps away all the others—a potential A-plus, far-reaching and dangerous; an idea people will recognize immediately as either a strikeout or a grand slam.

Having worked and re-worked the problem, your mind is poised at this point to make dazzling leaps of brilliance.

> "Whenever you think you have the answer to a problem, be greedy and reach for one more. Odds are, the next one will be even bigger!"
> – Richard Saunders

By removing yourself from the problem, you allow your brain to wander and free-associate.

If you need to, show your boss this chapter the next time she catches you at your desk resting your eyelids and doing those deep-breathing exercises the doctor prescribed.

Chilling Out in Action, if You'll Pardon the Phrase

The answer may well be in your unconsciousness. The problem is that we make so much noise in our conscious minds that the subconscious doesn't have much chance to speak its piece.

It's possible to program the subconscious mind. The key is to engage in an activity unrelated to the task at hand.

> "When I was stumped on a particularly tough engineering problem in college, I'd leave the room and spend 20 minutes juggling—not sim-

ple juggling, but difficult tricks with four or five balls or clubs, the kinds of stunts where, if you didn't focus your complete concentration, you'd get bonked on the head. Afterward, if I hadn't been seriously bonked, the gears in my brain would turn more smoothly."
– Austin T. McNamara, Group Vice President,
    Chiquita Brands International

I make it a point to go out for recess during the day, especially during group Eureka! sessions, when my mind has to be tightly focused for long stretches. Go outside and play, if it's a nice day. Climb a tree, bounce on a pogo stick, toss the old pigskin around, take a seventh-inning stretch.
Another way to make your subconscious work for you is to take a nap.

"I can usually see the answer in my dream, because I do a lot of lucid dreaming. Even if I've already slept and I'm not tired, I take a nap. And when I have a deadline, I just turn everything up and take shorter naps. It's sort of like sleeping quickly."
– SARK, friend and author

SARK is in good company. The ranks of history's stalwart nap-a-holics include Thomas Edison, Eleanor Roosevelt, Winston Churchill and Presidents Truman, Kennedy, Ford and Reagan. Not that SARK has taken naps with any of those people.
How do you Jump Start Your Brain?

"I take a nap."
– Jerry Mathers, "The Beav"

When I've got inventor's block, I sometimes find that if I close my eyes, relax and let my subconscious mind give me the answer, it will. Not long ago, I was stuck on a name for a new food product. The client liked the overall concept, but not the name I'd picked. I had 20 minutes to get back to her with alternatives.

I took a deep breath, wiped my conscious mind clean and waited. After a few minutes, the right name bubbled up from my subconsciousn. The client loved it, and consumers loved the concept. It'll be on store shelves by the time you read this.

11

TOP TEN
INDUSTRIAL-STRENGTH
JUMP STARTS

Feeling a bit of brain bloat? Is your train of thought stuck in the station? Do you sometimes feel as if your mind is on vacation but your mouth is working overtime? You may be suffering from mental constipation.

You heard me. Yes, mental constipation, a dreaded condition characterized by an absence of creativity, a lack of original thinking, and a general malaise and dullness of wit. Left untreated, mental constipation can lead to an overall deadening of the senses, eventually leading to total atrophy that leaves the patient in a drooling, zombie-like state, not unlike what you see in many mid-level management corporate types.

But there is a cure—10 cures, in fact, in this chapter. What you have here are my 10 industrial-strength ways to thinking smarter and more creatively.

Ironically enough, the greatest barriers to original thought are the thoughts you're already carrying around in your head. When your mind is filled with solutions, effective or otherwise, it's nigh impossible to conceive a newborn thought.

"For a tree to bear fruit, dead limbs must be pruned."
– Richard Saunders

As we grow into adulthood, we become mental pack rats. The passing of time deals out more and more facts to clutter our brains, starting with our Social Security numbers. Our minds become crowded with S.O.S.—the same old stuff. S.O.S. shuts down idea production. It puts a clamp on our ability to see new thoughts. It makes us mentally constipated.

Mental constipation occurs when you have old ideas knocking around in your head that prevent you from having new ideas and entertaining alternative points of view. The thing to do is flush out the old ideas.

Unfortunately, those who could benefit the most from a good flushing never get around to pushing the lever on the side of the tank. That's because the really insidious thing about mental constipation is that those who suffer most from it seldom know it.

Once upon a time, while working on a juice project with a major American food company, a senior god in a position superior to my own fell in love with an idea that would have brought together a beverage and the Huggies diaper trademark. Specifically, he wanted to license the Huggies name with a nutritional juice for nursing moms.

At first gasp, the premise was, well, breathtaking. It was also exciting, bold, and far removed from any existing consumer beverage in the civilized world. If our team could secure the Huggies name, we were convinced we could change the course history.

Hearts pounding, we plunged ahead, writing copy and designing packaging. Then we hit a snag. Someone raised the obvious question: What color should the product be?

Earth tones raised red flags. Lemon yellow was not so good, either. Once we began associating a real product with the concept, we kept finding negative connotations.

We reported our concerns to the Great One. We'd run into a problem with Huggies Juice. But there was good news, too. Our research had turned up five wicked good juice ideas that didn't involve Huggies.

The boss wouldn't hear of it. We weren't trying hard enough, he said. The problem was, we didn't get it. The problems we'd encountered were superficial, he told us. New mothers won't see it that way, he said. The love new moms feel for their babies will overcome our petty concerns, he added.

It turned out that the boss was about to become a father. He was, perhaps for the first time in his life, feeling something akin to an honest emotion. He was mentally constipated with it.

We pleaded with him to deep-six Huggies Juice. At the same time, out of reverence for his position, I led the team back into the marketplace wilderness four times to run the concept past everyday consumers, who unanimously turned up their noses. Each time, the boss told us to try again. The team's enthusiasm withered.

In the end, Huggies Juice died a horrible death. The five decent ideas from the earlier research and the spirit of the team went with it—all because of mental constipation.

A few months later, I was again called on to develop new products for the same boss. Once again, he'd had a vision—one based at the other end of the age demographic. I later learned he'd been spending a good deal of time with his elderly mother.

I greeted his proposal for Ex-Lax Juice, the high-fiber juice, with all the excitement I could muster. I returned the next day with what I hoped would have a laxative-like effect on his brain blockage: Ten package designs and a portfolio filled with advertising copy. He spent the afternoon preening the concept until it was to his liking.

Then it was time to test the concept—not a small base concept screener, but with a full-scale national $10,000 test sample.

Judgment day finally arrived. The boss was pumped, big time. But his excitement was short-lived, seeing as how Ex-Lax Juice, the high-fiber juice, had set new lows for poor taste and an utter lack of consumer interest. The boss was shocked and dismayed, but he couldn't argue with the findings. A jury of real people—real elderly people—had spoken.

I took advantage of his moment of vulnerability to offer a vision of new areas for development. It worked. He heard me. He authorized a new project based on real needs and actual consumer interests. Nine months later, a product you've heard of, one which I unfortunately am not at liberty to mention by name, was launched in test market with great success.

My point is mental constipation is a bad thing. It smothers new ideas. Avoid people who are suffering from it. If you think you might have it, avoid yourself. Here are some other symptoms:

- Your brain is doubled over with cramps.
- You're pretty sure you're engaged in a conversation because you see the other person's lips moving, but you don't hear any words.
- You have an uncontrollable urge to run an enema nozzle up your nostril.
- Your tongue is parched and swollen from incessant talking.
- You're seized with embarrassing bouts of verbal flatulence.

Mental blockage is not exclusive to corporate management. It also happens to everyday people everyday. You know how sometimes you get a song in your head and can't get it out?

Like, say, if you go to Disneyworld and take the "It's a Small World After All" boat ride? And hours later, the song is still playing over and over in your brain until you can't think of anything else and you're afraid you're about to go absolutely berserk help oh pleasesomebody-helpme?!?!?!?!?!?!?!?!?

It's the same with ideas.

> "When the ideas aren't flowing, I take a mental laxative by putting some distance between the problem and myself. That can mean starting a new project, taking a break, going for a run, playing with the kids, taking a nap … After my subconscious thrashes things around for a few minutes or a few days, everything falls into place and—Eureka!—Problem solved."
> – Kevin Knight, President, Knight Marketing
>   Communications

You can fall in love with an idea. A better idea may try to woo you away, but you don't know it because you can't take your eyes off the object of your affection. And until you have fully considered your idea, until you have brought it out into the light of day where you can see its big nose and jug ears and flabby thighs, you're its slave.

These are the kinds of ideas we all bring to the problem-solving process. The ideas aren't necessarily as all-consuming as I've portrayed. They come in varying degrees of intensity. But it's only natural for you to have them. It's normal for the human brain to anticipate and bring at least a few prefab ideas to the table. Sometimes, these ideas are wicked good and worthy of instant patenting—but mostly not. Still, they have to be gotten at before any others can be had. The slate has to be wiped clean.

> "Purging is like hog washing. Management people often have hogs of ideas that need cleaning,

remodeling, updating. These sacred hogs tend to be stale and old. It's important that they be washed out because they sap strength and steal motivation. They're so fat, they leave no sustenance for younger, leaner original ideas."
– Mike Katz, Entrepreneur & Eureka! Trained
  Brain

WARNING: The following Jump Starts are industrial-strength. They require deeper thinking and correspondingly result in bigger ideas for solving your creative challenges.

INDUSTRIAL-STRENGTH JUMP START NO. 1

Mind Dumpster

Mind Dumpster is the ultimate Roto-Rooter for breaking mental blockages. It flushes old ideas from your mind in minutes. It's also the first step in every creative effort I undertake. It's like a good stretch before a long run.

Objective: To quickly rid minds of preconceptions, prefab ideas, and blockages so original work can begin. Mind Dumpster is also a fast way to read the landscape of what's running through your mind and, if you're in a group, the minds of others.

How to do it: Get a stack of Flush Cards—3x5 index cards, preferably of varying colors—and a fat, juicy pen so that you can write in a bold, assertive hand. Scribble one thought per card. Unburden yourself of any miscellaneous mental luggage associated with the task that you brought to the creative effort.

Just move your pen—the words will follow. Let thoughts flow from the tip of the pen in a stream-of-consciousness fashion. Do it quickly, in three minutes or less. The idea is to let it happen, to flush whatever's inside out. That's why I call them Flush Cards.

Music is helpful. I like classic rock 'n roll or a rousing bagpipe medley.

Let your mind take off in whatever direction it feels tugged to go. Or delve into your own background for ideas. Sometimes I use the following to prompt the dumpster process:

- Graphic images relating to the area of interest
- Rumors and gut instincts about the problem
- Best and worst memories associated with the problem
- Sensory elements: sights, sounds, tastes, smells and touches
- Emotions, positive and negative
- Pet ideas, peeves and otherwise that your mind connects to the task

After blowing out the impurities from your mind, collect your cards and shuffle them. Let them ferment for 20 minutes or so. Now it's time to play blackjack; deal the cards into piles—which is perhaps a poor term to use in a discussion about mental constipation. At any rate, arrange the cards in stacks of associated thoughts. Then go over them again, adding bulges (oops—there I go again) as they occur to you. Watch out for flying sparks.

Mind Dumpster in Action

As part of the preparation for writing the first version of *Jump Start Your Brain*, I convened a dozen Trained Brains to spend a day talking about what ought to go into the book. The day began with a Mind Dumpster. I asked my team this question: "What comes to mind when you think of creativity, inventing and imagination?"

Here are a few of the thoughts written on the Flush Cards that came back to me:

Dr. Seuss	From darkness to light
Out on a limb	The little engine that could
Amaze yourself	Wild imaginings
Get more out of life	Alive—Alert—Awake
Why ask why?	Fear of speaking up
Caffeine/brain food	Fun (listed 10 times!)
Rev up. ... magic mushrooms	Kids
Jumper cables	Lots of color
Disneyland of the mind	Be open to all kinds
Make more connections	Bare feet
Fear of blank paper	Open up your brain nasal cavities
Question everything ... why?	Moan, groan, push ...
Reverse the effects of mind cramps	
Break, trash, destroy all rules	

These figments stimulated many of the thoughts in these pages. Such as:

- **Caffeine/brain food**: This got me to thinking about the impact of what you put in your body has on what comes out of your head. My first-level response turned out to be the earlier section on the power of caffeine, caloric reduction, and Maine lobster. On further reflection, I realized brain food could also be interpreted to include any external factor that affects the act of thinking, so I expanded the section to include environmental aspects that influence creative motivation.

• **Fear of speaking up**: This card helped me realize what a barrier fear is to the creative process and, conversely, how important it is to have courage. Hence, the chapter on facing fear.

• **Dr. Seuss**: This card set my antennae to twitching. The Doctor has always been one of my favorite authors. The card immediately conjured the Grinch in my mind, who called up Ebenezer Scrooge, who in turn recalled a number of CEO's I've known. I fiddled for a while on a section of Corporate Ghosts of Christmas Past, Present and Future, then decided that the true magic of Dr. Seuss' works lay in their use of utterly original, utterly outrageous characters to tell simple stories and teach simple lessons. I wanted to do that, too. The result is "Yink's Search for It!"—a children's story for grownups. It's at the end of the book. Think of it as the dessert after the main course. Don't peek. You might spoil your dinner.

INDUSTRIAL-STRENGTH JUMP START NO. 2

666

This is one of the most provocative, productive Jump Starts in my Eureka! repertoire. The name is rooted in the Trained Brains' warped senses of humor and disrespect for authority.

In the 1980's, you may recall that Procter & Gamble was besieged with an unfounded and vicious rumor based on a misinterpretation of its man-in-the-moon logo. It was the opinion of some rumormongers that certain elements of the logo were satanic and that, by extension, P&G was a nest of Satan worshippers. While I can testify that not all Proctoids are angels, neither have I met any Beelzebubs.

In any case, due to my P&G background, the Trained Brains dubbed this exercise in honor of my former employer, using a number that has biblical references to the anti-Christ. *Tsk.*

Despite repeated attempts to rename the exercise, the name stuck. The fact is the exercise is a crapshoot. It uses three dice, each of which has six sides. It's an unfortunate coincidence. So with apologies to those who find the name offensive, let's press on.

Objective: To force-associate related elements of the challenge in random sequence. To bring together the different elements with the roll of the dice and increase the number of mental connections that would not have been forged otherwise. To follow the dice wherever they lead.

How to do it: Divide your task into as many separate aspects as you can. List all possible areas of exploration, along with characteristics that might help define each area.

For example, when I was challenged to invent ideas for new board games, my list of areas of exploration included–

- Target audience (boys, teens, seniors)
- Types of game boards (cloth, three-dimensional)
- Theme (music, sex)
- Scoring devices (poker chips, dollar bills)
- Subject matter (politics, the future, the past)
- Materials (rubber, kites, masking tape)
- Types of power (electricity, brainwaves, muscles)

From your list of areas of exploration, select three to pursue in 666. In the case of my board game example, I selected target audience, theme and materials.

Now create six options for each of the areas of opportunity. 666 is most effective when the areas of exploration are related to your task. You'll find a collection of starter lists you can use to get going from 666's cousin, Dr. Disecto, later in this chapter.

Arrange your lists in columns, like so:

WHITE DIE THEME	BLUE DIE TARGET AUDIENCE	RED DIE MATERIALS
1. Food, food, food	1. Seniors	1. Invisible ink
2. Sex and rock 'n roll	2. Teens	2. Nylon
3. Laughter	3. College age	3. Masking tape
4. Best/worst	4. "Roseanne type"	4. Sponge rubber
5. Gossip	5. Yuppies	5. Kites/gliders
6. Family reunion	Couples only	6.Bouncing balls

You're ready to roll. Use three dice, each of a color to match the columns. Toss the dice and match the numbers on each die to the trait in the appropriate column. See what thoughts the linkages inspire. With each toss of the dice, you'll see a new pool of opportunities. When the well runs dry, roll again. When three consecutive rolls fail to yield any good ideas, move onto a new list of areas of exploration or another brain program.

In any case, use the combinations that emerge with each

toss of the dice strictly as starting-gate stimuli. They don't have to be taken literally. In fact, it's better if you don't.

At one Eureka! Inventing Session, I inadvertently let four Real World Adult clients form a group by themselves, without any Trained Brains to skew the mix. In no time at all, they were utterly discombobulated. They read their first three-item sequence out loud as if it were a sentence and began complaining it made no sense whatsoever.

Of course it didn't. The point of 666 is to trigger ideas outside the normal orbs of thought.

666 in Action

I wanted an idea for a new game. The roll of the dice, using the list shown above was 2, 2, 3. That added up to sex and rock 'n roll, Teens and Masking Tape.

What a combination. My thoughts unfurled along these lines:

Rock 'n roll had been done. That left sex. What do 14-year-old kids want? They want to touch members of the opposite sex.

How might they be allowed to climb all over each other without anyone getting too upset and/or pregnant? What if players were to get tangled up in each other a way that would be more humorous than amorous? What if they were to wrestle with their clothes on?

What if they tied themselves together with masking tape? Or something like masking tape? Something that would come off easily. Like Velcro.

The result was Octopus, a game that has parallels to Twister, but in 3-D. Players attach different colored Velcro bands to their wrists, ankles, and head. With a roll of a big foam die, the players attach and entwine themselves around each other—wrist to ankle, angle to head, and so on, depending on what colored band is where—until they're physically unable to make the next required connection. Random House liked it well enough to license it.

I wish I'd had Octopus when I was 14. Or I wish I'd had 666 so I could have thought of it.

The advantage to 666 is that it creates a context—albeit a twisted, bizarre context—that's almost always entirely new. So it almost always leads to fresh ways of bulging into the great beyond.

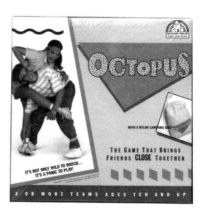

INDUSTRIAL-STRENGTH JUMP START NO. 3

Don't Sell Me

Don't Sell Me is based on the premise that people hate to buy things. What they want is to have their basic needs and desires to be satisfied. As in:

Don't sell me clothes ... sell me attractiveness.
Don't sell me shoes ... sell me feet that feel refreshed.
Don't sell me books ... sell me knowledge.
Don't sell me a lobotomy ... sell me peace of mind.
Don't sell me Barry Manilow. Please.

Objective: Hone in on the intangibles to identify higher-order benefits. Don't Sell Me asks you to think more about implications, less about the task itself. It moves your perspective away from things and more toward feelings, hopes, emotions. Don't Sell Me is the scenic route to new awareness of the essence of your task. It takes you right to your mission's core, but from a variety of emotional directions.

How to do it: Define your mission. What are you trying to accomplish? What are you trying to change? Who do you want to listen?

Now complete the following statement:

Don't Sell Me (your task in concrete terms) ... sell me (your task in abstraction).

Complete the statement as quickly as you can. Fill in the

blank a dozen times or more. Let your pen move. You're looking for soft stuff—the feelings, emotions, attitudes, results, consequences, secondary benefits, gut instincts, intuitions, and perceptions that drive your day-to-day existence.

When you've finished, set the list aside for 10 minutes and do something else.

When you return to your list, focus on each blank, one at a time. Concentrate on the pieces, not the aggregate. When you attack a problem in its totality, you can quickly become overwhelmed. Better to be underwhelmed. Or just plain whelmed.

Use each of your statements as a springboard to new ideas. What comes to mind? What new thoughts does each statement prompt? Look at each statement as an opportunity to solve a part of the task. Consider each as an element of the challenge—or a new direction from which to approach the challenge. Let each represent a separate need, like a moon orbiting the task. Address emotions, feelings, and perceptions. Look for weaknesses to fix and strengths to trumpet.

Don't Sell Me in Action

I love this technique. I had some friends over and we plugged it in to help invent this book. Here are some of the ways we filled in the blank:

> Don't sell me CREATIVITY BOOKS ... sell me "creative juice."
> Don't sell me CREATIVITY BOOKS ... sell me "a renewal of my childhood."
> Don't sell me CREATIVITY BOOKS ... sell me "success in the corporate world."
> Don't sell me CREATIVITY BOOKS ... sell me "a life I can be excited about."
> Don't sell me CREATIVITY BOOKS ... sell me "a blueprint for achieving greatness."
> Don't sell me CREATIVITY BOOKS ... sell me "spirit."
> Don't sell me CREATIVITY BOOKS ... sell me "enthusiasm and energy that last."

The ideas of "confidence in my brain," "spirit," "creative juice," and "enthusiasm and energy that last" helped me think about the importance of courage and enthusiasm, along with having the inspiration and wherewithal to challenge conformity. As a result, these pages have a certain element of evangelistic fervor, in case you hadn't noticed.

The ideas of "success in the corporate world" and "a life I can be excited about" underscored the importance of examples of creativity techniques in action in both professional and personal environments.

Once during a soft drink project for Pepsi-Cola, I completed the Don't Sell Me phrase with the following results.

Don't sell me SOFT DRINKS ... sell me "fun"
Don't sell me SOFT DRINKS ... sell me "good taste/flavor"
Don't sell me SOFT DRINKS ... sell me "outrageousness"
Don't sell me SOFT DRINKS ... sell me "refreshment"
Don't sell me SOFT DRINKS ... sell me "a break in the day"
Don't sell me SOFT DRINKS ... sell me "excitement"
Don't sell me SOFT DRINKS ... sell me "revolution"
Don't sell me SOFT DRINKS ... sell me "perpetual youth"
Don't sell me SOFT DRINKS ... sell me "a piece of America"
Don't sell me SOFT DRINKS ... sell me "thirst elimination"

I sat and pondered. I bathed my brain in these thoughts. While soft drinks are about flavor, taste, refreshment, and slaking thirst, they're also more than that. They're part of our lives, a reflection of Americana and a symbol of youth. Or youthfulness.

Hmmmm. I was drawn to "fun," "outrageous" and " perpetual youth." What could you do with a carbonated soft drink that would be outrageous and fun? What's the funnest, funniest thing a soft drink could do or be?

In a remote crack in my mind, I saw Larry, Curly, and Moe attacking each other with seltzer bottles. Eureka! I whipped out my trusty PowerBook and blew out the copy in 10 minutes. The next page details what the concept board and copy looked like:

Stooges ALL-NATURAL *Seltzer*

For Those Who Know How to Laugh

Pepsi introduces new Stooges ALL-NATURAL Flavored Seltzer. Named in honor of those classic Kings of American Comedy: Curly, Larry, and Moe. Just shake the product, push down on the special top and spray into your mouth for all-natural taste that can't be beat. Flavors include Citrus Curly, Lemon Larry, and Mandarin Orange Moe.

I faxed a copy to Pepsi's world headquarters in White Plains. The client laughed and approved it for testing with 30 other ideas. She told me she felt sure Stooges Seltzer would be either a big winner or a huge bust.

I held my breath during AcuPOLL's concept testing. A jury of honest-to-gosh real Americans was assembled to record responses on AcuPOLL computer terminals. In an instant, reactions to various concepts were translated into letter grades reflecting how the panelists' responses compared to previous tests of similar new products. A grade of "A" meant an idea scored in the top 20 percent of previously tested concepts. An "F" put an idea in the bottom 20 percent.

As the votes came over a central computer terminal, the

grade flickered from "A" to "F" and finally leveled off at "C." Rats. I hate average.

But at second glance, I found hope in how the votes shook out. The "C" grade was not reflected in a normal parabolic distribution of votes, but by a polarized combination of extremely negative and extremely positive reactions. Stooges Seltzer was clearly a concept that caused controversy. Hope drew a faint breath.

I asked AcuPOLL President Jack Gordon to look into what people liked and didn't like about Stooges Seltzer. The responses led us to what we would later confirm in statistical analysis. Stooges Seltzer was a concept with a clear male/female split. Men gave the idea an A+. Women gave it an F.

Later, I asked my wife whether this means that "those who know how to laugh" pretty much just includes men. "Don't think so," she said. "It means women are the ones who have to clean it up."

When the AcuPOLL report was presented to Pepsi, I put an emotional spin on the results, pitching Stooges Seltzer as an idea with magnum drama and excitement. Unfortunately, considering its average overall grade and the fact that another concept had scored an A+, more than spin was needed.

The A+ idea had set test records. It was about an idea for a cola with a new generation of taste, and its score shot off the top of the charts. It was called Crystal Pepsi.

I loved the Crystal Pepsi idea. In simple terms, it was meant to be "a more refreshing cola because it had no sticky caramel aftertaste!"

It had a clear Overt Benefit: More refreshing.

It had a clear Real Reason to Believe: No sticky caramel aftertaste.

Sadly, this idea never made it to market. The leadership of Pepsi was concerned about what impact the new upstart would have on the parent brand so they watered down the concept making it a "7-Up Wannabe"—no caffeine, no color, no nothing.

Oh well. In my heart, I still think Stooges Seltzer would have been more fun.

INDUSTRIAL-STRENGTH JUMP START NO. 4

Musical Chairs

Step outside yourself. Take a different seat. Forget who you are. Put on a different pair of shoes. Try a different hat. Slip into someone else's point of view.

> "When an idea has me stuck, I jump into the idea and pretend I'm inside on a micro scale. For example, when I was doing my doctoral research on aspartame (NutraSweet), I wanted to understand how the sweetener might behave in a food system and where it went during processing. So I would pretend I was a molecule of aspartame, and mentally visualize how I might react under a certain set of experimental variables. Many hurdles in my research were cleared once I got 'inside' the problem."
> – Jeffrey A. Stamp, Ph.D., Principle Scientist
>   Frito-Lay Inc.

Objective: To look at your problem from a different seat in the bleachers, on the bus or in the cockpit. To glean new insights from other elements of the task. To kick start your imagination with different points of view.

How to do it: Start with someone who has no understanding of your task. If you were your mom, how would you see it? How would you react at first blush? Where would you look for answers? What would be your concerns?

Get more specific. Look at the whole family. Consider the needs, desires, and spins of the middle teenage son, Aunt Gladys, Mom, sister Sue, and the family gerbil.

Do a double-take and look at it from the slant of someone who has been involved in the challenge for years. What mind ruts would you travel? What would you regard as immutable facts? What would be your beliefs? Which established mind ruts offer an opportunity to contradict history by contradicting them?

Amplify your challenge. Move the chair at the extremes. Exaggerate the issues by taking the most stuck-in-the-mud, right-wing conservative view, then the far-leftist, bleeding-heart, throw-money-at-every-problem liberal view. What are the stereotypes? What seemingly carved-in-stone perspectives are out there?

Put yourself in chairs from other lands. Imagine your challenge in the hands of Queen Elizabeth, a Sumo wrestler, an Inuit, a French chef, a Zulu chieftain, a Ukrainian peasant, a hula dancer, a Rastafarian, a desert sheik, a Norwegian fisherman, the Wildman of Borneo. What insights might they have to expand your perspective? What can you borrow from their worlds to make your challenge easier?

Put your chair in a time machine. How would Ben Franklin handle the challenge? George Washington? J. Edgar Hoover? John Wayne? Jed Clampett? Marat Sade? Sgt. York? W.C. Fields?

> WHEN I NEED TO JUMP START MY BRAIN ... "I call my mother. She has a knack for simplifying things in my mind and making the solution attainable. Getting back to a child-like mind set is easier if you are the child. So call your mother, even though you're all grown up, you're somebody's child."
> – Debbie DellaCave, Eureka! receptionist

Musical Chairs in Action

A great time to use Musical Chairs is when you're working on ideas for motivating and involving children.

I was faced with such a challenge when Procter & Gamble acquired Hawaiian Punch, a brand in serious need of jump starting.

First, I looked at the product from an adult's perspective. The line seemed complete, if somewhat complicated. Hawaiian Punch was available in 23 jillion flavors and colors.

Then I looked at the product as if I were a kid. To a child, it was simply Hawaiian Punch, a fruit drink that came in colors. Seated in the child's chair, I couldn't remember all those flavors and colors. In particular, I was confused by the four red flavors. I could never remember which red I liked.

Looking at the test data, one flavor stood above the others—Fruit Juicy Red. What if all Hawaiian Punch was Fruit Juicy Hawaiian Punch? Instead of changing the flavors from product to product, what if color was only thing? What if all Hawaiian Punch offered was Fruit Juicy Red, Fruit Juicy Green or Fruit Juicy Yellow? What if we had a Fruit Juicy Blue?

My adult self liked the simplicity of the idea. At least we'd be selling everybody's favorite taste. And from a kid's perspective, you could just ask for your color.

The change rolled national. Since then, Hawaiian Punch sales, as tracked by Information Resources, are up 16 percent. Moreover, the product is purchased by 19 percent more households than before—a figure that translates to an additional 3,000,000 homes. Which means a whole lot more kids are walking around with red moustaches, blue mustaches, and green mustaches.

I often invoke Ben Franklin's spirit for answers. Not long ago, I was tempted by an opportunity to hire hundreds of people for a business selling small—and medium-size companies one of our Eureka! services to discover new paths for growth. The opportunity was an exciting one. At the same time, the thought of having more people on staff, more overhead and more meetings turned my stomach. I'm an inventor, not a manager.

I wondered how Franklin would deal with it. Franklin kept his personal staff small, yet his business interests and wealth grew significantly. He did it through dozens of partnerships and joint ventures.

I took the same approach. Instead of hiring people, I found organizations that already had a network of consultants and licensed it to them.

Ben would have been proud. The Eureka! way is communicated to an important audience. And I stay focused on what I enjoy most—and do best.

INDUSTRIAL-STRENGTH JUMP START NO. 5

Lawbreaker

"Never underestimate the power of giving overt permission to break rules. Telling someone they can be open and creative on one hand and telling them to break the rules on the other are two different hands."
– Richard Saunders

We learn early on that rules are to be followed. Some rules, like the Golden Rule, teach us how to behave in a civilized manner. Other rules are Don't Rules, which are rules that have mostly come into being for our own good and are almost always handed down to us by individuals who have more authority than we do. Such as: "Don't touch that hot stove," "don't run through the house with my good scissors," and "don't talk back or you'll get a good spanking!" (As opposed to a bad spanking.)

But there's a disadvantage to following all the rules all the time. We can drift mindlessly on the Sea of Conventional Wisdom, to the point that we fail to notice the wicked good creatures of unconventional wisdom when their dorsal fins break through the surface of our subconscious minds.

"Patents are only issued to rebels and rule breakers."
– Richard Saunders

We sometimes need permission to break the rules in order to see what's behind, beneath, above, and beyond them. Unless you're given the okay to go ahead and vandalize a rule now and then, it can be hard to challenge your thinking and push your thought envelope outward. Indeed, the more knowledgeable you are about the task at hand, the more difficult it can be.

The exercises in this chapter are here to encourage the anarchist in you. They're here to tell you, hey, it's okay to break the rules.

> "I like to turn the problem inside out by asking myself seemingly irrelevant questions. For example: What if this were a place? What if it happened on the moon? What if they named a street after it? What if it had no top? These 'what if's' get me going. It's sort of like playing your own private party game. If this doesn't work, I eat chocolate. That never fails."
> – Liz Nickles, Author and Co-founder, Direct Dialogue

Objective: To consider your task in terms of the regulations, traditions, clichés, stereotypes, and/or popular conceptions attached to it. To examine what happens when you ignore, circumvent or twist the intent of those laws.

How to do it: List the laws, truths, perceptions, myths, and absolutes surrounding your task. Search for the most obvious facts, the ones that could never change. Here are a few examples of Great Laws through the Ages to illustrate:

- Fruit drinks are colored.
- The world is flat.
- The sun revolves around the Earth.
- Underwear has to be white.
- Nice guys finish last.

- If you keep cracking your knuckles, you'll get arthritis.

For each law, list one or two ways to break it. Twist the perceptions, shatter the absolutes, prove every "Thou Shalt" and "Thou Shalt Not" wrong. Break laws two at a time, three at a time, whatever presents itself. Be a rebel and break them all at once if you feel the urge. This is your chance to tweak the nose of conformity.

Now step back and examine the havoc you've wreaked. Where does it take you? How does it change the situation? In what ways does it liberate the task?

Lawbreaker in Action

One of our favorite examples of the success of lawbreaker is a part of the regulation Eureka! diet—specifically, dessert.

> "Ben and Jerry's Chocolate Chip Cookie dough is an integral part of any invention process, for that matter so is Cherry Garcia, Rainforest Crunch, Chocolate Fudge Brownie, Wild Maine Blueberry ... "
> – Richard Saunders

Ben Cohen and Jerry Greenfield broke all kinds of laws when they set out to sell ice cream.

If you were thinking about getting into the ice cream business and wanted to introduce a premium product—say, something about twice as expensive as anything else on the market—you would be advised to follow certain rules, among them:

- Stock your factory with gleaming, state-of-the-art equipment.
- Give it a classy, foreign name, like Haagen-Dazs.
- Use only imported ingredients, French vanilla or Swiss chocolate.
- Sell it in upscale places where goat cheese is more popular than Kraft Singles.

Ben and Jerry ignored the rules. Using an old-fashioned rock salt ice cream maker with a hand crank, they sold their first ice cream at an abandoned gas station in Vermont. They covered their cartons with handwritten labels and cartoon images. Their number one flavor is Chocolate Chip Cookie Dough. Picture the Queen Mother digging into a pint of that. They named a flavor after Grateful Dead lead guitarist Jerry Garcia and promoted it with tie-dyed T-shirts. They gave their employees roller skates to use on breaks and staged free music festivals.

They did everything wrong. But they created the No. 1-selling super-premium ice cream and frozen yogurt in America.

They may be chuckleheads. But they got the last laugh. In the end they sold the company for an estimated $326 million to Unilever, maker of Good Humor and Breyers ice cream.

Lawbreaker also has spiritual applications. I was wrapping up a lecture outside Washington D.C. when a man approached me, introduced himself as George and told me he'd learned about Lawbreaker from the first edition of this book. He said he'd made it work in his own life.

"When?" I asked.

"At church!" George said.

I retreated a few steps, keeping an eye out for lightning bolts of retribution. I wondered if George had taken matters too far. There are some authority figures you don't want to cross, after all. But George didn't appear too badly cursed. He told me this story.

His church was rapidly outgrowing its building. Its parking lot was overflowing. But it was located in an area where local zoning regulations required a fixed percent of the land to remain green space.

At a meeting of the church deacons, George suggested they look at the problem through Lawbreaker. They listed several laws:

- The parish had a limited amount of property.
- Churches are built on land.
- The church was at its capacity in terms of adding to the church.

• They didn't have enough land.
• Zoning laws require that you not exceed your current green-space-to-building-space ratio.

Once the laws were on paper, solutions to the problem began to present themselves. One, the church could buy more land, which would allow it to expand the building so that the ratio of developed land to green space would remain the same. Two, they could build underground.

It turned out that the church was able to purchase a few adjoining properties, tear down a few houses and add onto their church without running afoul of the city zoning inspector. Should the need arise, the deacons also have a plan to expand the church onto the parking lot and build an underground parking garage.

I was relieved. In this case, George's Authority Figure probably didn't mind a few laws being broken.

INDUSTRIAL-STRENGTH JUMP START NO. 6
Creativity Physics

For every diet, there's a dessert. For every fuel-efficient hybrid car, there's a mega macho sport utility vehicle. For every entrance, there's an exit. For every filet mignon, there's a slab of bologna. For every one-trick pony, there's a Secretariat. For every Stealth Bomber, there are a million paper airplanes. You get the idea.

Objective: To isolate trends and problem components, carry them forward to their extremes and then pull them as far as you can in the other direction. Stretch them.

Exaggerate them. Treat them like Silly Putty. Blow them entirely out of proportion. Somewhere between here and there is a rainbow of wicked good ideas.

How to do it: List overall trends or components related to your area of interest. Now apply Newton's first law of motion to each item on the list:

"A BODY IN MOTION STAYS IN MOTION."

Take each of your trends or elements to an extreme. Push it to preposterous lengths. Imagine what the world would be like if the trend continued for 1,000 years.

Turn around and take it the other way using Newton's third law of motion:

"EVERY FORCE HAS AN EQUAL AND OPPOSING FORCE."

Invent an idea that's the polar opposite of each of your trends or elements. Search for the mirror image. Take each of the extremes from earlier in the program and imagine if their opposites had been in effect for 1,000 years.

Creativity Physics in Action

In the summer of 1982, I was assigned at Procter & Gamble to work out a deal with the National Football League designating Coast soap the official NFL brand. At the time, the sports pages were dominated with headlines about the possibility of a players' strike.

Keeping in mind that a body in motion stays in motion, I asked the NFL representative with whom I was negotiating, a guy named Bill, about the likelihood of a strike. Bill said not to worry, it wouldn't happen.

I took it to the extreme.

"Are you sure?" I asked him.

"Yes, yes," he said.

"Can I be completely confident there will not be an NFL player strike?" I asked again.

Bill stayed in motion. "Absotively posilootly," he said.

It was time for me to take an equal and opposite tack.

"OK, then, how about if for every game the players do strike, just for the sake of argument, I get a rebate on my licensing fee?" I asked. "I mean, seeing as how you're so sure they won't strike and all."

To which Bill agreed, seeing as how he was so sure the players wouldn't strike and all.

The players went on strike. The strike lasted long enough so that, Coast Soap ended up paying nothing for its licensing agreement with the NFL that year.

Meanwhile, another Procter & Gamble product, a certain food and beverage brand, had entered into a similar agreement with the NFL. Unfortunately, the brand manager was ignorant of the laws of creativity physics and believed Bill's assurances that the players wouldn't strike. And that particular brand's manager paid the full licensing agreement for half a season's worth of games.

INDUSTRIAL-STRENGTH JUMP START NO. 7

System Solutions

Sometimes the right product or solution requires you to invent an entire system.

Perhaps the best illustration of this truth is the story of Thomas Alva Edison, who invented the light bulb, then invented the system to make it work, from the power plant to the utility poles to the point where your finger flicks on the switch.

Take away the power plant and the light bulb is irrelevant.

Edison understood the importance of having a total solution. In 1880, he formed the Edison Electric Company. His plan was to locate his first power plant near Wall Street, a move that would require the support of City Hall, inasmuch as it meant that streets would have to be ripped up to make way for power lines.

Imagine all the dominoes that had to be lined up for such a thing to happen. Obviously, the city fathers had to be part of the total solution. They had to see the benefit to agree to the aggravation that would result.

Edison invited the city fathers, probably not a particularly visionary lot, to his Menlo Park lab. With darkness approaching and the elected officials grumbling about the hour, Edison clapped his hands. A switch was thrown, and Menlo Park was flooded with light. The room was set for an elegant dinner party, with waitresses dressed in formal attire. The city fathers got the point, and Edison got his power lines.

Objective: To explore external factors that might influence your task. To identify the elements of the larger world of which your task is a part. To play with these elements with an eye toward improving the context and finding solutions.

How to do it: Diagram the Big Picture around your task on a sheet of paper. What forces, factors, requirements, constraints, and elements are at work? Neatness doesn't count.

Add new elements to your Big Picture. You might explore what could happen if you added, say, a double shift to your system. What would happen if you changed two or three forces or requirements at one time? What ideas does it generate?

Draw the interrelationships—the feed forwards and feed backwards.

Diagram all "if, then" relationships. As in, if we do X, then Y will happen.

Or maybe the solution lies in changing another part of the system. For example, if your small business has a problem getting part-time teen employees to show up on time, would you be better off hiring senior citizens?

Or if your flowers aren't growing on the north side of your house, can you change the type of fertilizer and the type of flowers to increase your odds of success?

System Solutions is about making multiple changes to realize a bigger result. It's about changing one piece of the puzzle to create a cascade of changes.

Chew on this: If all system constraints and requirements were met, the system would be in equilibrium. Now, make a dramatic change to one of the forces acting on your system, sending your system into chaos.

To return equilibrium, make the necessary changes to the other forces. This means some constraints will have to be removed or modified. Once you regain balance, take a close look at the newly created system. How does it look? Does it work? Can you see new opportunities?

System Solution in Action

When I launched my company, Eureka! wasn't the only entree on my menu. I had to invent AcuPOLL Research as well. Why? Because having a system for inventing 30 ideas in 30 days was of little value if clients had no objective way of knowing whether their customers would buy the ideas.

To be successful, we would have to offer a revolutionary research method as well as a revolutionary creative development system. This research method had to be (a) fast, (b) easy to understand, and (c) capable of providing pinpoint measurements of consumer responses to our ideas.

AcuPOLL meets all three requirements.

For speed, it uses a digital information-gathering computer network. Consumers log reactions to ideas on individual computer keyboards, making it possible to gauge the probable success of 30 new product concepts in three hours, compared to one concept in three months with traditional research methods. Wow!

And AcuPOLL results are easy to understand. Consumers grade concepts on a scale of 0 to 10. The numbers are translated to letter grades, A to F. Wicked good ideas are A's; ill-conceived, misbegotten ideas show up as F's, no matter how new and different they may be.

As for accuracy, AcuPOLL's predictions of new product successes and failures have been proven accurate 89 percent of the time.

The point is, AcuPOLL was the piece missing from a larger system. This same principal was applied when the Eveready Battery Company hired us to develop a product we called the Eversafe Child Locater Smoke Detector.

The task was to create a new smoke detector. We started there and worked backward, looking at the larger world in which smoke detectors come into play. We began with the obvious questions, which led to less obvious questions:

- What do smoke detectors do? Well, they detect smoke. Then they set off an alarm to warn people in the house so they can do something about the smoke—or wake them up so they can get the H-E-double hockey sticks out of there.
- What don't smoke detectors do? They don't tap you on the shoulder, they don't carry you out of the house and they don't light up.
- Who is warned? The people in the house hear the alarm, not the fire department or neighbors.
- What if you're a person who can't move? What if you're a baby? An alarm doesn't help you.
- So how could a smoke detector help those folks? Maybe it tells other people they're trapped. Like a fireman?
- What if you take it outside the house? What if you could show the fireman a child's exact location before he enters the house? A siren on the outside of the house might work. But a flashing light in the child's window would probably be better.

We thought so, anyway. We engineered a two-part system that included a smoke detector and a separate flashing light that mounted on the window. The client liked it, too.

INDUSTRIAL-STRENGTH JUMP START NO. 8

Do One Thing Great

Too often, we bite off too much. We try to create something that's all things to all people and ends up being nothing to anyone.

The truth is if you claim complete victory in one area, people will believe you can perform in other areas as well.

Let's say you want to genetically engineer tomatoes in your basement. But what's your scope? Instead of trying to create the world's greatest all-around champion tomato, let me suggest that you focus on a small bite. Consider the different purposes a tomato can serve. Make your product the best tomato for salads. Or ketchup. Or juice. Or spaghetti sauce. Or pizzas. Or throwing at politicians whose sentiments you do not share. Or heaving at mimes. Why do we hate mimes?

Do One Thing Great is about being best at something. When you're the best, you offer a solid reason to buy. It's much easier to get people to shout "Hooray for you!" when you're the best at something. Do One Thing Great is a ready answer to the question, "Why should I care?"

"A Jack of all Trades rarely gets to be King."
– Richard Saunders

Do One Thing Great is the shortest distance to blunt, highly concentrated only-an-idiot-could-miss-it focusing. It's a shortcut to locating and exploiting your advantages. It will give you new ways to define your assets and help you focus energy on the ones that can make you great.

Objective: To chart your area of brilliance, which is anyplace where you can wear the halo. To help you settle on a superlative and plan a route for making it real. To isolate one or two facets of the task you can use to burn hotter and shine more brightly than anyone. Do One Thing Great is a fast track to establishing:

- A clear point of difference between you and everyone else
- An area where you can make more money
- An area where consumers aren't fully satisfied
- An opportunity for growth
- An area of technological opportunity
- An area that's more fun
- A direction where no one has gone
- An area where you could stake your claim

How to do it: List your every asset, the small and the big, the fabulous and the silly. Fill an entire page using both broad and specific categories.

Consider the various components of your task. What is it now? Make a list of the obvious and the less obvious. Arrange these pieces under the heading "What is it now?"

Add an "est" or "the best" to each piece. Transform it into a winner under a second heading, Be No. 1. Address each piece under a third heading, "Ways to Realize."

Say you're inventing a new toilet bowl cleaner. Your "Be No. 1" sheet could look like this:

What Is It Now?	Be No. 1	Ways to Realize
Fragrant	Best smelling	Add Chanel No. 5
A toilet seat cleaner	The best cleaner	Build a brush into the bottle
A sanitizer	The most sanitizing	Changes color when germs are dead

Bulge and build on each of the items in the best list. Which are proprietary, original, exciting, gold medal winners? Repeat the exercise, listing new-to-the world benefits you could offer.

To build on the previous example:

What It Could Be?	Be No. 1	Ways to Realize
Safe for pets and babies	Safest for everybody	Organic formulation
Fun to use	The most fun to use	Add multi-color swirl dyes

Do One Thing Great in Action

Ken Eilers does one thing great. Around Cincinnati, he's known as the Screen Guy. He drives a Screen-mobile with the slogan, "We Screen at Your Place" stenciled on both sides.

Screens are his life. If you ask him to help you hang a window box or trim a sill, he shakes his head and says, "Sorry. All I do is screens. That's it."

Ken installs window screens, door screens, screens for screen-in porches and sun screens. But he doesn't screen films, and he doesn't screen calls—those are different kinds of screens.

> "I don't want to compare myself to a brain surgeon but if you do one thing, you tend to get good at it."
> – Ken Eilers, The Screen Mobile

Ken has established himself as an expert. Because of his expertise, he can charge more. If you want to leave your windows open without having to worry about bugs flying, he's the man to call. Otherwise, he can't help you.

INDUSTRIAL-STRENGTH JUMP START NO. 9

Dr. Disecto

Dr. Disecto is about transformation. In the literature on creativity, it's called "checklist." We think it's bigger than that. We think it's about taking your challenge and applying a statement of transformation.

Dr. Disecto exists solely to hack entities of all kinds into piles of small throbbing, squishy parts. He has a fetish for breaking down whatever crosses his path into its constituent pieces.

> "When I'm stuck for an idea or solution, I try to look at the problem from a different perspective. Tear it apart; turn it upside down."
> – Tony Bevilacqua, Vice President Marketing Eveready Battery Company, Canada

Objective: To discover solutions to your challenge through the application of transformational phrases.

How to do it: Take your challenge and add a transformational phrase. In mathematical terms, it works like this:

$$Task + Dr.\ Disecto\ Phrase = Eureka!$$

Favorite options of Dr. Disecto phrases at the Eureka! Ranch include:

• What would be the simple solution?
• What would contradict history?
• What would be the most outrageous solution?
• What would send fear into your competitors' hearts?

- What would leverage consumer perceptions?
- What would leverage consumer misperceptions?
- What would contradict trends?
- How could our competition scare us?
- How could we draw coverage from USA Today?
- How could we attract heavy users?
- How could we bring new consumers to our category?
- How could we steal the competition's best customers?
- How could we provide outrageous customer service?
- How could we turn our weaknesses into strengths?

Take a deep breath. Exhale. Now force-associate your task with the first Dr. Disecto question. Add them together and see what you get. Bend and twist until they start to make sense. When finished, move to the next question. Make yourself do each question. It won't be easy, but you can do it. Keep in mind that the longest stretches usually produce the best results.

Bob Eberle is credited with creating a mnemonic version of Dr. Disecto called Scamper. It breaks down like this:

S is for Substitute—swap out components, materials, and people

C is for Combine—mix your challenge with others, combine pieces and parts in new ways

A as in Adapt—change the function or alter the purpose of one element of your challenge

M means Modify—increase (or decrease) a component of your challenge; change its form or attributes

P or Put to another use—Change the purpose of one or more components

E as in Eliminate—Remove components, simplify, destroy, or eliminate a big piece

R is for Reverse—Transform your challenge; look at it from inside out, upside-down or side-ways-down

One of my favorite checklist systems was created by the University of Oklahoma's Andy Van Gundy. He calls it the PICL process. (Product Improvement Check List).

> "The human mind thinks of ideas using chains of associations. Many of these associations arise from random thoughts, with one concept leading to another. A simple illustration would be how we view an object such as a tree. We might think of leaves, then tables, then chairs, then eating and so forth. The PICL process builds on this tendency of the mind to free-associate by channeling your associations to resolve a problem. You select a word at random and then consider how the concept might suggest a solution."
> – Arthur B. VanGundy, Ph.D

The PICL list is available in poster form direct from Andy VanGundy or from on-line vendors. The list contains more than 700 stimuli. It's divided into two parts. BASIC PICL offers 102 questions oriented to product improvement and organized in such categories as:

Who ...
- Uses it?
- Doesn't use it?
- Would never even try it?

What ...
- Are its most important features?
- Do customers suggest?
- Is altered by consumers?

Where ...
- Is it used?
- Is it stored?
- Is it first tried by consumers?
- When couldn't it be used?

When ...
- Is it liked most.?
- Is it misused?

Why ...
- Is it better than a competitor's product?
- Do people stop using it?
- Was it developed?

The second part of the poster, called PICL JUICE, is a compilation of some 600 idea triggers. These are divided into four categories, each capable of spurring new thoughts and associations by the wheelbarrow-full. A few samples:

Try to	Make it	Think of	Take away or add
Bend it	Adjustable	Genetic research	Handles
Inject it	Pocket size	Hot coffee	Turbulence
Divide it	Self-destruct	Credit cards	Ball bearings
Weave it	Grow	Televisions	Baskets
Assemble it	Portable	Rain	Padding
Spread it	Collapsible	Turtles	Pipes
Wind it up	Magnetic	Toothpaste	Elastic
Dehydrate it	Unbreakable	Banks	Keys
Ventilate it	Striped	Disappearing ink	Accessories
Dissolve it	Triangular	Silent alarms	Decorations

Dr. Disecto in Action

Bob was looking for a way to save several million dollars a year in lost sales revenues. He made his living selling chemicals used to print newspapers. He was good at it. In fact, he was his company's national sales leader. But he had a big problem. One day, he dropped by the Ranch to talk about it.

The thing was, you see, Bob's product required him to provide huge helpings of technical assistance to his customers. He had no problem serving big accounts in major cities, but the smaller markets in the hinterlands were a different story. He couldn't tap them because his staff couldn't get to them as often as they were needed.

It was costing him plenty. Bob and I engaged in a stream-of-consciousness conversation that basically took this course:

> Me: "Okay, let's look at ways to provide outrageously good service."
> Bob: "How?"
> Me: "Give your customers instant service."
> Bob: "What?"
> Me: "Have a technician available for each printing plant."
> Bob: "Can't do it."
> Me: "Why?"
> Bob: "It costs too much to get there."
> Me: "Why?"
> Bob: "They gotta drive. It's a long way."
> Me: "What if we put a technician in each plant?"
> Bob: "How?"
> Me: "Beam them there, like they do in Star Trek."
> Bob: "What do I look like, George Jetson?"
> Me: "George Jetson with a Spacely Sprocket space phone."

Dr. Disecto had the answer. Bob's customers could sign a six-month contract for a free "Video Service Station," a two-way video telephone service. When his customers had a production problem, they could press a button and a technical support person would instantly appear on the screen to solve it. Because now, Bob's technicians could see the problems as soon as his clients saw them.

INDUSTRIAL-STRENGTH JUMP START NO. 10

Crystal Ball

"I never skate to where the puck is. I always skate to where the puck's going to be."
– Hockey great Wayne Gretzky

Research indicates that new product ideas that ANTICI-PATE THE FUTURE are 10 times more predictive of success than those that simply listen to the voice of the customer.

Think of it this way. No one ever asked for a Sony Walkman or an Apple i-Pod. Sony and Apple created the concept by looking into the future.

"Launching a breakthrough idea is like shooting skeet. People's needs change, so you have to aim well ahead of the target to hit it."
– Raymond Kurzweil, author, scientist, futurist

Objective: To anticipate customers future needs. To imagine the future.

How it works:

Step 1: Answer three or more of the following future-focused questions.

- The TRENDSETTING customer or expert would want the solution to be ...
- In the future, the big GROWTH area associated with my challenge will be ...
- A smart entrepreneur could create chaos with this challenge by ...
- Thinking outrageously, it could be in 10 years that ...
- In the future, it's likely that new technology will make it possible to...
- In the future, China or India could very well...

Step 2: IF X, THEN Y

Pick one of the Crystal Ball insights and free-associate on potential solutions. Force yourself to believe that this trend is an absolute. Believe that there is no question of it becoming reality.

If you knew for sure that this trend would happen, what would or should you do now, today? How can you capitalize? How can you use this trend to your advantage? How can you get ahead of the competition?

If you have trouble finding a sense of urgency, think about what you'd do if your competition invested time and money on leveraging this prediction? Would you be scared/concerned/frustrated? What would you do about it?

Crystal Ball NOT in Action: This is the sad story of two opportunities lost. In the early days of the worldwide web, one of the world's biggest companies asked for our help inventing a strategy for competing as an Internet provider.

This was before today's Internet icons. Looking into our Crystal Ball, we identified several areas we thought could generate interest and excitement for our client's future growth, among them:

1. A way to participate in auctions around the world
2. A way to make phone calls for free

3. A way to listen to the radio broadcast of high school or college football teams
4. A way to be your own NFL home announcer
5. A way to gamble on football games anywhere

Our team decided the best place to focus was on Internet audio broadcasting. A recommendation was written to buy Internet broadcast rights to all major league sports teams while creating an Internet phone system for international phone calls. The recommendation was more than a pipe dream; the client owned key technologies on audio compression and had on staff some of the world's experts in audio transfer.

A major presentation was assembled. I was charged with explaining the idea and reporting the research results, which were quite glowing. The team gathered together early that morning at the company office.

What we had in mind was a major shift in strategy. To date, management believed the way the company would win would be by providing more reliable service, leveraging the company's reputation in other telecommunications areas.

It was a long, hard day. Our meeting was delayed several times as the company leaders were tied up in other meetings. Finally around 8 p.m., we made our pitch.

I tried to paint a vision of the future. I spoke of the changes that were coming. I talked about how I had made an audio link to someone in the Middle East.

The Big Boss laughed. He said the company had achieved its success by staying focused on sound quality and clarity. In his view, the Internet could never provide the quality his network did. He also pooh-poohed such "gimmicks" as Internet football broadcasts.

I argued that, in the future, the Internet would have audio quality that matches classic phone networks—and it would be free. I urged him to buy up the rights to audio content—and to work to become known for world-class audio.

My client made even more emotional pleas for support.

There was no chance. The boss' opinion was clear:

"We're one of the world's most successful companies. We got here by standing for reliability—we'll win on the Internet because of that reputation."

Meeting over.

In the hallway afterward, the client was livid. "I can't believe it," he said. "We are so out of touch with the future."

I asked him what he was going to do.

He told me he was gone. He said the project had opened his eyes to new possibilities. His plan was to find a company that is more progressive. About a month later, he did.

Much of the future vision came true, not exactly as we envisioned it, but our big picture dimensions were pretty well on the mark. The Boss Man was good to his word—the company relied on it past reputation. It didn't work.

A competitor eventually acquired the company. And an opportunity for great victory was lost.

Over the past 30 years, I've experienced these types of challenges hundreds of times. A team envisions the future, only to be stopped by CEOs or boards of directors lacking the courage to move forward.

Over the past 10 years, since writing the first edition of this book, it has become even more clear to me that the key to megasuccess with creativity is a future focused outlook that anticipates the future. Net: **to the bold and the brave go all the big rewards.**

★ ★ ★ ★ ★ ★ ★ ★ ★ ★ ★ ★ ★ ★ ★ ★

12

TOP TEN GROUP
CREATIVITY JUMP STARTS

★ ★ ★ ★ ★ ★ ★ ★ ★ ★ ★ ★ ★ ★ ★ ★

Group Creativity Jump Starts are designed to help you tap into the ideas, insights, and wisdom of others. Historically, tapping into the wisdom of others has involved a brainstorming session where a group of people gather to share ideas.

> "None of us is as smart as all of us."
> – Japanese proverb

In today's world that process can also occur in a digital world. New technologies make it easy for people to gather in a virtual world.

Video conferencing is moving from high-end systems costing tens of thousands of dollars and requiring dedicated ISDN lines to a "free service" built into laptops and computer operating systems.

Portals like blogs, Facebook and Wikipedia make it easy for group collaboration. You can easily post a problem and wait for others to submit ideas for solving your challenge.

A key to success for these systems is the writing of responses. Writing makes each contribution clear to everyone and ensures organizational memory. When a community working on a challenge wrestles with a decision, the debate is recorded so it can be recalled later, hopefully avoiding the repetition of previous failures.

This last chapter of Jump Starts details ways to connect with others. Some are ways for you to simply gather the ideas of others. Some are methods that are made for group gatherings.

Note, in the case of a group meeting all of the earlier Jump Starts can also be used in meetings as too most of these can be used on an individual or paired basis.

GROUP CREATIVITY

JUMP START NO. 1: YOU GOT IDEAS

One of the most powerful ways to leverage the Internet may be the simplest.

E-mail lets us connect, while allowing a pause for thought. It also makes it possible to connect with a level of "distance" that allows for more honesty and clarity than is sometimes available on an interpersonal basis.

Research confirms the power of distant collaborations. A study reported in the *Creativity Research Journal* found that collaborations between authors working on academic articles at different locations were more effective than those convened in a single location.

Researchers studied the number of citations that 5,113 academic articles generated, using citations by other authors as a measure of impact the research had. They found that articles written by authors at different universities were cited significantly more than articles produced by authors at the same location.

My theory is that this "distance factor" works in two ways.

First, the mere fact of having different people in different environments adds diversity of thought to the challenge. With different thinking styles attacking the challenge, you're bound to generate higher quality thinking.

Secondly, having distance between members of a team allows for deeper thinking and more honest feedback. E-mail has a rhythm that can be quite effective. You can respond immediately if you wish. Or you can also take time to think through an issue before responding.

The ability to stop and think deeper about an issue increases the quality of feedback. Ben Franklin used a similar process. When writing an important letter, he would wait a day before sending. As his message percolated in his mind, he would find a better way to express his thoughts—or he would come to his senses and pitch the letter. His files are filled with letters that were never sent.

Objective: To think more deeply about an idea based on the feedback from others in your e-mail address book.

How to do it:

Step 1: Write the story of your challenge. Ideally in 200 words or less explain the who, what, when, why, and how of your situation.

Step 2: Identify the one to three most important questions for which you would like feedback. Be as specific as possible about what you need help with. Keeping your request clear and specific makes it easier for them to help you. Note—don't be surprised if they provide ideas that are far beyond your questions.

Step 3: Write an e-mail and send it to 10 people with different perspectives. In your e-mail, tell the story of your challenge and overtly ask your one to three questions. When addressing the e-mail, use as a subject: "Even just a couple minutes of your time would help me a lot. " This sets up the expectation that you are not looking for a major investment of time— simply their ideas and advice.

Step 4: When you get the responses, remember to write back and say THANK YOU. In the digital world, gratitude is not expressed nearly as often as it should be.

You Got Ideas ... in Action

When working on this book I sent out an e-mail to clients describing the purpose of this book and asked the simple question: When you're stuck for an idea, what do you do to jump start your powers of creativity?

Many of the responses I received are quoted on these pages—many more became ideas for chapter segments. The responses from some 100 Eureka! clients gave me a depth of understanding and perspective on the challenge of igniting fresh thinking that no amount of working on my own could have.

This morning, I received an e-mail from Jane, a friend of a friend. Jane is developing a sequence of college courses in applied creativity. In her e-mail, she outlined two options and asked what I thought was the better choice.

It so happened that I've been working with the University of Maine to create a new approach to teaching applied creativity that we've branded as Innovation Engineering. I responded to her challenge and attached a document detailing the Innovation Engineering approach. I copied Jane as well as the others on her copy list to spark more ideas.

An hour after I sent my response, another friend offered ideas that created even more choices, connecting my suggestions to Jane's choices. Within the 24 hours, Jane received a wealth of ideas and suggestions to help her make her decision.

Most importantly, I received the following response from her:

> Doug,
> Thank you for sharing your insights. I appreciate it!
> Jane

Dear Mr. President Variation of You Got Ideas ...

A simple variation is to use e-mail to engage an entire organization in a safari for new ideas called Dear Mr. President. Use the format from You Got Ideas. Start with a simple question and simple articulation of the challenge.

In a best case, have the request for ideas be signed by a

big cheese—the president, CEO, owner, someone with clout. Then use posters and e-mail to put out the word.

Dear Mr. President in Action

When I was brand manager for Safeguard soap, my team was looking for a new way to display the product in grocery stores without having to stack the bars by hand. While many grocery store products can be displayed in "cut cases," where the tops of cardboard cases are simply cut away, leaving them exposed in the resulting "bottom tray," you couldn't do that with bar soap. Or so we thought.

The company had recommended special shrink-wrap trays, a particularly expensive option. I remember discussing the problem at the soap plant in Quincy, Mass., with one of the technicians. We'd commandeered a conference room and, using my standard feel-it-touch-it modus operandi, we had before us 48 cases of Safeguard.

Thirty minutes and 15 cases of soap later, the technician blurted out an idea to split each case down the middle into two trays, like the two halves of a clamshell. One case could then be stacked on top of the other. The technician's idea was **10 times more efficient** than management's best recommendation, **at about a tenth of the cost**. Further, test markets showed the new case design increased Safeguard's sales by 40 percent over three months.

It was inspired. And it taught me that the people at the ground level, the ones who do the actual work, know what they're doing. They ought to—they plug away at it every day. Unfortunately, the corporate hierarchy usually is more interested in covering their backsides than opening their minds. Fortunately, it's hard to keep a truly good idea down.

"When I started at the plant, I suggested lots of new ideas for our production area. The bosses weren't interested. They wanted to do it the way they'd been doing it for 20 years. After being told no a dozen times, I stopped making suggestions. I still try out ideas, but only when the bosses won't notice what I'm up to."
– An inventive American who prefers to keep his name to himself

After a presentation to Monsanto Company, I was pleased to hear its Innovation Team had launched a three-month Dear Mr. President-style idea generation campaign called "It's in There Alright," in which employees were asked to submit ideas.

"We ended up with over 300 ideas. Of those, we have several that we're seriously looking into. One guy got so excited, he sent in 15 ideas. It's been great getting ideas in from around the world—India, Australia, Denmark, Korea, France, Japan … "
– Linda Moentmann, Monsanto Innovation Team

GROUP CREATIVITY

JUMP START NO. 2: HITCHHIKING

You're stuck. You can't break out of your thought pattern. Time to recapture innocent, uneducated raw thinking. But how?

Simple: Move your feet, and your imagination will follow.

You might try hitchhiking. Hitchhiking is a time-honored art at the Eureka! Ranch. Management Guru Tom Peters calls it "management by walking around." It's a process of hopscotching from one person to another to gather ideas.

Hitchhiking can be a spontaneous occurrence involving walking and talking to others. Or it can be encouraged, as in a group Eureka! session. Usually, in a free and open environment, it sort of just happens.

Objective: To unchain your brain. To grease the skids inside your head and build mental momentum. To let your imagination play leapfrog with the wit and wisdom of others.

How to do it: Push yourself away from your desk, head out the door, and hitchhike on the imaginations of others. Take a walk—through your office, down the hall, out to lunch, wherever. Talk to the waitress, the janitor, and/or the cab driver. Consult butcher, baker, and candlestick maker. Seek out common-sense people blissfully ignorant of the preconceptions, myths, laws and facts surrounding your task.

Tell them your problem.

> "The best ideas occur to me while I'm talking to someone else about the problem. If I can get someone else interested, then the process of explaining and defending my old moss-covered ideas causes new shiny ones to occur to me. Sometimes the old ones just get cleaned up, but they look new anyway."
> – Paul W. Farris Ph.D., Professor, Darden
> School of Business

Ask for a top-of-the-head, off-the-cuff, spur-of-the-moment, common-sense answer. Most of the time, most people are happy to help—especially if you're a high-profile corporate executive because then they can go home and tell their families about the poor schmoe they ran into that day who couldn't find his or her brain with both hands.

Lay out your situation. Let them in on what you're dealing with and what you're not dealing with so well. Then—and this is the tough part—listen closely. Let your mind drink in their fresh, naive thoughts and perceptions.

Listen in particular for pure gut reactions. Look for quick, instinctive snapshots of innocent thought. First perceptions often lead to the best solutions. You can mine gold from these virgin thoughts. That's because these people haven't been doing what you've been doing—over-thinking and overworking your task until your supply of common sense has depleted itself.

The same principle can come into play when you start a new job. More often than not, you experience a rush of ideas in your first week. As time passes, you become educated as to what you can and cannot say/do/be. You begin to over-think. You lose the ability to leap before you look.

As you listen to your innocent outsiders, pull back and ask yourself, "What's the obvious solution?" Get simple.

The key is to listen. Forget your education, knowledge, credentials, native intelligence, and the conformity facts of life. Seek ways to make innocent, virgin thoughts feasible.

TO JUMP START MY BRAIN ... "I talk to people. I think well if I talk things out, so I usually call someone or grab the first person that walks by and engage them in helping to find a solution.
– Barb Korn, Group Director, Ralston Purina

TO JUMP START MY BRAIN ... "I talk to someone who has no knowledge of my problem or situation. This translates into fresh, honest stimuli. And I sometimes wander through a grocery store and steal ideas, search and reapply or take various ideas and put them together to form a new idea."
– Bruce Hall, Procter & Gamble

The world is full of fresh perspectives just waiting to be consulted on any subject. And the naive, first-blush response is often the obvious solution — the one you'd missed because it was hiding in a secret place under your nose.

"Common sense is not so common."
– Richard Saunders

Hitchhiking in Action

While dreaming up the packaging and positioning for a new candy for Van Melle that we called "Great Unbelievable Tasting Sweets"—G.U.T.S., for short—I became what is known in the business as "stumped." G.U.T.S. was meant to be the Russian roulette of the confection world—red balls of hard candy, filled with either a concentrated cherry punch powder or concentrated red-hot cinnamon powder. The deal was, you didn't know what you're into until it's too late.

I was having a hard time finding a way to explain the difference between the hot candies and the cherry candies. I'd tried Fire 'n Ice, Hot Stuff 'n Cool Stuff, Flamers 'n Ice Cubes, Sugar 'n Spice. I was stuck in a rut.

Wandering through the Eureka! offices, yakking with staffers, I spilled my G.U.T.S. One staffer was reminded of cherries. But the taste was actually that of a red berry. To which someone else replied, "cherry berries!"

Not bad, I thought. It was fun to say, and it fit the product's sensory aspects.

Two flights of stairs led me to Randy Mazzola's office. We ping-ponged ideas back and forth, and Randy hit on a name for the hot candies: Cherry Bombs.

Cherry Bombs and Cherry Berries. Wow! Another nice fit.

Now I had to concoct a half-baked G.U.T.S. story to explain how Cherry Berries and Cherry Bombs got mixed up in the same box. I headed back downstairs to talk to others. I asked this person and that:

What do cherry bombs do?

They go boom!

Boom became Dr. Boom Boom. Once we had the doctor,

the story wrote itself. Here's what it said on the back of the G.U.T.S. package:

Hey Dudes and Dudettes!
The wild and wacky Dr. Boom Boom has invad-
ed the Van Melle candy factory.

Inside harmless looking, awesome tasting
Cherry Berry hard candies,
he's placed two different surprises.

In the center of most of the candies
you'll find gazillions of CHERRY BERRIES
that rock your mouth with awesome flavor!

BUT BEWARE!
In 2 to 4 of the candies in each bag, he's placed
HOT, HOT, HOT CHERRY BOMBS!!!!

The taste of Great Unbelievable Tasting Sweets
is incredible. But only try them if you've got the
GUTS!

Once again, I'd hitchhiked my way out of the abyss. The solutions to my problem were simple, as most great ideas are. But I was too deeply ensconced in my rut to find them on my own.

"Sometimes the best solutions come from those
not as closely associated with the situation or
those who are unfamiliar with everyday business
practices."
– Scott Becker, Brand Development Manager
Thomas J. Lipton Co.

Hitchhiking works with strangers. But spouses, friends and family members often make great sounding boards as well. I'm blessed with a fountain of insight, common sense, and originality in my own home—my wife, Debbie. When I'm twisted up in knot-ted notions, tangents, and peripherals, she cuts the cord for me.

GROUP CREATIVITY
JUMP START NO. 3: FLAPDOODLE

"Great Flapdoodle sheets are like great old Ford pickups. They're not gussied-up fashion statements. They're just plain functional. They do real work."
– Richard Saunders

To invent a wicked good idea, it helps to be able to see it. Or to put it another way, Flapdoodle it.

Flapdoodling is a process for display thinking. It's a way of collecting and structuring ideas so that they can go forth and multiply. It's a method for recording, free-associating and, most of all, making chaos work for you. It's especially helpful when you have a group of people working on an idea, as it makes it possible for others to see the connections as you see them.

Flapdoodling as presented here is a simplified variation of a display thinking system called Mind Mapping® invented by Tony Buzan.

The traditional approach to note-taking and outlining is to start at the top of a sheet of paper, work your way in a linear fashion to the bottom, and continue again at the top of the next sheet. You work in one dimension. Ho-hum.

You learned the outline format in the fifth grade. The problem is, it doesn't give your ideas much room to mingle, flirt or buy each other drinks. As a result, your ability to bulge on your ideas is limited. Opportunities for connecting, cleansing, and enhancing are lost.

A. Zzz Zzz
   1. Zxy
   2. Zwv

B. Yaz YAZ
   1. Xxy
   2. Xwv

Flapdoodling works in two dimensions. It has latitude and longitude. It's messy, free-form, alive, and dynamic. It's the next best thing to producing a printout of your brain.

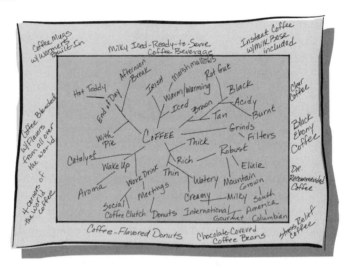

You can Flapdoodle in longhand on paper, with a hammer and chisel on a slab of granite, or on a half dozen computer programs that offer digital Mind Mapping.

Objective: To allow you to record ideas in such a way that they can bulge, build and hitchhike on one another. Flapdoodling is a way to invent ideas as well as a means of recording them. The process helps you see a range of alternatives. The discipline of Flapdoodling helps prevent you from simply taking the first path, the first idea that winks at you. The next idea is often a better idea.

How to do it: Get a nice big sheet of paper—say, 20 inches tall by 26 inches wide. I use king-size clipboards to make Flapdoodling more conducive to stretching out on a couch. Or you can lay a chart pad on a table like an extra-large placemat. Or spread a paper table cloth across a conference room table.

The first step is to define your objective. What is your task, mission or problem? Maybe it's just a word—a who, a how, a when, or a why. Write it in the center of the page using a juicy, squeaky colored marker with a nice, fat, assertive stroke. That's your epicenter, your point of departure. Draw a box around the task. Or, if you're feeling particularly mental, try a hexagon or other multi-sided gon. For each corner, push yourself to come up with one, two or more different areas of exploration—associations, ideas, or related elements.

Unleash your imagination. Send it skyward. Begin to free-associate outward in spokes from the epicenter, allowing each spoke to sprout spokes of its own as you work farther and farther from the center. The further you go, your thoughts will become less grounded in reality and move increasingly in the realm of new and different.

If necessary, prod your brain at bayonet-point. Through the act of forcing a variety of options, your mind will open itself to a wider spectrum of alternatives — as opposed to keeping a narrow perspective and limiting the scenarios you have to consider. You'll end up with a sheet that, at first glance, will look as if it was used to sop up an ink spill. But as you hopscotch out from the epicenter, your stream of consciousness will begin to flow. Connections will present themselves. Ideas will bubble to the surface, as if with wills of their own. The randomness of it can hardly help but reveal free associations that wouldn't otherwise emerge in a more logical, linear, lunkhead format.

Finally, dress the Flapdoole for stardom. Draw circles or boxes around wicked good ideas. If you're feeling particularly colorful, use different colored markers to make your thoughts pounce off the page. With Flapdoodling, you'll find ideas come in clusters, like grapes. Circle the ones that strike you as Aha! kinds of ideas. Draw stars and exclamation points around the ones that make your heart flutter.

Flapdoodling in Action

Here's a real world example of how I used Flapdoodle to come up with an idea for a birthday present for my wife Debbie.

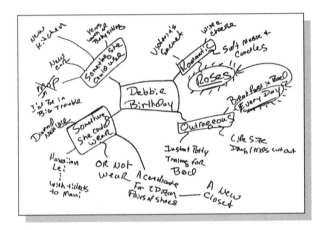

The epicenter of the Flapdoodle sheet was the question "What to get Debbie for her birthday?"

The first four spokes looked like this:

1. Something romantic
2. Something outrageous
3. Something she could wear
4. Something she could use

Each spoke provided a departure point of its own. The next level of the Romantic and Outrageous spokes sprouted these thoughts:

1. Something romantic
   - Roses
   - Soft music and candles
   - Wine and Cheese
   - Victoria's Secret

2. Something outrageous
   - A life size cut-out photo of me and the kids.
   - Breakfast in bed every day for a year
   - Instantaneous potty training for our son Brad.

As I scribbled thoughts out from the spokes, my mind started jumping the tracks back and forth from romantic to outrageous. "Roses" and "every day" connected themselves. So maybe I should buy her roses every day for a year? Nice idea, but too expensive.

Then again, a bouquet of fresh flowers lasts about a week. What if I had flowers delivered to her once a week for a year? That way, she'd have an unending stream of fresh blooms for the next 365 days. Eureka!

I arranged a frequent buyer delivery program with a local florist, setting up Wednesday as the delivery day to brighten the middle of the week. She loved them. Her weekly bouquet has since become a birthday staple each year. Truth betold, I intend to send her flowers every week for the rest of her life! (Isn't that romantic!) You'd think the thrill would wear off. Never.

> "One of the fundamental laws of interpersonal physics is that you can never give a woman too many flowers or a child too many stuffed animals."
> – Richard Saunders

Here's another example of a Flapdoodle sheet that led to the creation of a new chewy candy for kids who wanted to see what it's like to be a species other than human. It comes in a package shaped in their choice of bear, lion, pig or ape snoots.

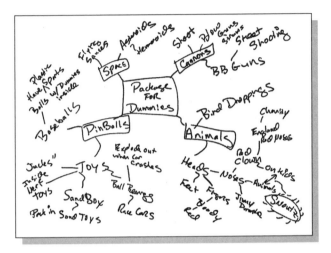

The task was to create a new packaging for a product Van Melle Candy Co. called Dummies, which took the form of small, chewy pellets. In this case, the Eureka! team had extra motivation. Dummies were a neat product, but sales were lagging. Unless we could come up with a way to salvage it, Van Melle was thinking about selling the equipment used to make the product and closing the line.

At the center of our Flapdoodle board was our target— "Package for Dummies." These four spokes radiated from it:

- Pinballs
- Space
- Animals
- Cannons

These smaller spokes sprouted out from animals:

- Heads
- Bird droppings

The heads spoke prompted still smaller spokes:

- Heads
- Feet

- Fingers
- Noses

Noses led us to Jimmy Durante, clowns and back again to animals. The Jimmy Durante tangent was too obscure, at least it would be to anyone under the age of 30. But clowns sparked discussion. What are clowns? Well, a clown isn't really a clown—it's a person dressed up in a costume, which usually includes some kind of fake nose. Kids like to dress up. What about clown noses?

But we wanted more variety. Clown noses, for the most part, are uniformly round red beezers. Animals come in a lot of different varieties. And they have noses. Well, not noses exactly. What is that thing animals have instead of noses?

"Snouts!" one of the Trained Brains shouted.

And that's just what we called it. Except we took away the "s" and added a "z." Snoutz is a soft blob of sweet candy that comes in a cup that's shaped like an animal snout. It comes in Apple-APE, PIGGY-Cherry Berry, Blue Rasp-BEARy and Lemon-LION. When you've finished the candy, you attach a string to the cup and strap it across your own snout.

Three months after the session, Snoutz was presented at a candy trade show in Washington D.C..

Later, when you go back over your Flapdoodle sheets, you'll be able to trace the lineage of each idea back to its organic roots. The sheets are like instant replay diagrams; they provide a play-by-play of the thoughts that led you to a certain destination, enabling you to work backward to earlier plays that may have been neglected in the initial blast of creativity but are often worth exploring later.

Part of the beauty of Flapdoodling is that it allows for continued growth. After your initial Eureka! effort, you can return to your Flapdoole and push the branches out further. You can continue to add ideas and new connections long after your initial spurt of creativity.

> "Linear lines on paper lead to linear ideas.
> Wicked good ideas come from coloring outside
> and across lines."
> – Richard Saunders

Try this variation on the Flapdoodle theme if you're working in a group. Divide into small groups of three or four people and give each group a Flapdoodle sheet. Let them work a few layers outward, then have them pass their sheets to the next group for continued layering. When your Flapdoodle comes back, you may not recognize it. But your initial ideas will have been enriched, fortified and polymerized to a high gloss under the buffing brushes of other perspectives.

Okay, it's your turn. Time to see it, feel it, touch it. Your mission is to create ideas for a weekend outing — for yourself, your nearest significant other or your whole family.

I'll get you started with the first spokes of your Flapdoodle. You can take it from there. Get a sheet of paper, oversized if you can, 8 1/2 by 11 if you have to. Copy the Flapdoodle spokes listed below on the sheet.

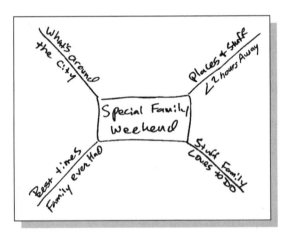

Want to learn more about display thinking? Learn from the display thinking masters. Check out the two best books on the subject.

- Mindmapping, by Joyce Wycoff Published by Berkley Books, New York, 1991

- Use Both Side of Your Brain by Tony Buzan Published by E.P. Dutton, Inc, New York, 1974

GROUP CREATIVITY

JUMP START NO. 4: DRAFT PICK

This Jump Start is all about shooting from the hip in its purest form. It's a good energizer, stimulates the creative flow and eliminates the middleman of the conscious mind. Draft Pick should be done at a full gallop. It's designed for doing in a group meeting. However, it could just as easily be done via a web chat room.

Objective: To energize minds through force associating unrelated elements.

How to do it: Divide into small teams of 4 to 6 people each. Ask folks to free-associate on the task at hand. Ask them to yell out their thoughts using the following as prompts.

- What comes to mind when you think of the challenge?
- What is the wackiest thing that comes to mind ?
- What is NOT part of the solution?
- What outrageous thoughts come to mind?
- What are the component parts of the challenge?

As thoughts emerge, write them on a white board or chart pad. Don't be neat. Write in random fashion, at angles, horizontally, and vertically. Once you've filled the sheet, let the Draft Pick begin.

Have each team in turn pick a word or a thought, then cross it off. Have each team make selections until each has three words or thoughts to work from.

Give each team 10 to 15 minutes to smash-associate its words or thoughts together to come up with one or more potential solutions. Then have each team present their original words and solution(s) to the broader group.

As with all Group Creativity efforts, keep it moving, keep the coffee flowing and keep the music cranked.

Draft Pick in Action

Draft Pick came into play when David and I were mapping out ideas for segments for our "Brain Brew" public radio show. The stimuli included "experts", "don't be boring" and "irreverent."

From that, we came up with something we initially called "The 60-Second Guru." The idea was to bring on an author or an expert in whatever area, then give that person 60 seconds to tell us the secret of success as he or she defined it. While our expert of the day would be talking, the listener would also hear a clock ticking, with a bell at the end of the 60 seconds to let the expert know his or her time was up. Then we'd ask a few questions, talk for a few more minutes and go onto something else.

That segment has become one of the show's most popular. But after a while, Dave and I got bored with it. So we changed it to "The 30-Second Guru." If you'd like to hear some of them, visit www.EurekaRanch.com.

GROUP CREATIVITY

JUMP START NO. 5:
THE OUT-OF-THE-BLUE
LIGHTNING BOLT CLOUD-BUSTER

This exercise pushes the playfulness button in your brain. It works well with small groups and better with larger ones. One day, I would love to do this exercise in a stadium full of people hundreds of thousands of airplanes.

You'll need paper airplanes. The Out-of-the-Blue Lightning Bolt Cloudbuster is piloted by the amazing Obatala, the  Yoruban diety of creativity, a mythical hermaphrodite who is held in high regard among members of the Yoruba people in Nigeria. He/she looks like this:

Obatala is not the world's best pilot. She/he has trouble landing, which can be an emotional strain for the passengers of her/his Out-of-the-Blue Lightning Bolt Cloudbuster, although it isn't a problem as far as she/he's concerned since, in some incarnations, she/he has wings in the middle of his/her back. To her/his credit, however, she/he's highly skilled at flights of fancy. Let Obatala be your co-pilot.

Objective: To give people a fun, immature, high-spirited way to build on others' thoughts on a confidential, one-on-one basis.

How to do it: Make up enough paper airplanes ahead of time to fill the runways at LaGuardia, O'Hare, and LAX. You can develop a model of your own design or, if you're a Real World Adult who has forgotten how to make a paper airplane, you can assemble a Lighting Bolt Cloud-buster from the following schematics:

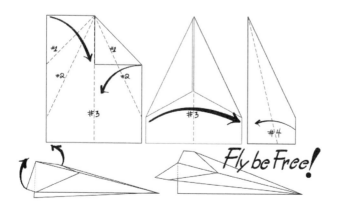

Crank up a lively piece of rock 'n roll to a ridiculous level and toss out the planes. Have your participants write their thoughts and or ideas onto the wings of planes. In particular, ask them to jot down ideas that, for whatever reason, they would like to see explored more completely.

Fill the air with aerodynamic origami. Ask each session-aire to pick up any planes that come his or her way, give it a quick read, and jot a note, an idea, or a bulge to the wing.

You're looking for gut reactions, not considered respons-es. You want people to feel as if they're flying by the seats of their pants. Each time an idea or bulge is added to an airplane, it should be relaunched within a few seconds. Allow enough time for each plane to take four or five flights.

Enough music, already! Gather up your planes for review and analysis another day or, if you must come to completion, ask everyone to take a plane and retreat to his or her team to enhance and refine the cargo of ideas from the various aircraft.

Remember that when the brain hears a good idea, it clings to it for a while, which keeps it from taking hold of new thoughts. Writing these ideas on paper airplanes helps reduce the risk of mental constipation. It also makes it possible to openly articulate your concerns and issues.

Out of the Blue in Action

The scene was an annual meeting of sales people from an indus-trial company. More than 200 people took part in flying air-planes around the room. It was pandemonium.

The client liked the energy and excitement this Jump Start generated at the meeting. He also liked the ideas it pro-duced. But what he like most was that it gave him fresh insight into what his sales people were thinking. By looking at what they wrote on the planes he discovered: 1) what his sales peo-ple wished for, 2) what they saw as flaws in the current offering, and 3) what they felt clients really needed.

Special thanks to Tracy Jo Duckworth, who inspired this Jump Start with her discovery of the Obatala legend.

GROUP CREATIVITY

JUMP START NO. 6: PASS THE BUCK

At some point in your search for the wicked good ideas, you're bound to slide into a slump, a slippery slope of a slimy slump, and you'll need a blast of energy to help you out of your rut and over the top.

When you sense a slump coming on, it's time to pull out Pass the Buck. This is genuine Acme TNT designed to blow away the blahs.

I like to accompany Pass the Buck with music. Not the chamber musings of Beethoven or Bach. I mean head-banging, pulse-pounding, rattle-and-roll of classic rock that makes your feet move and your arms flap. Whatever it takes to start your engine. Don't be shy. And for pity's sake, turn it up! The musical accompaniment to Pass the Buck is best played at a decibel level comparable to that of a 747 at take-off. You'll know you're getting the most out of it when your neighbors call the cops.

Objective: To transform the wild and whacked-out into practical, wicked good ideas. Sometimes, Pass the Buck produces a world-class idea. Other times, its value is simply as an energizer or as a means to show Real World Adults how to find brilliance in the bizarre. Either way, you can't lose.

How to do it: Divide into four groups. Give each group a Pass the Buck sheet. It looks like the diagram on the next page.

On your mark, get set, *GO!* Each team fills in the "Absurd, Bizarre, Exotic Idea" window, then passes the sheet to the next group, under the frantic exhortations of the Eureka!meister to move it, move it, move it!

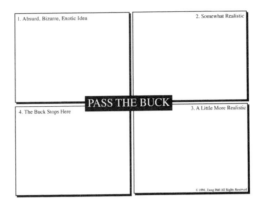

As the sheets are passed around the room, each team takes a turn refining the initial unrealistic ideas into concepts that are by stages more realistic.

After three passes, the buck stops with the final group, which has to turn the rough idea into a practical, tactical something that will send fear into the hearts of competitors.

Ask each team to read its sheet out loud, from beginning to end. See what falls out—you're sure to be surprised.

Pass the Buck in Action

I sprang a Pass the Buck at the Eureka! Party held to invent this book. The object of the exercise was to come up with an idea to land an appearance on the mother of all T.V. talk shows, Oprah Winfrey's syndicated TV show. My life will not be complete until I've been a guest on her program.

Included here is one team's sheet from that session. This team was not particularly respectful, either to Ms. Winfrey or myself. I apologize to Ms. Winfrey for their behavior. But the final idea is one I'm determined to carry out.

Goal: An idea to get Doug on Oprah

In the Absurd Bizarre Exotic Idea window, Group 1 wrote: "Doug naked on Oprah talking about 'The Naked Mind.'"

Group 2 made it somewhat realistic: "Oprah and Doug naked; they go on crash diets for 'Fat Head' program."

Group 3 made it a little more realistic: "Doug & Oprah on Brain Food Program featuring ultimate diet for your Brain/Life."

For Group 4, the buck stops here: "Doug & Trained Brains on 'Oprah' doing Eureka! Jump Starts live with kids who don't think they're creative."

Wicked cool! When I get on Oprah, I promise to wave. The idea stirs emotions for me.

I once ran Eureka! sessions with two distinctly different groups of 10-year-olds. The children in the first group were miniature Real World Adults, future corporate Americans and pre-preppies. They were from an upwardly mobile neighborhood with an upwardly mobile school, where they'd been enrolled in an upwardly mobile program for gifted students. They'd been convinced they were creative. Boy, were they smug!

The second group was made up of ordinary kids culled from an ordinary school, and that's how they thought of themselves. No one had told them they were creative, and they most definitely didn't think of themselves as such. They were shy, withdrawn, and untapped.

But when this latter bunch was given the proper Eureka! Jump Starts, stimuli, and sufficient emotional support from the Eureka! Trained Brains, ordinary children exploded into supernovas of raw creativity. Their faces beamed as they filled the session with glittering ideas that far outstripped those of the so-called gifted students.

The ideas that emerged have to remain shrouded in secrecy by the client. But I can tell you that, of the 20 ideas we presented, 15 had originated in the second group.

The Trained Brains fell in love with the ordinary kids. They told us they never got to do creative stuff at their school, reminding me yet again of the many ways the education system snuffs the creative spirit. I resolved one day to translate the Eureka! approach to creativity into a program for elementary and secondary schools across America. It is my life's mission. That and being a guest on Oprah's show.

Second Edition Note: OK, so this hasn't happened—*YET*. We have created a program called Great Aspirations! Designed to help parents inspire their children. See www.Aspirations.com for a free AUDIO CD Download.

But I haven't given up on Oprah. We once had an Oprah producer talk to us about helping women who were entrepreneurs, but the story died on its way up the chain of command.

With this second edition, we'll try again—on the original idea of putting Eureka! in classrooms and doing something to help real world entrepreneurial women.

GROUP CREATIVITY

JUMP START NO. 7: AS SEEN ON TV

Let's pretend. It's a great way to bend the world into whatever shape you want. It's a step or two beyond imagining. When you pretend, you put yourself in the picture. Pretending requires that you believe, at least a little. In that sense, pretending may be a bit pathological. That's OK. The important thing is that there are no limits when you pretend, as long as you pretend it's so.

At Eureka! inventing sessions, we've found that a powerful way to engage in productive pretending is have each group create and act out infomercials to sell this or that idea. You know what an infomercial is—brash, bold, over-the-top rambling commercials that usually air at 2 a.m., pounding the same message over and over.

At the Ranch, we give each of our four small groups a duffel bag filled with wigs, hats, and oddball stuff, which they use to invent characters for their infomercials. The groups get 15 minutes or so to throw together a rough script. Then it's show time!

Objective: To stimulate original thoughts through acting out an infomercial that inspires customers to call and order now. The tone should be urgent, urgent, urgent!

How to do it: Split your group into teams of four to six people each and challenge them to create a three- to five-minute infomercial that sells a solution to your collective challenge. Let them use any props they can find. At first, most adults aren't all that excited about acting a story line—it is total foolishness. But once they get into it, the ham comes out in a big way.

To help focus their thinking, use the following "keys to success" we've gleaned from interviews with actual infomercial producers.

- Make your benefit huge and easy to understand.
- Be blunt about your dramatic difference.
- Use numbers to quantify your advantage.
- Energy and enthusiasm rule—TV or no TV, people still buy from people.
- Bring your benefit to life with testimonials .
- Make your promise so amazing that a guarantee is an absolute necessity.
- Explain clearly that there's nothing else like what you're offering.
- It helps if you have a catchy name or slogan to repeat, repeat, and repeat again.
- Concoct persuasive scientists, experts, or research findings.

Then let the Infomercials Roll. If you listen closely as your groups act out their fantasy infomercials, you'll find a gold mine of language, ideas and insights.

After the infomercials, allow an equal amount of time for the small teams to huddle and discuss these points:

- What surprised them about the infomercials?

- How did they respond to the messages?
- How did they perceive the solution offered?
- How could the solution have been more clearly presented?

As Seen on TV in Action

The exercise draws lots of laughs—and some dramatic responses. There's something magical about standing up, making a simple, honest promise and then keeping that promise.

From Walt Disney to American Express to Johnson & Johnson, we've seen big results when teams get involved.

In this book's first edition, I explained how a negative reaction to this kind of role-playing in the end had a positive impact.

The challenge involved a $10 billion-a-year company, one with a history of posting double-digit growth in sales and profits. But sales had slid the previous two years as smaller, more entrepreneurial competitors surfaced.

We assembled a group of the company's best and brightest sales and marketing executives. To help them see their situation with fresh eyes, I invited them to role-play the selling process.

As the exercise began, it became clear that most of the team's members didn't believe in their products. Indeed, they admitted that they thought what they were selling was a sham and only a step away from stealing.

It was a disaster. The realization that their products were a scam seemed to dawn on them all at once, flattening their morale like a straw hut in a hurricane. The memory of the moment still sends a chill up my spine.

The group fell into a heated debate. I had to do something to shift the momentum—and quickly, before knives were pulled. I asked one of the few believers, a local market field rep, to give an emergency testimonial on the value of the company's products.

She spoke with passion about the impact the products had on real world people and how it made their lives better.

Slowly, the group's confidence returned. The tide of self-assurance brought with it a vision for a series of marketing programs in which the company offered bold new guarantees of performance and satisfaction. The ideas were refined and tested with customers, and the response was universally positive.

But more importantly, the company leaders experienced first-hand the lack of faith in the ranks of employees—and were able to do something about it.

GROUP CREATIVITY

JUMP START NO. 8: BATTLE OF THE MINDSETS

Battle of the Mindsets is a Jump Start that never fails to astound me with the energy and imagination it evokes. It always causes a big commotion. I don't know why. It must be just another of those things we're not meant to understand. But **when you OVERTLY segment people based on stereotypical dimensions you generate a different type of thinking.**

Objective: To stimulate new ideas and insights by leveraging distinct prejudices, perceptions and misperceptions.

How to do it: Separate your group into two or more teams that have a natural tension associated with their interaction. Examples:
- Men vs. women
- Marketing managers vs. product development managers
- Creative department vs. account services
- Field staff vs. office staff
- Management vs. workers.

Then ask each group to invent ideas based on their perceptions and misperceptions of:

- The perfect solution to the task from their perspective
- The perfect solution to the task from the perspective of those on the other side of the room.

Then stand back! Get set for major explosions. When you assemble like-minded groups and allow them to be overtly prejudicial, each group quickly takes on the camaraderie and spirit of a street gang. Their thinking becomes raw, focused, and overt. It often moves to the lowest common denominator. However, in the process, a new honesty is discovered. The ideas that emerge from Battle of the Mindsets have a vitality, energy, and realness that is all to rare in our politically correct world.

Battle of the Mindsets in Action

Our task was to build a winning concept for a new mouthwash. We divided up into "boys" and "girls."

The boys were asked to dream up the ideal mouthwash for women; the girls, the perfect mouthwash for their Neanderthal counterparts.

In casting about for a way to talk about why men would use mouthwash in the first place, the girls hit on the idea of "dragon breath." Their underlying premise: the only way to effectively detoxify the breath of the typical American male is to use a three-stage approach involving gasoline, a flamethrower, and an industrial-strength disinfectant.

The trail quickly led the girls to Dragon Slayer, a mouthwash for men with triple levels of cleaning, deodorizing, and freshening to make "the man in your life that much more kissable." Initial consumer research showed the idea a winner on both ends—female consumers immediately latched onto the idea of dragon breath, while male consumers were willing to do just about anything to make themselves more kiss-worthy.

GROUP CREATIVITY

JUMP START NO. 9: MOVIE MAGIC

Movie Magic is about using the digital world of music, photos, and video to spark fresh ideas and insights.

In less time than it takes to write a document—you can create a movie that features photos, customer quotes, video demonstrations, and other digital content that you can use to spark new connections in your team's brains.

DISCLAIMER and boast from an Apple Computer fanatic. Okay so you can create a movie instantly on an Apple Macintosh computer using Apple's iLife suite of programs—on other computers, good luck.

As the director of the video—you direct the team's creative thinking. The customer quotes you share, the images you use will focus your team's thinking and immerse them into the area of your desire.

Objective: To stimulate new ideas by focusing a group's thinking on a specific category, issue or target audience by providing them with focused stimulus.

How to do it:

Step 1: To prepare your Movie think like a Hollywood director. Think about what is the purpose of your film. What is the feeling or sensation or information that you wish to share with your audience? What do you want them thinking about as they're watching? What is the key point of "drama" in your story?

Step 2: Having defined your purpose your next task is to assemble the movie. The key is to keep it simple. Use text and still images as much as possible. The impact of a customer quote being read over a photo of your product is nearly as powerful as the consumer saying it on video—and the time and effort to edit it is significantly reduced. The master at making still photos come to life is Ken Burns. It's worth watching one of his documentaries on the Civil War, Baseball or other subjects to gain an appreciation for the impact simplicity can have. (Again a blatant plug for Apple iLife where you can automatically generate what is known as the "Ken Burns" effect with still photos.)

Where appropriate, take your audience to the "scene of the crime"—show them real people in real life situations dealing with the challenges. Tap into ideas and insights using the questions and prompts from the Candid Comments Jump Start.

Provide "space" in your movie for digesting what's been communicated. Leave a space here and there in video to allow your audience to digest what they've just heard or seen. Add some music and a few still photos before bringing up more

Step 3: Show the movie to your gathered group. Challenge them to write their ideas and insights as they watch. When the movie ends give them a moment to capture their thoughts then divide the group into teams of 4 to 6 people to explore the ideas that the movie sparked

After about 15 minutes of team discussion have a representative from each team report to the larger group on their ideas and insights. With the spark of each team's reporting another wave of ideas are often unleashed.

Movie Magic in Action

A company called asking if we could create a Eureka! program that could help companies make their products more environmentally responsible. As it turned out, the Ranch team had been thinking about creating a "Choices for Green Growth" program for a number of months.

To prepare for the meeting I asked the Ranch staff to assemble a quick movie that brought to life the need for "green." They assembled the movie from facts, images, quotes, and future forecasts that they found on the Internet, in books and magazines.

At the meeting we presented the movie. The movie plus presentation only ran about 15 minutes. When it was over the impact matched that of a Hollywood block buster.

The images and story transformed the meeting. The CEO of the visiting company was instantly inspired to think BIG! The facts and images brought to life the urgency of the issue. The charts on public opinion amplified the breadth and depth of opportunity.

The CEO of the visiting company became a volcano of new ideas. Inspired by the movie he sketched out ideas for partnership that I would have never imagined. With the spark lit— the Ranch team built on his ideas. Within an hour following the movie a clear vision for partnership was outlined. A week following the meeting we were already taking action on making the partnership real.

In comparison, alliances with other companies have taken months and months to get to the same place that this one has moved in just a week. The movie made the difference. It brought to life the facts and the emotions of the challenge and opportunity like no amount of talking could have generated.

GROUP CREATIVITY

JUMP START NO. 10: JUNTO

The Junto Jump Start is inspired by Ben Franklin's Junto Society. Ben conceived of the Junto as "a club for mutual improvement," whereby he could gather his brightest, most articulate, artistic and creative pals "to spend a social evening together discoursing and communicating such ideas as occur'd to us upon a wide variety of subjects."

The first Junto Society members were "leather-apron men"—artists, printers, explorers, barristers, and writers, all with a hunger for learning and a desire to improve themselves.

The Junto was one of the earliest adult education programs, a combination lecture series and party time. Franklin required "a pause between speeches so one might fill and drink a glass of wine." The wine flowed. So did the ideas.

The Junto Society was a boon to Philadelphians. It was responsible for the creation of America's first public library, the first fire department and the first plan for paving, lighting and cleaning the city's streets. The group also established Philadelphia's city hospital, the American Philosophical Society, and the University of Pennsylvania.

To be eligible for Junto membership, one had to observe four criteria, as Franklin defined them:

- "To love truth for truth's sake, and to endeavor impartially to find and receive it personally and communicate it to others, without fondness for rudeness or desire for victory."
- "To not harm any person in his body, name or goods, for mere speculative opinions, or his external way of thoughts."
- "To love mankind in general no matter what

the profession, beliefs or opinions."
- "To have respect for all other members and invited guests."

The concept is two centuries old, but the principles still apply. All you need is a place and people who are willing to expose their minds to the leading edges of philosophy, art, religion, politics, and any other area of thought you might wish to pursue.

The Eureka! Ranch convenes a modern version of the Junto Society the third Saturday of every other month, with a membership comprising about 40 friends and employees of the Eureka! Ranch, along with spouses and significant others. Speakers are culled from whatever fields the members care to explore—from paranormal psychology to square dancing, from yoga to sleep disorders, from computer law to politics.

Our approach is to invite two speakers to talk for 15 to 20 minutes each, then have an interactive discussion the rest of the evening. We find that we learn most from the two way discussion. Given the size and diversity of our group, it's not uncommon to have relatively heated discussions between believers and non-believers, Republicans and Democrats and many other Yings and Yangs. But we're careful to follow Franklin's example in these discussions and express neither fondness for rudeness, nor desire of victory.

One of the more memorable Juntos was the time we brought in a psychic to put us in touch with the spirits of Ben and Elvis, and to make a clean sweep of sundry spirits that some Eureka! staffers were convinced were inhabiting certain corners of the Mansion.

The psychic—she was one of those first-name-only types, like Cher, Charo and Madonna—impressed the Juntonauts with her ability to divine the names of their dearly departed family members. She conveyed to their various survivors that they were fine and generally enjoying themselves in the afterlife, which was rather nice of her.

Unfortunately, she was unable to draw the spirit of Elvis—a circumstance she felt was probably due to numerous other psychic efforts in other locations to contact the King, thus distracting his spirit.

Ben never actually appeared either, although I'm pretty sure I felt his presence. At least, I felt a definite tingling in my legs.

Late in the evening, our psychic invited 30 Juntonauts and a reporter from the *Wall Street Journal* to accompany her to a tiny office on the third floor, where she aimed to release the spirit of a young woman who, in fact, had become pregnant out of wedlock around the time of the Civil War and hanged herself in that room.

Except for the light of the moon shining through the windows, the room was dark. One woman in our group began weeping. She told the psychic of a soft, frightened female spirit who had been in the room for many years and was afraid to leave. At that, the psychic's voice deepened two octaves as she took on the persona of her "spirit guide," an American Indian she called White Feather, and directed the frightened spirit to, I don't know, some place else.

The Juntonauts were afflicted with goose pimples the rest of the night. I decided that at the next Junto, we'd explore the mysteries of square dancing.

The headline in *Wall Street Journal* gave the psychic the benefit of the doubt. "Elvis Is a No-Show," it read, "but Ben Franklin's in the Air."

Searching for Elvis might not have been the sort of subject matter Franklin had in mind when he created the Junto. But it was a lively evening, for believers and nonbelievers alike.

To ignite fresh thinking think about forming a Junto of your own. All you have to lose are your preconceived notions. Gather your friends, gather your family, and explore new elements of the world you were not previously familiar with.

Go to see an opera, see a ballet, see a heavy metal band, visit the art museum, the starving artists gallery, take a class in yoga, take a class in computers. Take a trip, try a new restaurant, rent a foreign film. Whatever you do, do something.

The key to Jump Start your brain is a spirit of adventure. To be truly alive you need to continuously be filling your mind with new stimuli and new experiences. From this comes a passion for life, learning, and love.

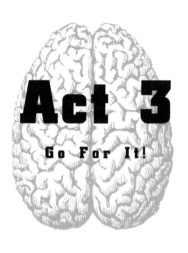

Act 3

Go For It!

13

REAL WORLD SURVIVAL GUIDE

The trick to surviving and thriving in the Real World is to be yourself. Insist on it. It's how to be your most effective. It's how to be fulfilled. Think of yourself as a product. You'll rise faster on your own abilities than you ever will by trying to fit the official "Real World Adult" personality mold.

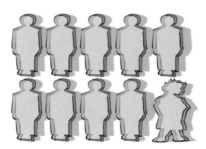

The more you establish yourself as an expert in a distinct area, the more valuable and successful you'll be. Average doesn't cut it. You have to be exceptional in some area.

"He that hath a trade hath an estate."
– Ben Franklin

Use your energy, enthusiasm, and smile like weapons. Sadly enough, most people in the corporate world lead what Henry David Thoreau called lives of quiet desperation. If you sweep in with high-voltage enthusiasm and a 100-watt grin, these people will gravitate to you. They will make you their champion. They will want to be like you.

Don't be afraid to take risks. Corporations have an amazing array of checks, balances and safety nets to prevent you from hitting the wall at 90 miles an hour. As long as you've looked at both sides and measured the risk against the benefits, be bold and brash. Develop a reputation for it. In big corporations, you'll encounter big obstacles. There are ways to get around them.

In my early days developing an all-purpose spray cleaner at Procter & Gamble, I was having trouble winning management support. So I arranged to have all senior management take home a bottle and test it on the domestic front. When their wives tried it, (a sad statement that they were all male) the logjam began to open up. Their reactions kept hope alive, laying the foundation for what a few years later became the highly successful Cinch spray.

In another case, a group of us were shackled with an unbearable boss, the kind of guy where, if you put a flashlight to one ear, the beam shines through onto the wall on the other side.

We had an idea. We decided to look on the bright side— and to trumpet his virtues to every executive recruiter we could find. We showered him with laudatory adjectives and let it be known to the recruiters that this guy wouldn't be around Procter much longer because he was just too danged sharp. We put the spit polish on him. We lathered him up thoroughly.

By the end of the week, our boss let it slip to me that, "Boy, I've been getting a lot of calls lately from headhunters." Really? I asked.

The upshot is, he was gone within a month. He got a big raise and, ding dong, the wicked witch was dead.

Be like Frank Sinatra. Do it your way. That means, among other things, not worrying about looking like everyone else. In my case, I gave up suits. People used to ask how I got the people upstairs to let me out of wearing suits. The answer is, I didn't ask. Whenever you ask **THEM**, whatever it is you want to do becomes **THEIR RESPONSIBILITY.** If you press forward on your own authority, they'll look the other way.

Once I stopped wearing suits, I became known as That Eccentric Inventor Guy. I was seen as a slightly mad step-cousin who was best left alone. By being myself, I came to define the corporate lunatic fringe.

Not long after that, the top brass decided to ease up on the corporate dress code and handed down a memo outlining the premise of "casual Fridays." The idea was to give employees the option of laying back, kicking out the jams, and, once a week between Memorial Day and Labor Day, wearing something to work other than the standard navy or gray wool suit. Naturally, casual Friday was not unqualified. Jeans and sneakers would still be verboten.

It confused me. But I adhered strictly to the policy and restricted my wearing of jeans and Nikes to Mondays, Tuesdays, Wednesdays, and Thursdays. In keeping with the letter of the law, on casual Fridays, I wore shorts and sandals.

Avoid fitting in. Whenever possible, make the structure adapt to you.

Got that? OK, time to start up the chainsaw and rip into the big bad world. Here are some tips to help you on your way:

The 10 Commandments of How to Succeed

COMMANDMENT NO. 1: MAKE IT REAL

Turn your idea into a tangible model that can be seen, felt, and touched. It doesn't have to be pretty. This isn't a pageant. The key is to rough it together so people can see your idea and put their hands on it.

Build "works like" and "looks like" prototypes. If your idea is for a new fundraising event, draw up a poster and draft a letter to explain it. If your idea is for a service, build a brochure around it.

Sketch it out and take a long, hard look. If your idea is a board game, cannibalize parts from Monopoly, Yahtzee, Risk, and Trivial Pursuit to make it work.

The cartoonist who dreamed up Garfield agrees:

> "If we have a truly different idea, the best way to sell it is to help the client visualize it. We'll take our idea, dress it up, draw it, paint it, set it to music and prototype it. We go to dramatic lengths to demonstrate our ideas. If our clients can see it as we see it, chances are they'll embrace it."
> – Jim Davis, Paws Incorporated

Building a prototype is a learning process. You'll learn about tradeoffs and challenges. Don't let them scare you. Keep your dream in focus. As you define your idea, you'll discover bumps in the road you hadn't been aware of—and probably wouldn't have if you hadn't embarked on a prototype.

"By making the thing real, you have a 'thing' to
do something with."
– SARK, "A Creative Companion"

Don't outsource your prototype's construction—involve
yourself in it. Doing so will help you understand the three-
dimensional dynamics of your vision. It'll also be your salvation
when it's time to sell your idea to the real world.

"Hammers and screwdrivers have built more
ideas than all the meetings and paperwork in
the world."
– Richard Saunders

Make a little, sell a little, learn a lot. Line up a small supply of prototypes, put them in stores, and watch the reaction.

Many times, I've talked a good line. But when I wrote it
down or built the prototype, many ideas that seemed great in
the abstract suddenly lost their luster. And I saved a lot of time
chasing wild geese.

"Before leaping from a plane, it's best to have
seen and felt the parachute."
– Richard Saunders

COMMANDMENT NO. 2: YOU GOTTA BELIEVE
You're the Gipper, with apologies to Knute Rockne and Ronald
Reagan, and you're the Gipper's team. You can't allow yourself
to stop anywhere short of the Best.

You must be willing to stake your name, your reputation
and the family jewels on your vision. You'll have to fight for it.
If you don't put your total energy behind it, if you aren't willing
to reach way down deep, no one will pay attention.

"If you don't believe, I don't believe."
– Richard Saunders

What's your dream worth? What are you willing to risk? The
cost of achieving is always greater than you expect it to be. At the

same time, the exhilaration is greater than you can imagine.

I marvel at the faith that my forefather, Lyman Hall, showed when he signed his name to the Declaration of Independence, agreeing to go to war against the most formidable power on the planet. In comparison, George Washington had no army, no arms, no uniforms.

But he had men who mutually pledged their lives, fortunes, and honor. Imagine the outcome at that meeting in the summer of 1776 if the heads of Chrysler, General Motors, and Ford had been asked to add their names to the parchment.

Nothing cheeses me off more than hearing corporate bosses whine about the raw deal they're getting from "fill in the blank" with anything or one. If they put as much energy into providing vision and leadership as they do to whimpering, they wouldn't have anything to mew about.

Short of winning the lottery, there's no such a thing as instant wealth. In order for greatness to occur, you have to do something great.

"Do nothing, and nothing happens. Do something, and something happens."
– Richard Saunders

Do you wake up ready to attack your task? Do you stay up late sweating details? If you do, you're sufficiently committed. If you have no trouble separating the task from the rest of your life, you probably aren't. I don't mean to suggest you should rip up your life. **But you'll never start the engines of a new-to-the-world idea with 50 percent effort and half a heart.**

It's worth it. No amount of money, fame or hedonistic pleasure matches the feeling of walking into a store and seeing a product you've created on the shelf. I can think of only four moments that surpass the rush I experience whenever I see a product of my own making awaiting shipment at the loading dock—namely, the day of my marriage and the births of my three children.

Still, when my first board game, "ONCE ... ," arrived on store shelves, I stood in the aisle of Swallen's department store in Cincinnati staring at the boxes for four hours. I spent two more hours pointing them out to anyone who happened down the aisle. I might have been a happy dad gazing through the big window on the maternity ward.

COMMANDMENT NO. 3: TAKE RESPONSIBILITY– NO WHINING ALLOWED

"Fish stink from the head down."
– Ben Franklin

You are the Chosen One. It's up to you, Geronimo, to blaze the trail as you head westward ho into the wilderness. As your own CEO, you're not merely the Chief Executive Officer. You're the Chief Energy Originator.

I'm merciless on CEOs. People want to do the right thing. They want to take pride in their work. If a business isn't performing properly, the fault lies with the person atop the pyramid.

"Corporations are like monsters; heads enough, but no brains."
– Ben Franklin

You alone are responsible for the success of your venture. By definition, you're responsible for making sure your people succeed. When they succeed, so will you.

Leadership is dangerous, scary, lonely, fun, and exhilarating. It's not for everyone.

The best of leaders are easy to spot. Wicked good leaders:
• Inspire people to perform above themselves.
• Create confidence with their customers.

- Are maniacs in regard to quality.
- Have the guts to get it done. Sometimes they have a gut, too.
- Have equal shares of heart and brains.
- Love people.
- Lead by example.
- Take responsibility.
- Accept neither praise nor money that aren't deserved.
- Are honest with themselves and with others.

Leading is not the same as managing. Managers are concerned with style and process. Leaders concentrate on substance and imagination. Managers shy away from aggression out of an inborn fear of chaos. Leaders know nothing gets accomplished without aggression. And although they direct their aggression at ideas, not people, leaders are willing to risk bruising a few egos. Leaders realize aggression is a necessary element in the chemistry of motivation.

"Trust thyself, and another shall not betray thee."
– Ben Franklin

I staged my first paid magic show when I was 11 years old. The gig was for the birthday party of a six-year-old at York Beach in Maine, and it paid $5.

I practiced for weeks, imagining my audience would react with wild applause and perhaps even hoist me up on their shoulders. In reality, my reception was tepid at best.

After the show, an elderly guy I sort of knew stopped by to ask me how it had gone. The guy was at the beach every day and had watched me teach myself to juggle. It turned out that, when he was younger, he'd traveled the vaudeville circuits in New England. So we had something in common.

"I was great," I said. "My audience wasn't so hot, though."

He smiled.

"Let me tell you something, sonny," he said.

"There's no such thing as a bad audience—only poor performers. If they didn't like you, it's because you didn't give them the right show."

He was right. **If you want it to happen, YOU HAVE TO MAKE IT HAPPEN.** If you make excuses, you'll never make anything happen. Excuses flow freely from the fountain of non-commitment.

COMMANDMENT NO. 4: HAVE A FULL GAME PLAN, AS IN A VISION AND PLAN OF ACTION

"The first step to greatness is believing you've already arrived."
– Richard Saunders

The Game Plan is what will sell your new-to-the-world idea. Game Plans include a vision of where you are going and an action plan for accomplishing it.

The vision should be vivid, clear, and compelling.

The plan of action should be tangible, clear, and reasonable. It doesn't have to be fully proven—but it does have to be sufficiently thought through to motivate others to take action on it.

"A vision without a plan is like a car without gasoline (or hydrogen or fuel cells). It may look nice, but it won't go anywhere."
– Richard Saunders

Your Game Plan has to depict your idea so that investors, customers, family, and friends can see your destination—or a reasonable facsimile thereof. Wicked good visions and plans of action breathe life into dreams.

The combination of a vision and a plan of action is as exciting as the idea it defines. It should dazzle, amaze, tantalize, and tease. It should swoop, plummet, and soar like a roller coaster. It should make your heart pound and your audience catch its breath.

No matter what your task, you must know where you're headed and have at least an idea for how it will happen.

Your vision can change along the way. Your plan will definitely change as you learn—if it doesn't change, it's probably because you aren't learning. Visions and plans aren't chiseled in granite. They're alive and fluid. The important thing is to have them. If you do, you'll be able to cash in on the serendipities. If you don't, vast networks of dead-end streets lay waiting to swallow you up.

"Without a vision, you'll never know if you're moving toward your goal or away from it."
– Richard Saunders

Another way to gauge your vision is to close your eyes and form a picture in your mind. Athletes routinely use this technique, imagining the ball falling through the hoop, sailing through the goalposts, catching the inside corner of the plate. I've used it to build my business and my clients' businesses.

When I was looking for a new headquarters for Eureka!, I decided on doing a custom-built plant. The Eureka! Mansion was a 180-year-old historic building, and it had been a great place to work. But it had its limitations. The old ballroom could fit about 16 people, and clients were talking about bringing 20 to 30 of their people to work with us. Also, the food-service facilities were limited.

I had plenty of land to accommodate a construction project. But it would be a major investment. Logical, rational advisors urged me to keep looking for existing space. But in my mind's eye, I saw a world-class invention facility, a place in the country that could be an island of originality. It took a few months to clarify the vision, plan a space in such a way as to improve the quality and quantity of ideas we were creating and draft a rough sketch of what it might look like.

The planning took a year, with another six months for construction. But the Eureka! Ranch is arguably the most excellent invention facility on the planet.

When you have one vision, you can develop dozens more. Once you have a vision of a potential solution, your mind will open, and other answers will come tumbling out. The first vision often turns out to be a mirage. But by then, it has served its purpose, stoking your confidence and providing direction.

COMMANDMENT NO. 5: CHECK YOUR MOTIVES

If your overriding motive is money or fame, you might as well call it a day. The journey is too hard, and there are too many other ways to make money or win fame.

> "'Tis easy to frame a good, bold resolution. But
> hard is the task that concerns execution."
> – Ben Franklin

Changing the world is hard work. It's fatiguing. And fatigue is a big hairy grizzly bear. To overcome it, you have to be internally motivated to make a difference. Otherwise, the first of the hundreds of obstacles you confront will drop you like a sack of ball peen hammers.

The kind of motivation I'm talking about comes from a profound conviction that you're doing the right thing—and that the right thing will make the world better. Never mind what the world thinks it needs—you have to believe the world needs your idea. The purity of your motivation is vital to your success. Procter & Gamble emphasizes the importance of doing the "right thing in the right way." That principle is presented as standard operating procedure to new recruits. It's a big reason Procter & Gamble is as successful as it is.

So your idea has to be the best in its class. The crowd—the bankers, the manufacturers, the sales staff, the storeowners and the average Joe—has to believe you have an idea that matters. If the crowd doesn't believe, they won't rally around you.

When your goal is pure, you won't have to concern yourself with looking for money and fame. They'll find you.

Before you blast off, you should know how to lead, manage, and sell to "Suits." A Suit can be a corporate executive or a banker or a client. A Suit is a RWA with sufficient money and power to make your idea happen.

If you have a job in a corporation, don't leave simply because you can't stand working within those hallowed halls. If you can't make things happen inside a corporation, the odds of succeeding on the outside aren't good. When you leave, you'll be substituting one kind of Suit for another. Instead of management Suits, you'll face client, banking, and governmental Suits.

Study your motivations. Why are you really leaving? If it's because the money isn't good enough or because you're angry, don't do it. If it's to accomplish a significant goal, to realize an inner passion, then what has kept you this long?

Never be pushed into anything. In America, you have the freedom of choice. You can be a slave to corporations, bankers, and investors only if you consent to it. Never run away from a Suit. Have the courage to run toward opportunity.

"Necessity never made a good bargain."
– Ben Franklin

COMMANDMENT NO. 6: SELL, SELL, SELL

"He that would catch Fish must venture his Bait."
– Ben Franklin

Your million-dollar idea isn't worth a dime until you sell it.
People have to want it. They have to see it's in their best interest to buy it. They must believe your product or service is better able to meet their needs than what they already have.

Your role is to help them see that. The process is a friendly mix of cajoling, inspiring, instructing, and wooing. The most important rule to remember when selling is to be likeable.

"If you would be loved, love and be loveable."
– Ben Franklin

People like to buy from likeable people. They like to buy from companies that are friendly and fun. They will occasionally buy from jerks, scum-balls and slime-buckets if they have no choice, but they'd rather not.

People will like you if you're reliable, honest, conscientious, relaxed, and friendly. Chances are, they'll like you if you're simply yourself.

Fun is fundamental to selling, just as life for most people is fundamentally boring. Most people don't have a lot of on-the-job fun. If you can add a little fun to their lives, they'll love you.

Friendliness is the key. And I don't mean a you-scratch-my-back-and-I'll-scratch-yours greasy kind of friendliness. Nor am I referring to the patronizing type of suck-up-brown-nosing friendliness so popular at used car lots and in corporate boardrooms. I mean a true, genuine, loyal friendliness, more along the lines of a do-unto-others-as-you-would-have-done-unto-you friendliness.

Unless you're selling trousers to aborigines, you and your idea are destined to encounter at least one Suit on the sales trail.

For the most part, the Suit has not arrived at its lofty position by embracing new-to-the-world ideas like yours. For the most part, whatever status the Suit has achieved has been by way of the safe bet.

By dint of your entrepreneurial spirit, you're an alien being to the Suit. You and your idea are out there on the lunatic fringe. You're living, eating, and breathing your brave new universe. The Suit, meanwhile, has little time and less tolerance.

So the question is how do you sell a Suit?

Suits come in two varieties. It's important to know which type you're dealing with to tailor your pitch. The key is in knowing what's beneath the Suit's suit.

> "Initially, you want to believe that under every suit, there's a T-shirt. You can tell immediately. You can tell when someone understands. All of a sudden, a light goes on and they say 'yeah.'"
> – Guy Kawasaki, author, Macintosh software evangelist

If your Suit's suit is hiding a T-shirt, summon up formidable supplies of energy, enthusiasm, and passion to paint the vision. This type of Suit will quickly get the picture.

If, on the other hand, the Suit has on a suit beneath its suit, the challenge is steeper. A Suit with a suit under its suit is a Suit through and through, even when it's naked. The spirit of such a Suit is governed by fear, doubt, and despair. Their natural posture is defensive. Their No. 1 priority is protecting what they have, which has little to do with risk-taking.

T-shirt Suits smile easily. They roll up their sleeves. They react. They offer you coffee and get it for you themselves. Suits with suits beneath their suits wear their suit coats as if they were bulletproof shields. They don't react. Their eyes are glazed, like doughnuts. They offer you coffee, then buzz an assistant to get it for you. Change is their enemy. It's the one dynamic they fear above all else. And since change is a fact of life, they live in fear. They're constantly looking over their shoulders, less concerned with what's right than how they're perceived.

It's not a pretty picture. Pity the poor double-suited Suit.

They're ususally mere conduits in the corporate plumbing, through which ideas percolate up from the bottom and bubble onward to upper management. They lack the power and, generally speaking, the initiative to make decisions.

Selling to this second type of Suit requires almost monumental strength. In fairness, they can grasp the incremental ideas—the unscented product, the new flavor, the idea that transforms pie into pie a la mode. But their minds are closed to any idea that makes a quantum leap forward. They must be spoon-fed the proper sensations in order to see, feel, and touch your new world order.

Always show a Suit your idea in three dimensions. Give Suits the experience. If it's a direct mail campaign, show them the mailing piece. If it's a new product, give them a sample. If you're selling cars, take them on a test drive. Once a Suit has experienced the wicked goodness of your idea, you're half way to making the sale.

COMMANDMENT NO. 7: NEVER, EVER, EVER GIVE UP

"If we are industrious, we shall never starve, for at the working man's house hunger looks in, but dares not enter."
– Ben Franklin

Sell like the wind. Do it over and over and over again until you break through. If your vision is good and you're calling on the right people, you'll prevail. Don't let quitting be an option.

It took three years to sell my first board game and two presentations to sell the second. Today, toy companies call me asking for ideas. The key is to keep looking for new clients. In most cases, sales(wo)manship is a matter of spreading the word and ringing doorbells. It's a tough, lonely road fraught with frustration. It requires equal measures of faith and courage. The only way you maintain sanity in the face of adversity is to develop an unshakeable faith in what you're selling. Otherwise, a mind is a terrible thing to waste.

"It is true that there is much to be done, and perhaps, you are weak-handed; but stick to it steadily, and you will see great effects; for constant dripping wears away stones; and by diligence and patience, the mouse ate in two the cable; and little strokes fell great oaks."
– Ben Franklin

Nothing is more important to your business growth than

a continuous marketing effort. Marketing is not something you turn on and off.

The effect of marketing efforts is cumulative. This letter illustrates this point:

> "Dear Mr. Hall," it read. "I was intrigued by an article I read in the Wall Street Journal regarding your business. Your whole creative approach struck me not only as novel but as fun. I clipped the article to put in a 'think-about-someday' file. Since that point, I've seen two further articles on you and your business and have decided I need to learn more."

COMMANDMENT NO. 8: INSPIRE WICKED GOOD PEOPLE TO HELP

You have to know yourself to be a wicked good leader. That means knowing your limitations. You have to know when to hold your ground and when to yield.

> "Three things extremely hard: steel, diamonds and knowing one's self."
> – Ben Franklin

Great leaders set examples that inspire people to perform above their abilities, to make them better than they could ever thought they could be. Prove to your team that they're champions. Once they believe it, they will be.

Instill a feeling of togetherness and support. Give your team players the strength to fend off armchair naysayers.

> "To be a good leader, you have to be nice. You have to be nice and take turns. Good leaders don't push and shove."
> – Kristyn Hall, age 5

You're a listener, not a dictator. Lead not just by example, but by collecting thoughts from those around you and incorporating them into the vision so they can achieve. Give them credit for having functioning brains. After all, you hired them. You didn't hire them because of their ability to say yes; you hired them because they're capable of greatness.

Understand that Lincoln freed the slaves. You're no one's master. America is a free country, which means that everyone who works with or for you is free to take a hike at any time. **Great leaders work with people, not at them.**

Success, it is said, is 10 percent inspiration and 90 percent perspiration. Ideas don't perspire, no matter how wicked good they are. People perspire. It follows, then, that your odds of success are tied directly to assembling the right people.

The important thing is not to hire the smartest, the most likeable, the most persuasive, or the fastest. It's more a matter of spirit, passion, and an ability to persevere in the dead of night.

The right people aren't your clones. The right people have a range of skills and strengths different from your own. Your team should reflect a wide portfolio of talents. But everyone on it should have the same values.

Think of it as a basketball team, where the key is consistency between the players. Some prefer a fast-break, run-and-gun style. Others like a slower tempo, where the ball is passed until someone has an open shot. Either is effective. Both aren't. When you begin to mix playing styles, you end up with chaos.

At the Eureka! Ranch, I look for people who want to move quickly. I look for a low tolerance for bureaucracy and a desire to change the world, as opposed to simply making money. And I look for confidence. In short, I look for people who share my values. A profile of the late Celtics legend Red Auerbach in the May 1990 edition of *Yankee* magazine put it this way:

> "Before Red drafts a player, he calls his coach, coaches who have opposed the player, his family, friends, teachers, anyone who can tell him not only how good that player's jump shot might be, but what kind of character he has — Red has never been a coach who judged per-

formance by scoring or rebounding statistics. 'You can't measure a ball player's heart, or his willingness to sacrifice by statistics,' he once said. 'I always had only one statistic. When this guy's in the game, does the score go up in our favor or down?'"

I look, too, for people with a yen for adventure. I tell my newly hired to expect thrills and chills, spiced with plenty of highs and lows. I tell them we'll make up the rules as we go and what exists today will look a lot different tomorrow. I tell them they'll be expected not only to do their job, but to look for ways to make it faster, smarter, quicker, and, yes, more fun.

COMMANDMENT NO. 9: SWEAT THE DETAILS

"Glass, china and reputations are easily crack'd, and never well mended."
– Ben Franklin

It's one thing to talk the customer into giving you a shot. It's another to keep him coming back.

It might surprise you to hear this, but the big issues aren't key to your success. The major screwups won't bring you down. You'll handle those. What will jump up and bite you in the throat are the tiny details. Your ability to deliver wicked good customer service hinges on your attention to details.

"A little neglect may breed great mischief. For want of a nail, the shoe was lost; for want of a shoe, the horse was lost; and for want of a horse, the rider was lost, being overtaken and slain by the enemy. All for want of a little care about a horseshoe nail."
– Ben Franklin

Customer service is non-negotiable. The customer is the boss. By customers, I'm referring to the blessed saints who give you the money to do what you do. In a corporate setting, the customer is the company management. If you're out there in the entrepreneurial stratosphere, the customer is your client.

You may fool a customer once with now-you-see-it-now-you-don't sales techniques. But once they learn your idea isn't as good as you said it was, you'll never trick them into coming back. And the cost of a lost customer is immense.

"Tricks and treachery are the practice of fools
that have not wit enough to be honest."
– Ben Franklin

It's no trick to get a satisfied customer to return. People want to believe their faith in you is well founded. It's human nature to want to be right. Your job is to prove them right.

When a customer feels slighted, it doesn't matter who's right and who's wrong. What matters is that you lose. And the expense of finding a new customer is far greater than the cost of maintaining one you already have. Stay focused on delivering the wicked good product or product that is your vision. If cost problems drive up your price, seek ideas to modify your vision, but stay focused on being great instead of compromising to mediocrity.

"Tis easier to prevent bad habits than to break
them."
– Ben Franklin

Demand excellence in all areas. Don't let a flimsy bottle cap, a crappy wrapper or a faulty whompus ruin a brilliant product.

"The worst wheel of the cart makes the most
noise."
– Ben Franklin

Sweat the details. Properly sweated details breed success. Suits usually notice sweaty details. Even if they don't, sweat the details anyway because it's the right thing to do. Otherwise, you won't be the best.

"If a consumer makes a mistake with your product, it may be the consumer's problem. But it's
your problem, too. Moreover, it's not the consumer's fault. The fault is yours."
– Richard Saunders

As a wicked good leader, you set the moral and spiritual
tone for your effort.

You're the lightning rod. You bear the blame when something goes wrong. Conversely, you share the credit when you
succeed. If you follow that pattern, your successes will far out-
number your failures.

The larger issues of ethics, customer-service standards,
and corporate culture all flow down from the top. If you accept
a 10 percent consumer complaint level, your team will see it as
an objective, not a maximum.

"There was a righteous man who walked a right-
eous mile,
He built a righteous fortune with a righteous
brainchild;
Then he started cutting corners,
His priorities grew confused.
So he lost his brainchild fortune,
which was righteous through and through."
– Richard Saunders

COMMANDMENT NO. 10: CHANGE QUICKLY

"When you're finished changing, you're finished."
– Ben Franklin

Whatever the pace of your marketplace is, double it. The
fact that most of those engaged in your area of interest are huge,
lumbering giants is a fact that can work to your advantage.

Consider the components of momentum. In physics,
momentum is a function of mass and velocity.

It doesn't matter how huge your competition is. If you're
quicker on your feet, you'll get the lion's share. If you and your

Momentum= MASS x Velocity

band of gypsies move fast enough, you can go out and test it and fail and try it again and fail again and keep failing until you get it right before the corporation knows what's happened.

There has never been a better time to change the world than now. You occupy a unique point in history. The key is to take action quickly. Then when you find mistakes, change and adapt—also quickly.

> "Few innovations fail because of shipping too quickly—but many fail because they weren't changed rapidly enough once problems were identified."
> – Richard Saunders

Listen to Your Heart

We've come a long way, you and I. Thanks for bearing with me. I hope this book helps you move a few steps closer to realizing your dreams.

I'd like to know what you think of it. If you'd care to, please send an e-mail to DougHall@DougHall.com and tell me your stories of success and frustration. I will try to respond to all of them personally.

As you sail forth into the Real World, please remember to listen to your heart. Regardless of what the experts say or what the accountants calculate, the most important elements to your success are faith, energy and enthusiasm.

If you choose to push forward, you'll experience higher highs and lower lows than you ever imagined. You'll work harder and longer than you ever thought you could.

> "God helps them that help themselves."
> – Ben Franklin

If you believe your task is right, don't hesitate. Look closely at the numbers, look closely at your strategy, look for a path, and, most of all, look into your heart. When you can see a path then go for it. If you can't see any path at all, put your plan on hold until you can.

As you survey the landscape, don't forget the rest of your world. Don't forget your family and friends. Work is supposed to make life better. The act of carrying a wicked good idea from dream to reality is courageous and commendable. But it's not worth your family, your friends, or your life.

> "Wealth is not his that has it, but his that enjoys it."
> – Ben Franklin

Keep a steady hand on the reins. You'll work 20 hours a day for days on end, but you'll need to take time to play and enjoy. Balance the two. Otherwise, Flash, you'll crash and burn.

> "Drive thy business, let not that drive thee."
> – Ben Franklin

Like Dorothy and her pals in the Wizard of Oz, you already have what you need: The heart, the courage, and the brains.

Deep inside each of us is a little voice. If we listen closely, it will tell us what we should do and what we must do. It's time to start believing in that voice. It's time to start believing that everything we do and don't do makes a difference.

Well, that's about it. The day is done. You've been good. Time to hit the sack. The appendix of the book contains a little story called *Yink's It!* We kicked around the idea of removing it from

this second edition. Then I remembered the 30-something New York executive who came up to me after a lecture to tell me how

Yink had inspired him to change his life and career and how thankful he was. He asked me to sign the title page to his daughter. The story of Yink is the essence of the Eureka! Way

To view a quick time movie of the story in color visit...
www.DougHall.com/JSYB2

ONE LAST THING...
The final sentiment for this book are the quote from Ben Franklin that I started the book with—a quote so meaningful to me that I use it to end every book and every lecture I give. It's so important to me that when I'm laid to rest in the cemetery beside the little church of St. Thomas in Springbrook on Prince Edward Island, it will be carved on my tombstone. It's how I lead my life and how I challenge you to lead yours.

As Franklin said more than 200 years ago ...

"Up sluggard and waste not life, in the grave will be sleeping enough."

MUSIC BONUS: The link below takes you to a special contemporary version of "Amazing Grace" performed by the faculty of the College of Piping and Celtic Performing Arts of Canada with Patricia Murray singing.

The Great Highland Bagpipe and Amazing Grace became forever connected to reflective events when it was played at the funeral of President John Kennedy. What is not often known is that the lyrics to "Amazing Grace" were intended as a celebration. They were written by John Newton, a former slave ship Captain, in recognition of his personal salvation on May 10, 1748 by amazing grace, from his sinful life.

This fresh interpretation of "Amazing Grace" is intended to celebrate similar feelings of optimism, hope and dreams for the future.

Visit www.DougHall.com/JSYB2

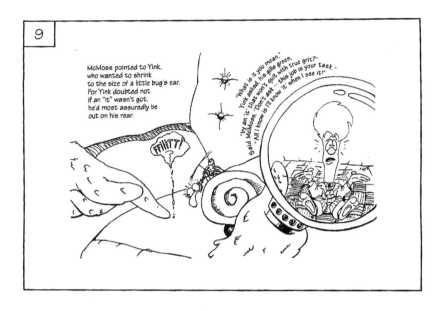

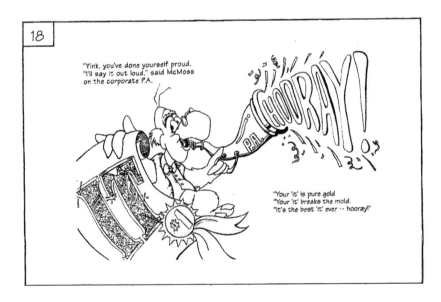

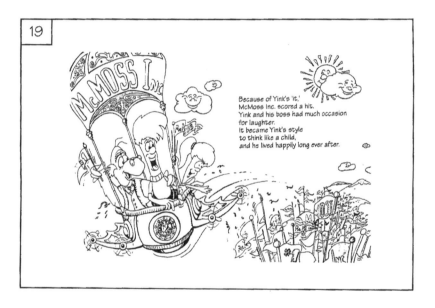

With respect to the greatest radicals in American history—among them, Ben Franklin, Thomas Jefferson, John Adams, George Washington, John Hancock and my forefather, Lyman Hall we declare our independence from conformity:

THE EUREKA! DECLARATION OF INDEPENDENCE
When in the course of human events, it becomes necessary for us to dissolve established patterns of thought that have connected us with the conforming world and beyond, a decent respect to the ruminations of mankind requires us to declare the causes which impel us to the separation.

We hold these truths to be self-evident, that all men and women are creative, that they are endowed by their Creator with certain unalienable rights, that among these are Wicked good Ideas Contradict History, Perception Is the Only Real Reality and Newborn Ideas Are To Be Respected, as well as and notwithstanding Life, Liberty and the Pursuit of Creative Freedom. That to secure these rights, Conformity to Conventional Wisdom is instituted among men, That whenever any form of Conventional Wisdom becomes Destructive of these ends, it is our right to alter or to abolish it and to Recapture Innocence, laying its foundation on such principles as shall seem most likely to give wing to Flights of Fancy.

And when a Long Train of Abuses And Usurpations intends to shackle us under the Absolute Despotism of Conformity, it is our Right, it is our Duty, to throw off Conventional Wisdom, and to provide a New State of Mind for our future independent, imaginative thoughts. The history of Conformity is a history of Repeated Injuries and Usurpations, all having an Absolute Tyranny over our Imaginations. To prove this, let facts be submitted to a candid world.

Conformity has enacted Political Correctness, discouraging fresh perspectives.

Conformity views passion, energy, and enthusiasm as lack of self-control.

Conformity puts out a Suggestion Box, but never looks inside.

Conformity discourages risk-taking, preferring instead the beaten path of least resistance.

Conformity believes in consensus to average instead of

debate to brilliance.

Conformity demands identical dress, identical talk, identical thoughts.

Conformity encourages us to toil in jobs we hate so we can retire and live the good life.

Conformity increments our salary upward till we're enslaved to maintaining the status quo.

Conformity confuses orderly, well-managed mediocrity for wicked good ideas.

Conformity regards change and chaos as a result of poor planning rather than a chance to grow.

Conformity whines and whimpers instead of taking responsibility.

Conformity rewards blind acceptance.

Conformity defends acting on precedent as risk-free.

Conformity views honesty, truth, and common sense as negotiable items.

Conformity believes that high-quality coffee is an unnecessary splurge.

Conformity believes overpriced French cuisine is superior to a cheeseburger.

Conformity believes money is a stronger motivator than pride and craftsmanship.

We, therefore, the Representatives of Original Thought and Unfettered Imagination, appealing to the Supreme Judge of the world for the rectitude of our intentions, do solemnly publish and declare, that we are and of right ought to be, Eureka!-ized; that we are absolved from all allegiance to Conformity, and that all ties between us and Conventional Wisdom are and ought to be totally dissolved, not to mention that we no longer wish to wear ties or panty hose; and that as free and independent thinkers, we have full power to imagine, reason, contemplate, create and otherwise use our brains as we see fit for the good of mankind.

For the support of this Declaration, with a firm reliance on the protection of Divine Providence, we mutually pledge to each other our lives, our fortunes and our sacred honor.

Thank You

Thank You, Debbie, Brad, Tori, Kristyn Hall—The source of my energy and my greatest teachers. Thank you for your patience with my slow learning.

Thanks, Jean Hall and Hazel Hall—You're no longer with us, but your spirit lives in these pages. You're the soul of the Eureka! way.

Thanks, Bruce & Beth Hall, Pam & Mark Twist and Buzz & Lois Hall—I look forward to many years together on our beloved Prince Edward Island.

Thanks, Eureka! Ranch Staff, Trained Brains and Clients—Your wisdom, irreverence and spirit have created The Eureka! Way.

Thanks, David Wecker & Kari McNamara—When I get down, the two of you pick me up. When I get too full of myself, you pull me down. I look forward to many, many more grand adventures together.

And thank you, Richard Hunt: The publisher of my books, my friend and kindred spirit.

Now a Word from David . . .

Thanks, Karen, for being amazing.
Thanks, Sam & Betsy, for growing up so beautifully.
Thanks, Bud & Dottie, for bringing me up, and Ken Fields, for continuing the process while you could.
Thanks, Kari, for making great things happen,
Thanks, Doug, for this wonderful ride,
And thank you, God, for all of the above.

The Legend of Brain Brew
Official Coffee of the Eureka! Ranch

Travel east on U.S. Route 32 out of Cincinnati and you'll come to The Eureka! Ranch, home to a small group of bold and brave thinkers known as the Eureka! Ranch Trained Brains.

One day, the Trained Brains noticed that a lusty cup of java cleared their heads and helped them embark on fanciful & vivid journey of the imagination. At great expense, they culled coffees from every roaster and importer they could find. They blended, ground, brewed and tasted from sunrise to sunset. Thousands of cups later, they arrived at their choice for the world's greatest blend. Out of respect for its ability to fuel the creative spirit, they named it Brain Brew.

Brain Brew combines an overwhelming amount of rich coffee aroma and robust coffee flavor without the bitterness, burn or bite of gourmet coffee "imposters." Its flavor is so smooth, visitors to the Ranch often remark that it tastes of chocolate. But there's no chocolate—just a near-perfect blend of pure Colombian Java from Java, Hawaiian Kona and the exotic single bean peaberry from Mount Kilimanjaro, resulting in an invigorating cup of pure aromatic pleasure!

Throughout history, the likes of Franklin, Voltaire, Twain, Bach, Beethoven and Brahms have sung the praises of coffee. The brew itself may be dark, but its power is clear.

> With coffee, all things are possible. Coffee enables us to endure the hardships and weather the tempests of life. Coffee helps us rise to challenges, overcome obstacles and at the end of the day, savor our victories.
> – Richard Saunders

If you care to order a pound or two or whatever, visit www.DougHall.com.

About the Author/s

DAVID WECKER

David Wecker is a storyteller. He sharpened his eye and ear over 20 years with *The Cincinnati Post* and *The Kentucky Post*, telling stories about real people, their values. their struggles and their victories. His stories showed again and again how the most outwardly ordinary people can be, at second glance, extraordinary and inspiring.

Wecker has also worked with Hall over the past 16 years creating ideas for Fortune 500 companies. As chief concept writer at Hall's Eureka! Ranch, he has written roughly 5,000 new product concepts in nearly every conceivable category for such clients as Nike, Disney, AT&T, American Express, Procter & Gamble, Johnson & Johnson, Pepsi, Coke, Chrysler and Ford.

DOUG HALL

Doug is a professional inventor. He began his inventing career at age 12, inventing and selling a line of magic and juggling kits. After earning a chemical engineering degree from the University of Maine he joined Procter & Gamble where he rose to the rank of Master Marketing Inventor—inventing and shipping a record 9 innovations in 12 months.

In 1986 Doug founded the Eureka! Ranch in Cincinnati Ohio. **The Ranch's mission is to help corporate executives and real world entrepreneurs develop MEASURABLY SMARTER choices for growth.** Eureka! services are available through a world-wide network of licensed Growth Coaches.

DATELINE NBC described Doug as *"an eccentric entrepreneur who just might have what we've all been looking for...the happy secret to success."* He is one of the world's top speakers on creativity, innovation and marketing. Doug has authored national newspaper/magazine columns and has starred on network radio and television programs. In recognition of his success, Doug has been awarded an honorary Doctorate from the University of Prince Edward Island, the George Land World Class Innovator Award, The Ned Herrmann

Spirit Award, the YMCA Character Award and the Ernst & Young Entrepreneur of the Year award.

For more information on Eureka! Ranch services or Doug's lecture and event availability visit **www.EurekaRanch.com**.

To contact Doug directly e-mail DougHall@DougHall.com.